A Vice for Voices

A Vice for

UNIVERSITY OF MASSACHUSETTS PRESS AMHERST AND BOSTON

Voices

READING EMILY DICKINSON'S CORRESPONDENCE

MARIETTA MESSMER

Printed in the United States of America

First paperback printing 2010
LC 2001002481
ISBN 978-1-55849-773-3

Designed by Kristina Kachele
Set in Monotype Bell by Keystone Typesetting, Inc.
Printed and bound by Lightning Source, Inc.

Library of Congress Cataloging-in-Publication Data
Messmer, Marietta.
A vice for voices : reading Emily Dickinson's correspondence / Marietta Messmer.
p. cm.
Includes bibliographical references (p.) and indexes.
ISBN 1-55849-306-9 (alk. paper)
1. Dickinson, Emily, 1830–1886—Correspondence. 2. Poets, American—19th century—Correspondence. 3. Women and literature—United States—History—19th century. 4. American letters—History and criticism. I. Title.
PS1541.Z5 M38 2001
811′.4
2001002481

British Library Cataloguing in Publication data are available.

For Roland and Helen Hagenbüchle

Contents

Acknowledgments

IT IS A SPECIAL PLEASURE for me to thank the many people who have helped in unique ways to make this book possible. For her unfailingly wise guidance in first formulating this project, my warmest thanks go to Lesley Higgins. Her keen intellectual challenge and unwavering support constantly gave me the courage to reach for new horizons. It was a great privilege for me to have Cristanne Miller and Paul Crumbley, two superbly knowledgeable readers, as my guides through the publication process. For sharing so generously her own thoughts on editorial matters, for offering a wealth of invaluable suggestions, for asking incisive questions that encouraged me to think further and probe deeper, I am deeply indebted to Cris, who has contributed so much to giving this book its final shape. Paul Crumbley's astute readings, stimulating comments, and eminently useful recommendations proved no less indispensable for the book's completion. It is a pleasure to remember the contributions of two of my first and most generous readers, Bob Adolph and Marlene Kadar. To Mariantonietta Fitzsimmons and Nancy Johnston I am grateful for their untiring willingness to "talk Dickinson," and Cindy Mackenzie, I trust, knows how much I appreciated receiving a draft of her impatiently awaited concordance to Dickinson's letters. I would especially like to thank Carol Betsch of the University of Massachusetts Press and Nancy Warrington for their expert editorial work.

Most of these are debts I can never repay. Yet I cannot even begin to measure what I owe to the boundless knowledge, inspirational teaching, and infinite generosity of Roland Hagenbüchle. His unfailing belief in me, his wise guidance and warmest support throughout the years helped me in more ways than he can ever know. His exceptional example shall always remain before and beyond me.

I thank York University, Toronto, for providing a scholarship that allowed me to devote a full year of my time and energies to this project and made repeated visits to the Dickinson archives possible. To Leslie Morris, curator at the Houghton Library of Harvard University, and John Lancaster, curator at Amherst College Library, I am grateful for their kindnesses and their assistance in enabling me to work with Dickinson's manuscripts.

Harvard College: MS Am 1118 (1); bMS Am 1118.95, box 12; bMS Am 1118.99c; MS Am 1118.5 (B24), (B33), (B34), (B54), (B78), (B79), (B123), (B126); MS Am 1118.2 (32), (46), (75); MS Am 1118.10 (12); MS Am 1118.3 (H83), (H84), (H93); L41, L58, L213, L229, L235, L240, L247, L250, L532, L745, L809, L832, L1020, L449, L517. Quotations from the Emily Dickinson manuscripts in Archives and Special Collections at the Amherst College Library are identified as "Dickinson ms. [number], Amherst" throughout the text and are included by permission.

M. M.

A Vice for Voices

I have a vice for voices.

—EMILY DICKINSON

INTRODUCTION

Two Centuries of Critical Responses to Dickinson's Letters

READING EMILY DICKINSON at the beginning of the twenty-first century has become a daunting enterprise indeed—not least because so much can depend on whose Dickinson we are reading. Thomas H. Johnson's typographic representations of *Poems* (1955) and *Letters* (1958), for example, invite us to trace the poet's chronological development as a writer of individual, isolated lyrics and letters. Building on Johnson, Ralph Franklin's impressive and monumental 1998 variorum update of *Poems* strives to capture and convey even more of the complexity of Dickinson's poetry. Franklin's facsimile reproductions of her fascicles in *The Manuscript Books* (1981), on the other hand, provide the foundation for our understanding of Dickinson as a compiler of hand-sewn booklets of thematically or otherwise potentially related groups of poems, drawing our particular attention to the multiple unresolved variant readings. These fascicle representations, however, while displaying Dickinson's poems as they appear in manuscript, tell us nothing about the various forms and formats in which they reached her friends and family. They also tell us nothing about Dickinson's habit to incorporate poems into and intertwine them with her letters. A glimpse of the latter can be caught from Ellen Louise Hart and Martha Nell Smith's *Open Me Carefully* (1998), an edition of Dickinson's correspondence with her sister-in-law, Susan Gilbert. By organizing a selection of Dickinson's materials not according to the traditional criteria of genre and chronology but according to the audience to whom they were addressed, Hart and Smith challenge our familiar notion of Dickinson "the poet" by displaying an array of letters, poems, and letter-poems resisting easy generic classification. Yet these epistolary exchanges with her sister-in-law—in many ways, according to the editors, reflective of poetry workshop activities, including the exchange of draft poems—also differ markedly from, for instance, Dickinson's late writings to Judge Otis Lord and other late fragments as (re)presented respectively in Marta Werner's *Open Folios* and her *Radical Scatters*. And as soon as we turn away from published, mediated versions of Dickinson's texts and instead approach the manuscripts themselves, we are confronted with additional hitherto unexplored configurations. To address this challenge, the Dickinson Editing Collective, founded in 1992, plans to represent electronically *all* of Dickinson's materials based on the groups in which they were left at her death (manuscript volumes, individual correspondences, ungathered poems and drafts) as well as *all* available print editions. Yet in many ways, this will only increase the necessity to decide: whose Dickinson should we read? And what are the consequences?

In this book, I am interested in reading the "public" writings of this most private of authors. Focusing on those texts that Dickinson specifically prepared for and circulated among her friends and family, I proceed from the belief that an examination of her correspondence as an interpretive unit can throw a fresh light on many aspects of her highly innovative poetics. Since Dickinson did not "publish" any of her materials in the traditional sense, her correspondence (poems, letters, and letter-poems addressed to various recipients) constitutes her only "letter to the world." It is also the only part of her oeuvre that was systematically "authorized," that is, prepared for an audience by Dickinson herself. Although those versions of her poems collected in fascicles more often than not were left in various states of incompletion (featuring multiple variants, cancellations, and unresolved alternative readings), all documents mailed to correspondents left Dickinson's desk as fair copies.[1] This difference between fascicles as spaces for gathering nonfinalized (draft) versions of poems, and correspondences as sites for exhibiting finalized versions of contextualized lyrics that merge with or, alternatively, enter into an intergeneric dialogic exchange with their letter context, leads me to propose an argument for "correspondence" (rather than "poetry") as Dickinson's central form of public artistic expression. It also leads me to disagree with Martha Nell Smith's claim (shared by Sharon Cameron and Jerome McGann, among others)[2] that *all* of Dickinson's manuscripts constitute her private form of publication (Smith, "Manuscripts" 117). The fact that, as far as we know, Dickinson never disseminated her fascicles—thus adamantly resisting sharing them with an "audience" while carrying on a prolific exchange of poems, letters, and letter-poems with a large number of people—suggests the potentially differing function and significance of these two bodies of materials. In this sense, even though the fascicle collections may illuminate Dickinson's creative or compositional processes, it is her correspondence, I am proposing, that may tell us more about the ways in which Dickinson chose to present her innovative poetics to her readers.

Placing "correspondence" at the core of Dickinson's literary production does, of course, require first and foremost that we suspend our traditional notions of this writer as primarily a "poet." It also requires that we suspend our traditional notions of Dickinson's letters as "subsidiary" or as predominantly "autobiographical" background materials. Yet owing to their audience orientation, it is her letters and letter-poems—rather than her (fascicle) poems alone or in isolation—which seem to be most representative of Dickinson's fundamental choices about literary production. Agnieszka Salska has highlighted this central significance of her letters by emphasizing that "the importance of Dickinson's correspondence for any appreciation or study of her work cannot be overestimated; her epistolary output constitutes an intrinsic part of her literary achievement" ("Dickinson's Letters" 163). This is of course not to say that *only* those materials mailed to correspondents are artistically meaningful, or that the poems Dickinson sent to her friends and relatives should *only* be read in the form(s) in which they were incorporated into her letters. It *is* to say, however, that the significance of Dickinson's correspondence in the context of her entire oeuvre has frequently been underestimated because of our predominantly poetocentric notion of this writer.

Dickinson's epistolary output, addressed to 99 known correspondents, and comprising 1,049 extant letters and 124 prose fragments,[3] in addition to "more than six hundred [poetry] manuscripts representing a few over five hundred poems" (Franklin, *Poems* 1:29), constitutes more than 60 percent of her entire textual production. Yet, in my view, what has contributed substantially to occluding the significance of this part of her work is a rigid generic differentiation—often hierarchically inflected—between "poems" and "letters," accompanied by a critical marginalization of the latter. This dichotomy, rather than being an intrinsic aspect of Dickinson's materials, is largely a critical construct, in part perpetuated by the editorial formats in which her texts have been represented since their first publication in 1890. Jerome McGann confirms the extent to which the physical shape, the arrangement of a text on the page, profoundly influences the way it is received by its audience: "reading Rossetti (or any other author) in a particular editorial format means that one has already been set within a definitive hermeneutical horizon" (*Textual Condition* 24).[4] That the traditional, generically dichotomous editorial format of Dickinson's "poems" and "letters" frequently results in an analogously dichotomous interpretation of "poems" as "literature" and "letters" as "autobiographical background material" is illustrated by the following brief sketch, which traces the interrelation between nineteenth- and twentieth-century editorial representations of Dickinson's texts and their concomitant critical receptions, both suggestive of readers' generic preconceptions about epistolary writing in general.

IN 1890, Dickinson entered the literary marketplace as a "poet." The enormous popular success of her *Poems*, First Series, as unexpected as it was unprecedented for a first volume of poetry, stirred the interest of readers, critics, and biographers alike in this hitherto completely unknown author.[5] The demand for biographical information, as well as for the publication of additional poems and letters, was intense. A note in the *Concord People and*

Patriot (February 1892) illustrates this strong curiosity on the part of Dickinson's readers: "the world will not rest satisfied till every scrap of her writings, letters as well as literature, has been published" (Buckingham, *Reception* 295, item 343). Moreover, Thomas Wentworth Higginson's 1891 introduction to his correspondence with Dickinson, published in the *Atlantic Monthly*, "arouse[d] interest in the forthcoming Second Series of *Poems*. But even more it aroused interest in the possibility of a volume of Emily's letters. A search for them was already under way before the Second Series of *Poems* was issued" (Bingham, *Ancestors' Brocades* 166). Two volumes reproducing a total of 345 letters, arranged in groups according to ten recipients, and edited with an introduction by Mabel Loomis Todd, were finally published on November 21, 1894.[6]

Sales of Dickinson's *Letters*, however, matched neither those of her poetry nor the expectations of her editor. The First Series of *Poems* had sold 10,000 copies, but the *Letters* only reached a total of 2,000 (Buckingham, *Reception* xiv); of the 1,500 copies issued in December 1894 as a second edition, 1,200 were still unsold by 1898. This surprising lack of public interest in Dickinson's letters can at least in part be attributed to a discrepancy between readers' expectations and the editorial format in which Todd chose to present them. Prompted by reviewers' depictions of the poet as a somber recluse, Todd intended the letters to showcase more of Dickinson's "enthusiasm and bright joyousness" ("Letters" 40). She was convinced, however, that the *Letters* would fulfill this purpose without major editorial explanations: "We [Todd and Higginson] felt that in publishing her letters all comment except what was absolutely necessary should be avoided" (qtd. in Bingham, *Ancestors' Brocades* 321). Her main editorial concern was to highlight the chronological development of Dickinson's epistolary style: "Nothing is perhaps more marked than the change of style between the diffuseness of girlhood and the brilliant sententiousness of late middle life, often startlingly unexpected; . . . all the variations in the evolution of a style having hardly less interest for the student of human nature than of literature" (Buckingham, *Reception* 341, item 418).

The general public, however, had expected something other than a study in epistolary style when picking up Dickinson's *Letters:* in keeping with Roland Barthes's premise that "the *explanation* of a work is always sought in the man or woman who produced it" ("Death" 143), readers and critics were hoping for an explicatory "companion to her poetry" (Buckingham, *Reception* 362, item 429). But, above all, the publication of Dickinson's letters as "the only record of her life" (ibid.) led readers to expect a key to the person behind the poems, one that would allow them to understand more fully the woman known primarily as "the myth of Amherst." As it became clear that Dickinson's *Letters* provided neither, the ensuing critical disappointment was widespread; it is best summed up by Caroline Healey Dall's comment in the *Boston Evening Transcript:* "Four years we have waited for these 'Letters,' hoping to find in their pages a clue to the whole life, and now we are as much at a loss as ever" (Buckingham, *Reception* 391, item 464).[7]

I contend that the disappointment expressed by these reviewers is, to a large degree, reflective of their strict generic and conceptual differentiation between Dickinson's letters and her poems, accompanied by implicit expectations about epistolary writing as unmediated confessional discourse, as autobiographical revelation.[8] This view is explained by the nineteenth-century poet, critic, and biographer Henry T. Tuckerman, who suggests in his 1851 discussion of the nature and function of private correspondence that "apart from their direct utility, letters are chiefly interesting as exponents of character, . . . of the heart and mind of the writer" (87, 102). In this way, they can prove to be particularly useful as source materials for biographers: "Biographers of poets wisely connect the narrative of their usually uneventful lives with letters chronologically arranged" (Tuckerman 87–88).[9] Characterizing personal letters as "printed talk," Tuckerman outlines the problems resulting from their publication: "They are either too unreserved to be read by a third party without indelicacy, too strictly private to interest the world, or so sacred in their revelations and tone that the glance of a careless eye would be profanation. On the other hand, stripped of all individuality of feeling, devoted wholly to generalizations, conveying no echo from the heart and animation from the real life of the writer, published letters are vapid" (80).[10]

Tuckerman's reservations about the publication of private letters were echoed by many of Dickinson's first readers. In her introduction, Todd had attempted to forestall criticism for publishing "intimate correspondence" too soon after the writer's death by emphasizing the audience-conscious, actor-like quality of Dickinson's epistolary voices.[11] In publishing Dickinson's correspondence, "the sanctities were not invaded. Emily kept her little reserves, and bared her soul but seldom, even in intimate correspondence. It was not so much that she was always on spiritual guard, as that she sported with her varying moods, and tested them upon her friends with apparent delight in the effect, as airy and playful as it was half unconscious" (Buckingham, *Reception* 341, item 418). Yet many reviewers tended to ignore Todd's differentiation between Dickinson's histrionic epistolary strategies on the one hand and the "sacred . . . revelations" (Tuckerman 80) of more conventional private correspondences on the other. As one reviewer remarked: "It is not only a mistake, but a mean trick to publish private correspondence. . . . There is a feeling all the time of base spying and peeping on the part of the reader" (Buckingham, *Reception* 377–378, item 450). And E. Winchester Donald told Todd: "Frankly, I turned from the Letters to the Poems to escape & recover the sense of unmixed happiness. Poetry is public, letters are—well, private . . . the letters are *published*. I wish they hadn't been. Still, I am glad you brought them out, for, by them, new readers may be led to the Poems, which justifies anything of this nature" (qtd. in Bingham, *Ancestors' Brocades* 314–315).

If reviewers were prepared to recognize differences between Dickinson's playfully enacted epistolary voices on the one hand and generic expectations of letters as unmediated revelations of the writer's soul on the other, they invariably faulted Dickinson for not conforming to their preconceived notions of nineteenth-century epistolary conventions. In his generally favorable review, E. Winchester Donald, for example, continues: "The early [letters] are quite human; that is to say, a good deal like other people's letters. . . . The later ones are, so to speak, *exposed*. . . . [T]he fourth [letter after Elizabeth Holland's death] shows the writer is recovering her grasp on her *style*. . . . Not that she was a *poseuse;* that implies an audience—but she did attitudinize for her own pleasure" (qtd. in Bingham, *Ancestors' Brocades* 314). Morton Dexter is struck by the "artificiality" of Dickinson's letters, "as though the writer were posing for literary effect" (Buckingham, *Reception* 395, item 466). And the tone of Atherton Brownell's review in the *Boston Home Journal* suggests his surprise at the nonreferential quality of Dickinson's correspondence: "Most of her letters are strangely impersonal, coming from a recluse whose solitude must largely have been spent in introspection; and yet, while they contain so little of self, they contain still less of the affairs of the great world outside of her home" (Buckingham, *Reception* 354, item 423).

Yet ironically, despite a frequently deplored absence of biographical revelations in Dickinson's letters, many nineteenth-century reviewers nonetheless insisted on mining them for biographical information: "They [the letters] help us to interpret this strangely realistic and impassioned woman" (Buckingham, *Reception* 362, item 429). And, echoing Tuckerman, the *Outlook* draws a sharp distinction between Dickinson's "letters" and "literature": "It is chiefly as a revelation of character that we attach importance to them, and the two volumes of the *Letters of Emily Dickinson* form a contribution to our knowledge of human nature rather than to our literature. They are psychological documents" (Buckingham, *Reception* 424, item 488). Thus the critical reception of Dickinson's letters during the 1890s resulted in a curious paradox: critiqued for failing to provide sufficient information about their author's life, Dickinson's letters were nonetheless read and reread as nonliterary, strictly biographical documents that would help unravel the mysteries with which her person had become invested. As Bingham has summarized: "Interest in the letters themselves was subordinated to preoccupation with the personality of the writer. This was a disappointment to my mother [Mabel Loomis Todd]. She had thought that the letters were great enough, as she said, 'to absorb the reader in the sentiments expressed'—great enough to lift him above inquisitiveness about the facts of Emily's life" (*Ancestors' Brocades* 320).

From the outset, then, readers' responses to Dickinson's correspondence reflect a discrepancy between largely implicit but widely shared critical preconceptions about epistolary writing as nonliterary and personal, intended to provide "a more or less direct relation of factual truth" (Mansell 64), and a stubborn resistance on the part of Dickinson's letters to conform to these generic expectations. The vast majority of twentieth-century approaches to the writer's correspondence can be read as attempts to address—without, however, fully resolving—this paradox.[12]

Following the pioneering efforts of Mabel Loomis Todd and Thomas Wentworth Higginson, almost all subsequent editors of Dickinson's writings (Martha Dickinson Bianchi [1924, 1932], Millicent Todd Bingham [1945, 1954], Theodora Ward [1951], Thomas H. Johnson [1955], Johnson and Ward [1958],[13] William H. Shurr [1993], as well as Ralph Franklin [1981, 1998]) have chosen to reinforce a more or less strict generic distinction between "poems" and "letters"—for the most part inspired by then-current critical genre conceptions, such as Johnson's New Critical privileging of (isolated) lyrics as objects of inquiry.[14] Yet this editorially foregrounded generic dichotomy, in addition to encouraging a poetocentric reception of Dickinson by directing her readers' primary attention to her lyrics in uncontextualized form, has also had an additional consequence. Since—until the most recent revisionist focus on Dickinson's manuscripts—the majority of twentieth-century readers have never had any reason to question this generic subdivision, they, like their nineteenth-century counterparts, approached Dickinson's epistolary writings as completely separate from her poems, which has frequently contributed to their marginalization as mere "background materials." William H. Shurr's recent edition of *New Poems of Emily Dickinson* (1993) is a case in point. It features Shurr's attempt to "excavate" metrical passages from Dickinson's prose in order to prevent their being buried beneath the artistically "inferior" epistolary context. In his introduction, he justifies this editorial decision with the following argument: "The epigrams and poems which are excavated and presented below are too overwhelmed by their contexts in the letters. . . . [I]t is questionable whether the letters—written to specific individuals concerned with the minutiae of everyday life—are really suitable context for these poems. They seem to transcend such limiting contexts. It is only when they are isolated and presented as freestanding poems that we can focus on them as the works of art they are" (Shurr, *New Poems* 10)

Although Shurr's hierarchically inflected dichotomy between "isolated" lyrics as "works of art" and their "limiting" epistolary contexts is certainly extreme in its condemnatory force, he is nonetheless representative of the majority of twentieth-century critics who, influenced by such editorial differentiations, also draw formal and functional distinctions between Dickinson's "poems" and her "letters." Since Dickinson did not leave any journal or autobiography proper, biographical critics, in particular, frequently read her "letters" as supplementary factual source documents providing information about the (psychological) "life" of the "poet" (rather than as works of art in themselves).[15] Theodora van Wagenen Ward, for example, who in 1951 edited Dickinson's correspondence with Josiah and Elizabeth Holland, analyzes these and other letters to draw a Jungian psychobiography of the poet in *The Capsule of the Mind.* And in *My Life a Loaded Gun: Female Creativity and Feminist Poetics,* Paula Bennett, echoing John Cody's 1971 theory of Dickinson's psychological breakdown, uses the poet's correspondence to construct a narrative consisting of a suicide, withdrawal, and reemergence cycle linked to Sue Gilbert's marriage to Dickinson's brother, Austin: "After 1853 Dickinson's letters travel a steady downward path toward suicidal depression" (38).

Some biographers thus unquestioningly presuppose a direct, revelatory link between Dickinson's "life" and her "letters," though others attempt to justify their strictly biographical readings by invoking the very dichotomy that had been assumed by Dickinson's editors. Nancy Walker (" 'Wider Than the Sky' "), for example, draws an explicit distinction between Dickinson's "autobiographical writings" (274) and her poems: "The distance between writer and reader afforded by the artifices of poetry and fiction—devices such as metaphoric and symbolic structures—is nominally absent [in her letters], and the writer translates thought into direct dialogue with self or specific others" (273). Aligning poetry with distance, artifice, and fictionality, letters by implication thus become unmediated factual documents that provide a "direct" access to the author's "self." A similar emphasis on the unmediated referential quality of Dickinson's letters can be found in Lewis Turco's 1993 claim that "it was in her letters that the poet spoke most often in her own personal voice" (*Woman of Letters* 1).

Increasingly, however, such strictly dichotomous positions have been complemented by more ambivalent ones. Some twentieth-century critics have begun to echo their nineteenth-century colleagues' complaints about the fact that Dickinson's letters more often than not seem to resist such a facile alignment between her own "personal voice" and her epistolary forms of self-representation. As a consequence, they ultimately argue that the writer's correspondence is situated somewhere in between "factuality" and "fictionality." Jean McClure Mudge (*Emily Dickinson and the Image of Home*), for example, introduces the term "hybrid" to describe this composite quality of Dickinson's epistolary self: "The 'I' then is a hybrid self, derived from both the poet's life and her poetic invention. It is a being at once existential and literary" (*Home* xvi). Mudge's perspective highlights the crucial function of Dickinson's letters as sites for complex negotiations between "existential" elements ("life") and "invention"/"art." S. Jaret McKinstry ("'How Lovely Are the Wiles of Words!'") aptly describes this generic mix as "something between autobiography and poetry, a unique genre that Dickinson creates in order to balance the poetic self-expression . . . and the female self-repression" (193). Not infrequently, however, the tension inherent in this generically ambivalent classification eventually gets resolved by shifting the balance toward the autobiographical side. For McKinstry, for instance, Dickinson's correspondence ultimately still is "biography" (195).[16]

Such privileging of the "factual" element in this generic mixture of "life" and "art" is occasionally also combined with a notion of art that often merely connotes a certain degree of "artfulness" or even "artificiality"; rarely are Dickinson's letters embraced as *literary* works of art, on a par with her poetry. The first book-length study of Dickinson's correspondence (*Portrait of Emily Dickinson: The Poet and Her Prose*), by David Higgins, for example, highlights the "artfulness" of Dickinson's letters: "Emily Dickinson was audience-conscious; she carefully adapted each correspondence to her estimate of the reader's capacities. . . . Emily Dickinson lived deliberately and preferred to present herself to the world only by deliberate art. . . . [Her letters] . . . can be deliberate creations from salutation to signature, and . . . show a great deal of 'stage presence'" (5–6).[17] Higgins's repeated references to Dickinson's "deliberateness" and his use of stage-related terminology ("audience-conscious," "stage presence") implicitly reveal his uneasiness about Dickinson's histrionic self-constructions. Presenting them in this way, he seems to draw attention to their unusualness in an epistolary context. And indeed, in the end Higgins clearly privileges a more strictly biographical reading of Dickinson's letters by relegating discussions of stylistic issues (the *art* of letter writing) to the introduction while providing a biographical portrait of "the poet" throughout the rest of the book. Unable to relinquish his expectations of a direct link between letter writing and autobiography, and unwilling to pursue the complex implications of his crucial observations about Dickinson as "audience-conscious" actor/persona, Higgins ultimately claims to find the "real" Dickinson in and through her letters: "The letters Emily wrote were part of her art, but the life she chose made them also her conversation and autobiography. . . . Now that more than a thousand of her letters are in print it is possible to follow with some accuracy the course of Emily's life in her prose expressions of it, and in the letter-poems she sent to friends. There are still gaps—some as long as a year—but the real Emily Dickinson, far more interesting than the legendary one, has begun to emerge from generations of myth and misconception" (24).

Higgins's important emphasis on the histrionic quality of Dickinson's letters is also echoed by Brita Lindberg-Seyersted and Dolores Lucas. Lucas argues that Dickinson "approached letter-writing and life in much the same way—as an artist who chose to present herself deliberately to an audience" (87), while Lindberg-Seyersted regards the letters as a stage upon which her epistolary self dons various masks and adopts multiple poses or disguises: "Reading through her letters, especially the early ones, one cannot help observing in them a fair amount of posing, another method for achieving detachment and disguise" (27).

"Artfulness," "posing," and "disguise," terms reminiscent of E. Winchester Donald's 1894 critique (qtd. in Bingham, *Ancestors' Brocades* 314–315), have become recurrent critical metaphors, especially in describing Dickinson's strikingly divergent epistolary "selves" in letters written to different addressees. Yet whereas Higgins and others had primarily expressed surprise at this seemingly "un-epistolary" quality—only to return to a direct autobiographical reading in the end—other critics attempt a more indirectly biographical approach by trying to explain Dickinson's choice of epistolary "roles" or "masks" in psychobiographical terms. In *The Art of Emily Dickinson's Early Poetry*, for example, David Porter analyzes the writer's "several public selves" (1) in view of her "confident self-regard" (8) in her letters to Elizabeth and Josiah Holland on the one hand, and the "pervasive humility" (6) in her contemporaneous correspondence with Higginson on the other. And in his "Dickinson's Letters to Higginson," John Stuart Mann regards Dickinson's awareness of her "audience" as being at the root of these "several public selves," maintaining that "they demonstrate how her words function in a stunning psychological game calculated to develop masks which enable the poet to meet the world and people in a highly dramatic and individual way" (4).

These emphases on Dickinson's epistolary personae or "masks"—expressive of a "psychological game" she plays with her addressees—have come a long way from earlier interpretations of her letters as unmediated revelations of the writer's soul. Yet more often than not, even such acknowledgments of Dickinson's dramatic strategies of self-fashioning inevitably end in autobiographical interpretations—albeit different kinds. Although on the one hand critics acknowledge the high degree of control and deliberateness manifested in these rhetorical strategies, they also tend to regard them as unconscious revelations of the writer's psychological needs. Robert Graham Lambert's *Critical Study of Emily Dickinson's Letters*, for example, posits an indirect (i.e., "unconsciously revealing") relationship between Dickinson herself and her epistolary self-constructions: "her finest letters are viewed both as conscious works of art—her drafts and revisions reveal the pains she took over them—and as unconsciously revealing statements about her soul" (xiv). In this way, Dickinson's actor-like personae both reveal *and* conceal the "true" Dickinson: "her letters often turned into a testing ground where she could try on various poses, masks that—although certainly a deep part of her personality structure—were also to a large extent assumed roles, mannered parts that concealed as much as they revealed the true Emily Dickinson" (1). Yet similar to Higgins and others before him, Lambert is most interested in unraveling the "true" Dickinson and her psychological personality structure when he insists that "analysis, explications, and judgments of Emily Dickinson's prose should be especially rewarding: she was a private poet without biography. All that happened was internal, and the letters provide a window on her maturing sensibilities" (xiii).

Deepening the explorations of the complexities inherent in the interrelation between Dickinson's epistolary acts of self-presentation and their significance as psychological gestures of self-revelation, both Suzanne Juhasz and Cristanne Miller have also emphasized the extent to which language itself inflects representations of material or experiential reality. Hence Juhasz is the first to explicitly discuss Dickinson's epistolary "selves" as discursive constructs, or, in Dickinson's own words, as "supposed person[s]" (L268):

"she [Dickinson] is always a supposed person, because she always uses language to represent herself" ("Reading" 190).[18] Focusing specifically on the poet's letters to her brother, Austin Dickinson, and to Sue Gilbert, Thomas Wentworth Higginson, Elizabeth Holland, and "Master," Juhasz examines in detail the different roles Dickinson chooses to play in each of these relationships—characterized by "ambition," an "aesthetic imperative," "poetic ambition," filial friendship, and dramatized desire, respectively—pointing out that the speakers in these letters represent different *personae* specifically adopted for each correspondent: "The letter creates and projects the self in terms of a particular interpersonal relationship" (171). Ultimately, however, Juhasz also returns to the psychology of the person behind the personae when suggesting that " 'posing' tells us as much about the real person as some kind of absolute candor would" (170). In the end, Juhasz thus argues for an autobiographical reading—albeit a highly sophisticated one—of Dickinson's correspondence: "We can indeed read Dickinson's letters as autobiography when we recognize that the mode and manner of self-representation is itself an essential self-revelation" (170).

Cristanne Miller takes Juhasz's position one step further by extending the notion of Dickinson's textually constructed "supposed person[s]" to include her addressees, emphasizing the high degree of control this affords the writer: "Through letters, the poet can control relationships, meeting her correspondents in a literary or aesthetic union—union that can only with difficulty or by death be taken from her because she has constructed it herself through and in language" ("A Letter" 35).[19] Yet like Juhasz and others before her, Miller also attempts to draw a highly complex link to the writer's "psychology" or "self." Referring to Dickinson's poems enclosed in letters, Miller's words can also be applied to the letters themselves:

> Dickinson uses the experience of her life and world to create what Weisbuch has called a "sceneless" poetry. The poems stem from her life but they do not point to it; there is no direct reference to a particular act of the poet or even necessarily to her real voice in the statement or voice of a poem. Dickinson's "I" is always a character stemming from her experience, and in that way reveals her character, but no "I" is simply the poet. Nonetheless, patterns of posing reflect the disguised self: Dickinson's varied poses and

strategies of indirection are as illuminating of her psychology as a more straightforward account of her life would be. Although the poet's language is not transparent, we do see her in it. ("A Letter" 34)

While Juhasz and Miller thus attempt to explicate Dickinson's epistolary "patterns of posing" primarily in terms of the psychological needs of her "self," Judith Farr and Martha Nell Smith have concentrated on identifying some of the cultural or literary models for these epistolary self-constructions. In *The Passion of Emily Dickinson*, Farr argues that Dickinson stylized her life according to contemporaneous modes of painting and iconography. Suggesting that in Dickinson's poems life and art thus come together, Farr analyzes how the poet acts out artistic and aesthetic modes of her time (modeled, in particular, on Tennyson, the Pre-Raphaelites, and Thomas Cole): "In her allusions to herself as a nun, by her assumption of white and her repeated association of herself with lilies, Emily Dickinson was participating in a finely articulated iconographic tradition" (*Passion* 39). Highlighting thus the aesthetic—rather than the psychological—qualities of Dickinson's epistolary self-configurations, Farr can ultimately also read these letters as "works of art" in their own right: "her letters themselves are, from about 1858 on, conscious and conscientious works of art" (*Essays* 8).[20]

In a similar way, Martha Nell Smith emphasizes the more strictly literary aspects of Dickinson's correspondence—in particular of her so-called Master letters—by reversing previous explanations; Dickinson's *literary* constructions are now characterized by verisimilitude: "In her production of these love letters, the writer Dickinson participates in a long-established literary tradition by making both the addressee and the writer seem real, even present to the readers. Studying the letter 'Master' in the context of one of her favorite Dickens texts, which sports similar incoherent epistolary rhetoric, argues for interpreting the letter as consciously paralleling fictional expressions of the period and not simply as authentic emotional exclamation" (*Rowing* 122). Smith's resistance to reading these (and other) letters as "authentic emotional exclamation" is no doubt in part predicated on the fact that she is the first to consistently abandon any generic subdivision of Dickinson's oeuvre into "poems" and "letters." Instead, she privileges an organization of these texts according to the audience to whom they were addressed. Specifically focusing on all materials that Dickinson exchanged with her sister-in-law, Sue Gilbert, Smith notes the blurring of boundaries between "fact" and "fiction" in these writings, highlighting the transformation of homoerotic desire into "compelling literature" (38). At the same time, Smith is fully aware of the attractions a biographical interpretation holds for readers of these letters: "Dickinson's choice of form especially lends itself to interpretations that confuse the speaker with the author" (77). She insists, however, that a "classification as fiction or nonfiction remains stubbornly indeterminate" (122), since the "degrees of fictionality blend practically indistinguishably with degrees of nonfictional expression" (125). Carefully attempting not to privilege either side of this dichotomy, Smith characterizes Dickinson's writings as being akin to "epistolary fiction" ("Manuscripts" 131) or fictional autobiography. They are thus *not* to be taken as a "faithful" revelation of the writer's "self": "The selves revealed by her letters and poems, then, are Dickinson's literary identities or ways of being, informed, to be sure, by the emotions of the actual woman who lived and wrote in Amherst but not faithfully representing them or revealing her. If they script an autobiography, it is a portrait of the artist" (*Rowing* 108). Interestingly enough, however, even Smith—like so many before her—seems to tip the precarious balance again when devoting the major parts of her studies to establish Sue Gilbert's central role as Dickinson's reader-critic, collaborator, and potential lover.

Farr and Smith were thus among the first to explore the more strictly aesthetic and "literary" sources and aspects of Dickinson's modes of epistolary self-fashioning, but Agnieszka Salska ("Dickinson's Letters") goes one step further by highlighting the significance of Dickinson's letters as literary products, equal to her lyrics. According to Salska, Dickinson's letters "became the territory where she could work out her own style, create her poetic voice, and crystallize the principles of her poetics" (168). Even though earlier critics had occasionally referred to the letters as "stylistic workshop," Salska's approach is no longer hierarchically inflected to view Dickinson's epistolary writings as a mere "testing ground" for her poetry. Emphasizing the merger of emotional and literary concerns in these letters ("Dickinson's Letters" 172), and observing that Dickinson "lived in a culture that persistently encouraged the fusion of literary and personal experience beyond the need and, really, the possibility of separating the two" (166), Salska points out that Dickinson's letters "are unique creations in which the formality of a poem and the informality of a personal communication reflect on each other" ("Letters" 29).[21] Situating them "on the border of personal and artistic expression," Salska is thus among the first *not* to tip the scale: she reads these letters as Dickinson's attempts "to keep in balance the personal and the aesthetic perspective" ("Poetics" 17). Abandoning earlier dichotomous interpretations, Salska thus best highlights the dialectical dynamic between "life" and "art" inherent in Dickinson's correspondence. Letters and poems become two manifestations of one artistic project.

FROM the start, then, the history of critical responses to Dickinson's letters has been dominated by various attempts to explore and explicate the discrepancy between generic conventions and preconceptions of epistolary writing as self-revelatory, referential accounts of "real-life" events on the one hand, and the largely nonreferential, "actor-like" quality of Dickinson's epistolary "poses" or "masks" on the other. Even though many studies display an acute, occasionally uneasy, awareness of the degree to which Dickinson's letters resist a strictly autobiographical reading, most of them nonetheless end up privileging this very aspect in one way or another. In several instances, the notion of an unmediated direct link between "life" and "letters" has been replaced by an insistence on the—at best—*indirect* referentiality between the psychological needs of the person and the choice of her epistolary personae. In all cases, however, these roles, personae, or masks are interpreted as manifestations of a single, unified self. Such references to the "psychology of the disguised self"—insightful as they are—are nonetheless historically predicated on a belief in the centrality of a coherent self that can be "identified" beneath the various forms of epistolary strategies of self-fashioning. I believe, on the other hand, that current theories of discursively constructed and textually enacted subject positions may be able to throw a fresh light on and offer new insights to this discussion of the forms and functions of Dickinson's epistolary voices.

Revisiting Dickinson's epistolary acts of self-fashioning from a contemporary feminist-poststructuralist perspective, and building on earlier propositions of the discursive constructedness of these personae (especially

Smith and Farr) yet striving to go beyond predominantly psychobiographical explications of the writer's negotiations between "life" and "art," I have been prompted by the following questions: In what ways exactly and through what strategies do Dickinson's letters resist explicit or implicit autobiographical readings, or render them at least highly unsatisfactory? How and on what grounds can we move beyond a dichotomous approach to Dickinson's texts in terms of "letters" versus "poems," "fact" versus "fiction," or "referentiality" versus "nonreferentiality" toward a more dialogically interactive model? To what extent can Dickinson's multiple epistolary subject positions, in addition to being understood as expressions of a personal need, also be interpreted as cultural and discursive critiques on a larger scale? And finally, what, exactly, does Dickinson mean when she tells us, "I have a vice for voices" (PF 19)?

In this book, I propose to revisit and reread Dickinson's correspondence as a performative act in which she effectively appropriates a multiplicity of discursively constructed voices that engage in an intergeneric dialogic exchange in order to critique prevailing gender constructions (in particular as they manifest themselves in the narrowly circumscribed subject positions available for women during the nineteenth century), rewrite existing power relations, and challenge traditional forms of author(iz)ed and authoritative patriarchal discourses. Such a feminist-poststructuralist framework enables me to go beyond a predominantly dichotomous or psychobiographical interpretation of Dickinson's writings and allows me to throw into relief the complexity of her epistolary art, including the dialogic polyvocality as well as the high degree of performativity within her texts. Since Dickinson's correspondence (in its form and function) explicitly engages with nineteenth-century epistolary conventions, and since, as both Juhasz and Miller have pointed out, the epistolary genre is centrally concerned with questions of self-representation, current theories of self-representation—as developed in related genres such as autobiography and biography—can, in my view, contribute productively to a revised understanding of Dickinson's epistolary voices and their sociopolitical significance.

My concept of discursively constructed subject positions is predominantly based on Roland Barthes's definition of the "author" as part of a linguistic game rather than a psychologically consistent, unified self: "Linguistically, the author is never more than the instance writing, just as *I* is nothing other than the instance saying *I*: language knows a 'subject,' not a 'person,' and this subject, empty outside of the very enunciation which defines it, suffices to make language 'hold together,' suffices, that is to say, to exhaust it" ("Death" 145). One consequence of this challenge to an "author's" stable identity outside of discourse is, as Foucault emphasizes, the elimination of any *direct* referentiality between the "person" and her/his textual subject positions: "The writing subject cancels out the signs of his particular individuality" (142–143); and "it is a matter of depriving the subject (or its substitute) of its role as originator, and of analyzing the subject as a variable and complex function of discourse" (158).

In the context of Dickinson's letters, such a concept of discursively constructed epistolary voices prevents what Adrienne Rich, quoting Dickinson, calls the "victimization" of a "life" by shifting the focus away from the writer's *bios* toward what James Olney describes as "the significance and the effect of transforming life, or *a* life, into a text" (6).[22] With Domna C. Stanton and Jeanine Plottel, I thus excise "the *bio* from *autobiography*" in order to "bracket[ ] the traditional emphasis on the narration of 'a life' and facile assumption of referentiality that has sustained the notion" (vii). The autobiographical "self"—and, by implication, also the epistolary self—thus becomes what Sidonie Smith terms "a convention of time and space where symbolic systems, existing as infinite yet always structured possibility, speak themselves in the utterance of a *parole*. The autobiographical text becomes a narrative artifice, privileging a presence, or identity, that does not exist outside language" (5).[23]

This notion of the text as a "narrative artifice" that lends prominence to discursive presences captures in a striking way the forms and functions of Dickinson's epistolary selves. By speaking in and through a wide range of different voices, Dickinson regularly, to use Sidonie Smith's terms, fractures "the narrated 'I' into multiple speaking postures" (47). On the one hand, these strategies of self-fashioning are adapted to individual correspondents in order to interrogate various addressee-specific gender-inscribed power relations. In these instances, Dickinson adopts a wide range of (largely fictional, highly gendered) identities mostly identifiable by name and taken from a variety of literary, biblical, or historical contexts. Yet the proliferation of voice configurations in Dickinson's letters is at once more pervasive and more complex than that. She not only *adopts* a wide range of fictional personae, she also *speaks* in and through a multiplicity of "borrowed" or appropriated voices that enter her texts primarily in the form of quotations. In fact, Dickinson's entire epistolary output constitutes a densely woven network of intertextual relations, including direct quotations from her own and other texts as well as other discursive gestures such as newspaper clippings or flowers. Dickinson's letters thus closely resemble Kristeva's and Barthes's definitions of "text." According to Kristeva, "any text is constructed as a mosaic of quotations; any text is the absorption and transformation of another" (*Desire* 66). Similarly, Barthes describes "text" as a "multi-dimensional space in which a variety of writings, none of them original, blend and clash" ("Death" 146). Michael Sprinker highlights the implications of such a notion of "text" for our understanding of the autobiographical "self": "Every text is an articulation of the relations between texts, a product of intertextuality, a weaving together of what has already been produced elsewhere in discontinuous form; every subject, every author, every self is the articulation of an intersubjectivity structured within and around the discourses available to it at any moment in time. It is in the context of this critique of the subject that the investigation of autobiography as a particular species of writing can most fruitfully be undertaken" (325).

In Dickinson's letters, these intertextual relations, or more specifically, the intertextual interactions between multiple discursive voices, are best captured in terms of Bakhtin's notion of dialogic polyvocality as outlined in his *Problems of Dostoevsky's Poetics*. For Bakhtin, lyric poems almost always "tend toward becoming monologues" (*Problems* xxii), but prose can also exhibit monologic tendencies if its heterogeneity "is subordinated to the unity of a personal style and tone permeating it through and through, the unity of a single world and a single consciousness" (15).[24] Successful dialogicity, on the other hand, is accomplished by "keeping the opponent alive" (xxxvii), by maintaining a "plurality of unmerged consciousnesses" (11), since the annihilation of heterogeneous voices always also entails the annihilation of the dialogic sphere. One way to ensure utmost heterogeneity and polyphony is thus to highlight "dramatic juxtaposition[s]" and "counterposition[s]" of heterogeneous voices (28).

The proliferation and juxtaposition of heterogeneous voices in the form of direct quotations in Dickinson's letters does indeed suggest the presence of a high degree of dialogicity and polyvocality in a Bakhtinian sense. At the same time, both Bakhtin and Manfred Pfister have emphasized that it is the degree to which a direct quotation has been modified in the quoting process which ultimately determines the quoting text's heterogeneity and hence dialogic intensity: "For what matters here is not the mere presence of specific language styles, social dialects, and so forth . . . ; what matters is the *dialogic angle* at which these styles and dialects are juxtaposed or counterposed in the work" (Bakhtin, *Problems* 182). In Dickinson's texts, this "dialogic angle" of juxtaposition can frequently be described as a highly complex negotiation between subtle strategies of monologic control within demonstrative gestures of dialogic polyvocality, in this way mirroring her highly complex generic negotiations between "lyric" and "epistolary" voices. Thus, Dickinson's texts frequently approximate what I shall call monologized dialogues or dialogized monologues. In addition, it is also crucial to note that Dickinson's voices are not merely directed toward the reader of her letters but are also addressing *each other*, in this way initiating an intergeneric dialogic exchange and acquiring an additional semantic potential. They can thus be described as a modified version of Bakhtin's notion of "double-voiced discourse," which he had defined as "directed both toward the referential object of speech, as in ordinary discourse, and toward *another's discourse*, toward *someone else's speech*" (185).

This approach to Dickinson's correspondence distinguishes itself from previous discussions in three vital ways. First, a poststructuralist concept of the textually enacted subject heeds Dickinson's own warning that she has "a vice for voices" by opening up the possibility to read specific forms of self-representation not merely as veiled acts of "self-revelation," but also as larger strategies of cultural and discursive critique. Placing dialogic polyvocality at the core of Dickinson's strategies of epistolary self-fashioning thus allows me to move beyond the dichotomy of factuality versus fictionality and to concentrate instead on the dialogic negotiations and critiques of patriarchal discursive formations and traditional author(iz)ed discourses. In the second place, this attempt to free Dickinson's letters from the classificatory constraints of unmediated "personal writing," (psycho)biography, and "nonliterature" challenges their generic marginalization as mere "background materials" or "vehicles" for her poems and provides the basis for a reconsideration and reevaluation of their status within Dickinson's canon. In particular, the multiple ways in which Dickinson's letters and poems are intertwined both formally and functionally illustrate the extent to which any editorial separation mutilates them both. Third, such a reevaluation of Dickinson's letters explains my claims to regard "correspondence" (rather than "poetry") as her major form of artistic expression and to read her "poems" and "letters" contextually as two complementary modes of writing engaged in an intergeneric dialogic exchange.[25]

In many ways, my approach to Dickinson's polyvocal epistolary subject positions shares conceptual considerations with Paul Crumbley's discussion of poetic polyvocality in *Inflections of the Pen*. In his study of Dickinson's dashes as "nuanced visual signals" that "introduce polyvocality as a direct challenge to the primacy of a single unified voice" (1, 2), Crumbley explains that "Dickinson's practice of occupying and then vacating a variety of voices becomes her means of demonstrating that within the house of language exist many mansions, none of which can accommodate the polyvocal self" (77). Referring to Dickinson's use of dashes in both poems and letters, Crumbley argues that the latter also "propose that Dickinson used language to claim plural identity and in that way elude entrapment in monologic consciousness" (77). I submit that, analogous to Crumbley's notion of Dickinson's polyvocal self deploying a "plural identity" and his suggestion that "standardized rules of grammar could not accommodate the self she sought to express" (77), standardized rules of generic conventions likewise could not accommodate the multiple epistolary selves that Dickinson sought to express in ever changing proliferations of alternative voice configurations.

In chapter 1, "The Context of Nineteenth-Century Epistolary Conventions," I analyze the extent to which Dickinson's epistolary polyvocality manifests itself on the physical level of manuscripts. I maintain that Dickinson's manuscripts themselves make it impossible to support a facile distinction between "letters" and "life" on the one hand and "poetry" and "literature" on the other by radically challenging the concept of fixed generic boundaries. Such boundaries, however, were constantly reinforced by nineteenth-century epistolary manuals. Based on an essentialist concept of genres, these handbooks define personal letters as "social duty" and as sites for the emotional outpourings of the *woman* writer's heart, while explicitly distinguishing them from poetry and other male-dominated *literary* modes of expression. Yet it is exactly against this notion of the personal letter as "women's writing" that Dickinson's correspondence constitutes a powerful statement. In both form and function, Dickinson's manuscript letters constantly blur the distinction and hence interrogate the differentiation between poetic and epistolary discourses, thus challenging a generic marginalization of her letters as "nonliterary" or "confessional" and a consequent limitation of critical interest to their autobiographical value.

At the same time, however, Dickinson's generic borderblur has, until very recently, been obscured by almost all nineteenth- and twentieth-century print editions of her writings, an aspect I examine more fully in chapter 2, "Editing Dickinson's Correspondence, 1894–1999." Contrary to manuscript evidence, most editors of Dickinson's texts presuppose the existence of a clear demarcation between the writer's "poetry" and her "letters." Employing Jerome McGann's notion of editing as sociohistorical reconstruction, I argue in chapter 2 that an editorial insistence on what Celeste Schenck has called "idealized generic . . . purity" (285) has contributed to a perpetuation of nineteenth-century essentialist connotations of epistolary writing. Ultimately, such an editorial separation of genres constitutes a prescriptive, predominantly patriarchal gesture that forms the basis for a hierarchical classificatory system in which specific genres such as personal letters—traditionally favored by women—can be denigrated. The generic transgressions at work in Dickinson's correspondence, on the other hand, encourage a revised understanding of the function and importance of these texts within Dickinson's project of liberating women's writing from patriarchal traditions, and will prepare the way for an exploration of her letters as fictional sites for enacting multiple, discursively constructed subject positions.

In chapters 3 and 4, I analyze such constructions of epistolary polyvocality on the level of individual correspondences, that is, letters, poems, and letter-poems mailed to specific recipients. Here I examine how Dickinson's epistolary personae function as textual performances, with different strategies of self-fashioning functionalized in different correspondences to different effects, while at the same time illustrate Denis Donogue's statement that "the question of voice is always a question of authority" (qtd. in Crumbley, *Inflections* 88). Chapter 3, "The 'Female' World of Love and Duty," concentrates on letters written to five of Dickinson's closest female friends. Drawing on both Felicity A. Nussbaum's and Betty Bergland's discussions of the construction of identity as dependent on and governed by prevailing sociocultural discursive practices, I investigate Dickinson's critique of some of the discursive models that inform her epistolary self-presentations. Nineteenth-century friendships among women frequently depended on a shared acceptance of socially sanctioned yet narrowly circumscribed female subject positions modeled on the "ideology of true womanhood," and Dickinson's earliest letters chronicle her negotiation of and gradual resistance to these roles. It is this resistance that finally initiates a breakdown of her early friendships and in turn induces Dickinson to transform her epistolary self-presentations to Elizabeth Holland and Sue Gilbert into carefully controlled acts of self-fashioning. In order to maintain her friendship with these women despite ideological differences, Dickinson rewrites these relationships discursively, ascribing fictionalized, often hyperbolically stylized roles to both herself and her respective addressees (inhabiting the role of perpetual "child-woman" in her letters to Holland while turning Holland into her "surrogate mother," for example; and mapping her relationship with Sue onto the discourse of courtly love). Ultimately, it is in and through these rewritings that Dickinson not only maintains but also orchestrates and controls these friendships, in the process transgressing the narrow strictures imposed on women by the "ideology of true womanhood."

In her correspondences with female friends, Dickinson's letters and poems for the most part complement each other in order to blur the boundaries between "fact" and "fiction," but her epistolary and poetic voices in her correspondences with male friends more frequently initiate intergeneric dialogic exchanges to negotiate gendered power relations. Thus, in chapter 4, "The 'Male' World of Power and Poetry," I analyze the writer's critique of gender inscriptions inherent in different configurations of power and dominance. Most of Dickinson's adopted personae in her letters to male friends tend to exhibit a high degree of ambivalence toward gendered forms of status, power, and authority by combining claims to superior (literary) authority with gestures of self-disempowerment, a strategy that frequently results in a dialogic juxtaposition of voices of dominance and submission, of conflict and conformity. Dickinson's ambivalent poses range from highly subtle forms of self-affirmation almost completely overpowered by self-abnegation (Master), to rebellious stances undercut by apologetic humor (Austin), to a careful balance between the self-confident voice of the poet and the submissive voice of the pupil (Higginson). It is ultimately this high degree of dialogicity and double-voicedness that specifically characterizes her letters to male correspondents. However, rather than remaining unmediated revelations of the writer's soul, all of Dickinson's polyvocal letters thus become performative acts that, on a discursive level, allow the writer to destabilize cultural gender norms and regulate ensuing power relations. Rather than expressing a stable gendered identity, Dickinson presents us with a proliferation of alternative voice configurations, a strategy that might be explained by what Crumbley has called her "fear of entrapment by social and linguistic conventions" ("Art" 79).

Yet Dickinson's textual role-playing and polyvocality goes beyond an *adoption* of specific (fictional, literary, biblical, discursive) identities in order to negotiate individual relationships in specific correspondences; she also simultaneously critiques the gender-inflected inscriptions in the very voices she appropriates. The ways in which Dickinson's modification and assimilation of "borrowed" voices (which enter her letters primarily in the form of direct quotations) ultimately challenges traditional notions of literary authority, the status of patriarchal discourses, and conventional processes of (literary) authorization are the focus of chapter 5, "Manipulating Multiple Voices." Drawing on Kristeva's definition of intertextuality and Bakhtin's concept of the dialogic and monologic, I examine how strategies of dialogization and monologization complement each other in Dickinson's methods of integrating, appropriating, and assimilating a proliferation of discursive voices (including direct quotations, newspaper clippings, and nonverbal gestures such as dried flowers) into her letters. On the one hand, Dickinson's correspondence thus becomes a "tissue of quotations," "a multi-dimensional space in which a variety of writings, none of them original, blend and clash" and interact in dialogic polyvocality (Barthes, "Death" 146). This results in dialogues between a wide range of socioculturally divergent texts, which contribute to a dismantling of the hierarchy between published and unpublished writings, and between "high" canonized literature and "popular" women's texts. Yet, on the other hand, "lyric" focal voices also exert monologic control over these intertextual gestures by subtly "editing" the wording of specific quotations, in particular those from traditionally patriarchal discourses. Analyzing Dickinson's citations from Higginson's writings, the Bible, and Shakespeare's plays, I explore how this functional integration and modification of other voices enables Dickinson to critique some of their specific historical and gendered resonances while appropriating them for her own purposes.

Ultimately, it is my contention that an analysis of all these textual gestures—the redrawing of generic boundaries, the construction of multiple subject positions, and the monologizing control of intertextual dialogicity—significantly contributes to a revised understanding of Dickinson's correspondence. Yet more than merely illuminating Dickinson's "poems" by restoring them to their epistolary context, such a contextual approach to all her "published" writings also highlights the extent to which Dickinson's "poems" and "letters" become complementary modes of writing that participate in a radically experimental, gendered critique of specific discursive formations. This, in turn, contributes to our overall understanding of the profoundly innovative quality of Dickinson's writings, or, in Salska's words: "Reading the poems in the context of her correspondence makes us see Dickinson's need for innovative freedom as much more radical" ("Dickinson's Letters" 178).

La lettre, l'épître, qui n'est pas un genre
mais tous les genres, la littérature même
[The letter, the epistle, which is not
a genre but all genres, literature itself].
—JACQUES DERRIDA

When is a letter a poem?
When is a poem a letter?
—MARTA WERNER

1

The Context of Nineteenth-Century Epistolary Conventions

AN UPPER-MIDDLE-CLASS WOMAN living in nineteenth-century New England, Emily Dickinson was steeped in a dynamic epistolary culture. The large number of etiquette books and, in particular, letter-writing manuals appearing with ever greater frequency throughout the century testify to this fact. Thomas E. Hill, himself the author of the successful *Handbook of Etiquette*, which includes a substantial section on letter writing, has pointed out that toward the end of the century an average of five new titles in adult etiquette appeared each year ("Preface" n.p.). And it was these manuals, I maintain, that played a central role in circumscribing the status and function of women's letters within the traditional generic canon, especially in relation to poetic and other literary forms of composition.

Outside the context of nineteenth-century letter-writing handbooks, epistolary prose had frequently been endowed with literary status. Samuel

Phillips Newman's *Practical System of Rhetoric*, for example, emphasizes the close affinity between "poetry" and "epistolary prose": "The word literature is most frequently used in distinction from science. In this sense, it refers to certain classes of writing. Such are Poetry and Fictitious Prose, Historical, Epistolary and Essay writing" (65).[1] Whereas Newman thus suggests how epistolary prose, alongside poetry, may be classified as a branch of "literature," letter-writing manuals, on the other hand, begin to insist on a hierarchically inflected differentiation between epistolary and poetic discourse in general, and between female "personal" and male "literary" letters in particular. Both strategies ultimately contribute to relegating women's correspondences to the realm of "occasional," socially useful, "nonliterary" activities.[2]

John Bennett's *Letters to a Young Lady*,[3] for example, introduces the topic of poetry writing as an aspect of epistolary etiquette, devoting an entire section to circumscribing the female letter writer's proper treatment of poetry: "Poetry I do not wish you to cultivate, further than to possess a relish for its beauties. . . . Besides, a passion for poetry is dangerous to a woman. It heightens her natural sensibility to an extravagant degree, and frequently inspires such a romantic turn of mind, as is utterly inconsistent with the solid duties and proprieties of life" (123). Because of these dangers, Bennett claims, a woman's involvement with poetry should be restricted to a passive appreciation of the great canonical masters: "Though I do not wish you to become a poet, it is however necessary, that you should not be wholly unacquainted with the writings of many inimitable bards. They will certainly refine your taste, and spread a very elegant repast for your private amusement" (125).

With poetry thus declared off-limits, epistolary prose becomes the woman's proper sphere of writing. According to the *Young Lady's Own Book*, for example, it is the only genre in which she is allowed to take an active part: "Various are the occasions on which ladies are called upon to exercise their skill in the art of epistolary composition: this, generally speaking, is the only style of writing of which they will find it inconvenient to be ignorant. Few persons are ever obliged to produce a treatise, or a poem; but there is scarcely any one who is not occasionally compelled, by the circumstances of life, to write a letter" (105–106). Apart from its social use value, it is also the close relation between a woman's emotional "nature" and the prescribed characteristics of the epistolary genre, as Henry T. Tuckerman suggests in 1851, which explains women's innate aptitude for this particular genre: "The superiority of women in the epistolary art has often been noticed, and may be readily accounted for. No form of literary development is so natural, so directly the offspring of feeling and observation, and so akin to and associated with the interests and diversions of home" (104). Frequently, this "natural," emotional style of writing is further differentiated from more formalized—and, by implication, more sophisticated—types of composition:

> To write *letters* is a very desirable excellence in a woman. . . . It is an office, particularly suited to the liveliness of your fancy, and the sensibility of your heart; and your sex in general much excels our own, in the *ease* and graces of, epistolary correspondence. Not cramped with the shackles and formality of rules, their thoughts are expressed *spontaneously*, as they flow, and become, more immediately, (what a letter always should be) a lively, amusing, written conversation. A man attends to the niceties of grammar, or well turned periods; a woman gives us the effusions of her soul. (Bennett 102, 103)

Such prescriptive notions of the ideal epistolary style as "emotional" and "effusive" eventually result in a classification of letter writing as an almost "mindless" activity. In praise of an unnamed female letter writer, for example, Bennett comments: "Imagery, taste, pathos, spirit, fire, and ease . . . should be the most *conspicuous* feature[s] in the productions of her pen. They came not from the *head;* it was the *heart* which wrote them.[4] They were not faultless, but they were impassioned. They had defects, but they had likewise beauties, which must have warmed the coldest critic that ever existed. They were interesting to an high degree, and left this conviction strongly on my mind, that we often labour only to be dull, and, in the search of distant ornaments, chill the natural fervours of the soul" (103).[5] The same mind-heart dichotomy was adopted by Thomas Wentworth Higginson in his "Women's Letters." Joseph G. Cogswell is quoted approvingly: "To preserve the true spirit of friendly correspondence, I conceive, requires more exercise of the affections of the heart than of the powers of the mind, and it is for this reason that ladies commonly excel us in epistolary writing" (qtd. in Higginson, "Women's Letters" 110–111). And, somewhat patronizingly, Higginson continues: "We may almost say that every woman writes better letters than we should expect of her; that a third-rate woman writes better than any but a first-rate man. Whence this difference?" ("Women's Letters" 111). For Higginson, one explanation is the different demands that letters, on the one hand, and conceptually more complex and methodical types of composition, on the other, place on the writer: "Now details are what we need in a letter; for philosophy and general grasp we go to a book. Method, order, combination, are quite unimportant in a letter; . . . the logic and the deductions may come in separate packages" ("Women's Letters" 112).

Yet, as the title of Higginson's essay already suggests, this distinction is carefully reserved for *women's* letters. Letters written by men are systematically differentiated from "artless," daily, occasional missives. Whereas women seem naturally predisposed to write good "emotional" letters, men are believed to excel in the *art* of letter writing. In her discussion of women's letters in seventeenth-century France, Katharine Ann Jensen refers to La Bruyère as an early example of such generic double standards:

> La Bruyère infers that while women introduced emotion into letter writing and surpassed men in facility of emotional expression, men with "long labor" and "painful searching" could approximate this feminine expressiveness. More than that, if women, writing spontaneously through emotion, also wrote incorrectly, then however much "we" may praise women's epistolary gift, this gift did not win women any literary prize. Conversely, if men, after much thought and work, were able to imitate women's letters, these imitations from the standpoint of literary correctness could only be an improvement on women's texts. The implications, then, in La Bruyère's theories are that femininity produces imperfect epistolary models of a superior emotional quality, models upon which masculine stylistic travail can improve. Men, then, can turn women's social art into literature, if they choose. (*Writing* 30)

This differentiation between women's letters as social art and men's letters as literature is also exemplified, according to Jensen, in François des Rues's collection of model correspondences. Des Rues presents letters written by a man to a woman as modeled on Petrarchan (i.e., "literary") conventions, while those written by a woman to a man are without literary models (i.e., "authentic") (*Writing* 34). And Abbé Cotin, in his *Galant Works in Prose and in Verse* (1665), "situates women's letter writing in the social domain while his own is carefully shown to extend to the literary realm" (Jensen, *Writing* 30). In this way, Jensen concludes, collections of female letters edited by men have a long tradition of positioning these texts either in the nonliterary social domain or in a private (erotic) space: "Women's purported epistolary excellence principally concerned the practice of the genre as a social art while men, however less predisposed toward the genre, exercised it socially *and* literarily" (*Writing* 28).

This effort on the part of letter-writing guides and etiquette books to define epistolary discourse against poetic (and other, rhetorically more sophisticated or "literary") discourses on the one hand, and to relegate *women's* letters to the social realm on the other, contributes to a lack of appreciation for the artistic quality in female epistolary composition, thus placing it outside the confines of the male-dominated literary canon. As Jensen summarizes: "By theorizing about woman's natural talent for letter writing, male epistolary theorists and editors sought to limit women's writing to the letter genre and to marginalize it as nonliterary" (*Writing* 10). Consequently, "by limiting women's epistolary expertise to its social practice[,] . . . men succeeded in reclaiming literature as an exclusively male province" (*Writing* 5). The continuation of this nonliterary, predominantly social and utilitarian concept of women's letters into the nineteenth century has been examined by Stephanie Tingley, who outlines the alignment of the nineteenth-century female letter writer with the role of nurturer: "Since letter writing provided one way for a Victorian woman to follow her culture's dictates to subordinate her own needs to the needs of others, it became one of a myriad of household tasks and responsibilities regularly assigned to the female realm because it was useful, private, and an essential means by which women could fulfill their duty to nurture relationships and strengthen familial bonds" ("'Letter'" 2). Thus, when the purpose of the personal letter was restricted to its sociocultural use value (regarding it as a form of nurturing), nineteenth-century letters written by women were, by definition, also relegated to a position outside the *literary* canon.

It is against this classification of women's letters as being emotional, nonliterary, and endowed with a primarily social, utilitarian function, as well as against the concomitant strict separation between poetic and epistolary discourses, I argue, that Dickinson's correspondence constitutes a powerful statement. Analogous to Jonathan Monroe's claim that "to choose to write in or on a particular genre is also to choose a particular mode of social, not just narrowly aesthetic intervention" (22), Dickinson's correspondence intervenes at the point of generic gender inscriptions and generic hierarchies. She continuously challenges the dichotomy between (superior) poetic and (inferior) epistolary discourses that had been reinforced by nineteenth-century letter-writing manuals through two complementary strategies: (a) she redefines her "letters" as "literature," and (b) she turns her "poems" into artistic "letters."

LETTERS AS LITERATURE

Even in her earliest epistolary exchanges with schoolmates, Dickinson wants her letters to be different and "uncommon": her long delay in answering Abiah Root's note, for example, is explained with the words, "I thought as all the other girls wrote you, my letter if I wrote one, would seem no smarter than any body else, and you know how I hate to be common" (L5). At first, this desire to distinguish her letters from those of other people still takes place within the confines of established epistolary conventions: "You know it is customary for the first page [of a letter] to be occupied with apologies," Dickinson observes, "& I must not depart from the beaten track, for one of my own imagining" (L23). Very soon, however, Dickinson does "depart from the beaten track" by radically redefining the form and function of letter writing itself. One step in this process is to remove the activity of letter writing from a woman's sphere of responsibilities and hence from the level of daily mundane activities to which it had been relegated by contemporaneous letter-writing manuals. This observation has been made by Stephanie Tingley, who points out that Dickinson "redefined letter-writing as a pleasure rather than a dreaded duty or household chore" ("'Letter'" 12). In fact, in L30, Dickinson describes how letter writing *interferes* with her other household duties: "and my two hands but *two*—not four, or five as they ought to be—and so *many* wants—and me so *very* handy—and my time of so *little* account—and my writing so *very* needless—and really I came to the conclusion that I should be a villain unparralleled if I took but an inch of time for so unholy a purpose as writing a friendly letter" (L30). Focusing on the expression "unholy," Tingley comments on this letter: "Dickinson alludes to her Puritan forbears' suspicion of creative writing, which they believed was 'evil' because it was designed to entertain rather than instruct. . . . By describing her letters as 'evil' therefore, Dickinson suggests that she considers her letters to be places where she can exercise her creativity and powers of invention, as a means of escape from the drudgery of huswifery" ("'Letter'" 13). As a means of escape from women's household chores, letters for Dickinson thus approach the realm of creative fiction, that is, literature.

In addition, this redefinition of letter writing as an "unholy," "creative" activity rather than a household duty also manifests itself in the fact that, for Dickinson, epistolary exchanges become a self-indulgent (as opposed to a primarily socially useful), and hence an almost illicit act that has to be concealed from other family members: "I have written *those* at night—when the rest of the world were asleep—when only God came between us—and no one else might hear. No need of shutting the door—nor of whispering timidly—nor of fearing the ear of listeners—for night held them fast in his arms that they could not interfere" (L30).[6] And the "sinful" nature of Dickinson's epistolary activities becomes even more pronounced when she substitutes letter writing (pleasure) for church attendance (duty): "I am at home from meeting on account of the storm and my *slender constitution,* which I assured the folks, would not permit my accompanying them today. It is Communion Sunday, and they will stay a good while—what a nice time pussy and I have to enjoy ourselves" (L54). Although Dickinson rarely dates her letters, her notes and letters marked "Sabbath eve" or "Sunday morn" constitute a disproportionately large group, thus indicating that (a) she habitually wrote her letters while the rest of her family attended church, and (b) that she wanted the recipients of her letters to be aware of this act of transgression.

A second revisionist strategy concerns the use of self-consciously introduced rhetorical tropes and figures, especially in her early letters. One central way in which epistolary manuals defined the generic boundary between personal letters and literary texts was by insisting that letters should be "natural," "emotional" outpourings of the female writer's heart, and therefore completely "artless." As Thomas E. Hill explains: "The writer has only to study perfect naturalness of expression, to write a letter well" (*Horse* 54). The best way to achieve this "naturalness" is, as Newman points out, an avoidance of rhetoricity: "Letters of friendly intercourse should be written in an easy, artless style. Sprightliness of thought and vivacity of expression, are appropriate to this class of writings; but the more formal ornaments of style should be rarely introduced" (198). H. W. Bilworth concurs: "When you write to a friend, your letter should be a true picture of your heart; the style loose and irregular; the thoughts themselves should appear naked, and not dressed in the borrowed robes of rhetoric" ("Introduction" n.p.).[7]

This insistence on the avoidance of rhetorical elements in epistolary discourse is based on the assumption that a letter should stylistically approximate spoken conversation: "A letter is but talk on paper" (Hill, *Horse* 54). The gendered implications underlying this demand for "conversational artlessness" are made explicit in Tuckerman's explanation: "The advantage of the letter as an exponent of a woman's nature is, that it is, after all, only written conversation, the artless play of her mind, the candid utterance of her sentiment" (105). The *Young Lady's Own Book* gives a more elaborate description: "A correspondence between two persons, is simply a conversation reduced to writing. . . . We should write to an absent person as we would speak to the same party if present. . . . But it will, perhaps, be observed by some that 'there is such a difference between talking and writing':—truly so; the great difference is, that in this, the pen,—in that, the tongue,—is the agent of expression. Whatever we should say to a person present, we may write if absent" (107; 112).[8] Yet Dickinson makes it quite clear that, for her, there is a vast difference between the written word in a letter and the spoken word in conversation: "A Pen has so many inflections and a Voice but one" (L470).

Preferring the "many inflections" to the "one," Dickinson regards her letters as carefully designed rhetorical constructs rather than "spoken conversation." This particularly manifests itself in her habit of drafting even short notes. An 1886 letter to Susan Gilbert, for example, reads in its entirety, "Thank you, dear Sue—for every solace—" (L1030). A draft fragment for this letter is quoted by Johnson (HCL L24) as: "Dear Sue, / Thank y[ ]." Far from being "spontaneous outpourings of the heart," her letters thus become meticulously revised products. In this way, they violate the advice of letter-writing manuals such as Hall's, which insists that "copying is to be deprecated, as it is apt to make letters stiff and formal" (*Social Customs* 241).[9] In addition, if Dickinson's style does become "loose" and "irregular" at times (especially in her early letters), she inevitably apologizes for this—in her opinion—inappropriate carelessness. In an 1852 letter to her brother, Austin, she explains: "I have got a great deal to say, and I fancy I am saying it in rather a headlong way, but if you can read it, you will know what it means" (L72). At the same time, she admires her brother's careful organization of his letter: "Should think you must have some *discipline* in order to write so clearly amidst so much confusion" (L72). A similar apology appears approximately two years later: "I'm so tired now, that I write just as it happens, so you must'nt expect any style" (L165).[10] In these early letters, Dickinson's concept of "style" refers primarily to a combination of careful composition, elaborate rhetoricity, and extravagant verbal play, all of which stand in marked contrast to the widespread demand for a woman's letter's "natural" tone and "artlessness."

Generally speaking, Dickinson's early letters are the most rhetorically conscious ones, often featuring explicit comments on her stylistic strategies or her methods of integrating rhetorical tropes into her prose. It is in these letters that the blurring of generic boundaries between poetic and epistolary discourses is particularly evident; her later letters more fully transform this reattribution of generic properties into an intergeneric dialogic exchange whose artistic quality lies in Dickinson's very attempt to make it sound artless. An explanation for such a development is provided by Bakhtin: "The better our command of genres, the more freely we employ them, the more fully and clearly we reveal our own individuality in them . . . the more flexibly and precisely we reflect the unrepeatable situation of communication" (*Speech Genres* 80).

Some of the rhetorical tropes used in Dickinson's early correspondences are considered particularly unsuitable for an epistolary context. Her own handbook, Newman's *Principles of Rhetoric*, discourages the use of metaphors in letters (86). It is specifically this trope, however, that Dickinson emphasizes in an 1850 letter to George Gould. Having suggested that "I am Judith the heroine of the Apocrypha, and you the orator of Ephesus," Dickinson then draws attention to her strategy by explaining: "That's what they call a metaphor in our country. Don't be afraid of it, sir, it won't bite" (L34). By thus explicitly throwing into relief her use of figurative language, Dickinson highlights her letter's transgression of the generic confines of epistolary discourse.

In addition to metaphors, however, Dickinson's most frequently used rhetorical trope is synecdoche. A good example is the "heart": "I hope the hearts in Springfield are not so heavy as they were—God bless the hearts in Springfield!" (L205).[11] Such rhetorical tropes are frequently combined with alliteration, anaphora, internal rhyme, assonance, consonance, as well as passages cast in iambic rhythm. An 1851 valentine to Elbridge G. Bowdoin, for example, contains assonances ("weave," "evening") and internal full rhymes ("I," "mine," "twined," "while"; "swift," "gift"; "Life," "wife"): "*I* weave for the Lamp of *Evening*— | but fairer colors than *mine* are twined | while stars are shining. | *I* know of a shuttle swift—I know | of a fairy gift—mat for the 'Lamp | of *Life*'—the little Bachelor's wife" (Dickinson ms. 795 and ms. Tr74, Amherst; L41). In L832, the use of internal rhymes ("sea," "be," "lovingly," "Emily") is combined with anaphora ("how") and incremental repetition ("how slow," "how slow," "how late"): "How slow the | Wind—how slow | the Sea—how | late their Feathers | be! | Lovingly, | Emily" (Dickinson ms. 46, Amherst). And L911 displays an intricate interweaving of internal rhymes ("Fang," "Pang"), assonances ("Dear," "Peace"), and alliteration ("Fang," "Flowers"; "Pang," "Past," "Peace"): "Choose Flowers that have no Fang, Dear—Pang is the Past of Peace."[12]

The most striking and pervasive poetic feature Dickinson inserts into her "letters," however, is iambic rhythm.[13] Though the extent of rhythmical prose in the writer's correspondence is much more widespread than Lambert's list suggests, I concentrate here on drawing examples from one subcategory of letters that Lambert fails to mention, but which contains a disproportionately large number of iambic passages: Dickinson's notes of condolence.[14] In his *English Composition and Rhetoric*, Bain advances an explanation for this quite common phenomenon: "In strong excitement, we are unable to adapt ourselves to the varying exigencies of a prose rhythm, and accordingly feel the simplicity of a poetic measure to be a great relief. The greater the excitement, the more simple usually is the metrical scheme" (273). Bain continues to define the precise effect of measured language on the writer: "In the effusion of intense feeling, the regularity of metre may act as a controlling or moderating power. The ebullition of excitement is made calmer and more continuous by the adoption of a measured step; so that, when the subject is of an impassioned nature, the proper accompaniment is verse" (273). That Dickinson shared Bain's understanding of the controlling effect of meter on the writer/reader becomes explicit in a letter to Higginson, in which she explains: "I felt a palsy, here—the Verses just relieve—" (L265).

In her metrical notes of condolence, Dickinson frequently falls into a combination of iambic trimeters and tetrameters, as in L1020: "October is a | mighty Month, | for in it Little | Gilbert died. | . . . Quite used to | his Commandment, | his little Aunt | obeyed, and still | two years and | many Days, and | he does not re- | turn. | Where makes | my Lark his Nest?" (Dickinson ms. 52, Amherst; L1020).[15] L868 (to Sue Gilbert, upon her son Gilbert's death), more specifically, alternates between catalectic iambic tetrameters and trimeters, thus falling into a variant of Dickinson's common hymn measure: "He knew no | niggard moment— | His Life was | full of Boon— | The Playthings of | the Dervish were | not so wild | as his— | No crescent was | this Creature— | He traveled from | the Full— | . . . I see him in | the Star, and | meet his sweet | velocity in every | thing that flies— | His Life was | like the Bugle, | which winds | itself away, | his Elegy an | echo—his Requiem | ecstasy—" (Houghton MS Am 1118.5 [B79]). An example of a regular hymn measure (alternating iambic tetrameters and trimeters) is the following letter to Samuel Bowles: "We voted | to remember you— | so long as both should | live—including Immortality. | To count you as | ourselves—except sometimes | more tenderly—as now— | when you are ill— | and we—the haler | of the two—and so | I bring the Bond—we | sign so many times— | for you to read, when | Chaos comes—or Treason— | or Decay—still witnessing | for Morning" (Dickinson ms. 677, Amherst; L229).[16]

Such instances of iambic prose constitute a key element in Dickinson's transgression of generic boundaries, as they allow her, in Bakhtin's terms, to move her letters—a genre traditionally associated with (dialogic) prose—closer to the pole of (monologic) poetry. According to Bakhtin, it is meter that strengthens the "hermetic unity" of a text—and thus its lyric quality—by "destroying all traces of social heteroglossia" that frequently characterize prose (*Dialogic Imagination* 298). In this way, Dickinson's letters thus partake of both monologic and dialogic generic properties.[17]

Simultaneously, the presence of rhythm within a prose context also "destroys" traditional notions of generic purity. For Edmund Stedman, who draws a distinction between "poetical prose and the prose of a poet" (58) and maintains that "a real poet usually writes good prose, and rarely rhythmical prose" (57), such a transgression of conventional generic boundaries constitutes a form of contamination: "As a drop of prosaic feeling is said to precipitate a whole poem, so a drop of sentimental rhythm will bring a limpid tale or essay to cloudy effervescence" (59). It is precisely the impossibility of "classifying" rhythmical prose generically that Stedman objects to most: "These illuminati [writers of rhythmical prose] leave firm ground, but do they rise to the upper air? There is something eerie and unsubstantial about them as they flit in a moonlit limbo between earth and sky" (58). Though rhythmical prose may temporarily be successful, Stedman admits ("it may catch the vulgar ear" [57]), "true" and "permanent" art, on the other hand, manifests itself in maintaining clearly definable generic boundaries: "See how definite the line between the prose and the verse of Milton, Goethe, Landor, Coleridge, Byron. . . . There is a class of writers, of much account in their day, whose native or purposed confusion between rhythmical and true prose attracts by its glamour, and whom their own generation, at least, can ill spare. . . . But it is to be noted that these after a time fall into distrust, as if the lasting element of true art had somehow escaped them" (58).

Dickinson's strategy of including poetic features in her letters—thus partly removing them from the realm of spontaneous, artless correspondence by increasing their "poetic" quality—is complemented by her omission or redefinition of conventional epistolary features in her letters, thus reducing their degree of "epistolarity." One formal component of epistolary discourse whose function Dickinson frequently redefines is the letter-writer's signature. *Aids to Epistolary Correspondence* stresses the importance of the signature, recommending that "in addressing any but intimate friends the name should be signed *in full* at the close of the letter" (22). In the context of a business letter, C. A. Fleming even suggests: "An important part of a letter is the signature, a small part it may appear, but one that should have more care bestowed on it than any other of a business letter" (52). Although Dickinson sometimes omits her signature altogether, or encloses it on a separate sheet of paper (L260), her most innovative strategy, from a generically subversive perspective, is to endow this epistolary feature with a "poetic" function. L208, for example, which consists of J222/Fr49 ("When Katie walks"), is a case in point. In its manuscript form, the last six lines of the letter-poem produce a series of internal assonances and end rhymes, of which the signature constitutes an integral part: "When Katie kneels, their loving | hands still clasp her | pious knee—Ah! Katie! | Smile at Fortune, with *two* | so *knit to thee*! Emilie" (Houghton bMS Am 1118.95, box 12). A similar example can be found in L745: the letter concludes with J1546/Fr1568 ("Sweet Pirate of the Heart"), which includes the signature in its rhyming pattern: "Sweet Pirate | of the Heart, | Not Pirate | of the Sea, | What wrecketh | thee? | Some Spice's | Mutiny— | Some Attar's | perfidy? | Confide in | me— | Emily" (Dickinson ms. 42, Amherst). Again, the signature (originally an epistolary feature) becomes, phonetically speaking, an integral part of the poem, thus assuming a "poetic" function as well.

A second element that letter-writing handbooks emphasize as being essential for a formally correct letter is the identification of date and place of writing. James D. McCabe, for example, insists that "the name of the place from which the letter is written and the date should always be carefully written at the head of the sheet" (239).[18] Hall is even more specific: "The address and date should always be put either at the beginning or at the end of a letter. For notes, the latter is usually preferred. It is better, in dating, to use both the day of the week and the day of the month, though for a note the day of the week is sufficient. In a letter, the date of the year is given; in a note, it is not" (*Social Customs* 233).[19]

Dickinson's earliest letters (written prior to the 1850s) are most likely to conform to these requests for specifying both time and place of writing. L2, for example, is fully dated "Amherst May 1, 1842." In agreement with several epistolary manuals, some of Dickinson's letters to her parents and close friends contain the time and day of the week only ("Thursday noon" [L16 to her brother, Austin]; "Saturday. *P.M.*" [L19 to Austin]; "Friday morning" [L93 to Susan Gilbert]). Occasionally, Dickinson metonymically redefines the place in terms of its specific meaning for her, substituting the school she was attending for the town itself ("Mt Holyoke. Seminary. Nov[r] 6. 1847" [L18]). Toward the end of the 1850s, however, Dickinson becomes increasingly more creative in her modification of temporal and spatial indicators, frequently omitting one or the other (her letters to Higginson, for example, are often only dated "Amherst") or both.

Although throughout her correspondence Dickinson shows differing degrees of accuracy in indicating time and place of writing (ranging from exact specification to complete omission of any date or place coordinates), she often also redefines this epistolary feature by assigning it a metaphorical function. L490, for example, dated "Saturday Night" and addressed to her close friend Elizabeth Holland, seems—on the surface—to conform to the rules set out in letter-writing manuals. On closer examination of the manuscript, however, the dateline appears centered on the first line rather than in the top right margin, thus suggesting the alternative interpretation that it forms part of (possibly the title of) the following letter. The letter itself contains the message "Austin will come tomorrow," followed by the poem " 'Tomorrow'—whose location | The Wise deceives" (J1367/Fr1417). The ambiguous status of this date marker, as possibly *both* a concrete reference to the time of writing (a particular Saturday in a specifiable month and year) *and* a self-referential (intratextual) title for Dickinson's message, is revealed by the two different ways it was interpreted. Elizabeth Holland, reading it as a conventional letter date, had expected Austin's visit the following day. When Holland inquires as to why he had not come, Dickinson replies: "Will my little Sister excuse me? . . . I am ashamed and sorry. I meant hypothetic tomorrows—though are there any other?" (L491). Holland's reaction illustrates that she interpreted "Saturday Night" in its traditional (epistolary) function of marking a fixed point of reference *outside* the letter (the time at which the letter was written), which would then allow her to interpret the purely referential indicator of time *within* the letter ("tomorrow") as having a specific ("fixed") meaning. Dickinson's reply, however, suggests that in combining "Saturday Night" and "tomorrow," she had played with the ensuing ambiguity by encouraging both a potentially referential interpretation as well as a purely metaphorical, intratextual (and thus self-referential) reading that undercuts any attempts to link these two temporal terms to a specific external point in time.

The fact that in her later letters Dickinson increasingly omits one or both references to date and place, is, I argue, an intensification of this effect, which contributes to a reduction of the referential potential of her letters and discourages readers from establishing specific links to a time or place outside of the text itself (that is, to the "life" of its writer)—in this way rendering "autobiographical" interpretations more difficult at best. That such links to extratextual referents are characteristic of and even necessary in epistolary discourse has been pointed out by Janet Gurkin Altman: "To write a letter is to map one's coordinates—temporal, spatial, emotional, intellectual—in order to tell someone else where one is located at a particular time and how far one has traveled since the last writing" (*Epistolarity* 119).[20] And Barbara Herrnstein Smith suggests that in a letter composed as a historical act, "some of its meanings [are] *historically determinate*, at least theoretically locatable in the historical universe" (140). By omitting or redefining the function of indicators of time and place, Dickinson thus reduces the "locatability" of her letters as well as their degree of epistolarity, while privileging the more "permanent" (because strictly intratextual) existence of her correspondence independent of its specific time and place of writing.[21] Simultaneously, she discourages her readers from interpreting the contents of a letter exclusively within the context of the particular life circumstances of its writer. In this way, many of Dickinson's letters signify in ways beyond—and in addition to—the purely autobiographical, occasional event that prompted their conception by foregrounding their nonreferential, non-occasional, non-event-specific aspects, thus effectively blurring the boundaries between "life" and "art." One way of challenging this boundary consists, as we have seen, in endowing letters with "literary" features, but Dickinson also practices the complementary strategy of functionalizing poems as letters.

POEMS AS (INTEGRAL PARTS OF) LETTERS

"When [Dickinson] started writing poems," Agnieszka Salska observes, "she treated them from the very beginning like letters" ("Dickinson's Letters" 173). This epistolary focus of her creative endeavors becomes even more pronounced when, after 1866, according to Salska, Dickinson's "poetic creativity clearly decreased . . . , and letters took over as the dominant form of her writing" (178). Yet even before the mid-1860s, Dickinson had begun to endow poems with epistolary features and functions. Within Dickinson's oeuvre, we can distinguish between two different kinds of poems-as-letters: poems that were enclosed with, incorporated into, or at times even fused with a specific "prose" letter, and poems without prose context that were designed and functionalized as letters. Yet although it has become critically commonplace to talk about the formal aspects of Dickinson's practice of "incorporating" or "enclosing" poems in or "fusing" them with their *prose* context,[22] many critics still tend to overlook their concomitant *epistolary* functionalization, as well as the *epistolary* elements in poems mailed without any accompanying prose contexts. In addition, poems included within letters are frequently still regarded as autonomous interpretive units and are hence discussed separately from their epistolary context. Yet Dickinson's manuscripts suggest that such a subdivision of her correspondences into their "prose" and "poetry" components is often arbitrary at best, and at worst tends to mutilate both parts by obscuring their intergeneric dialogic exchange. A contextual reading of Dickinson's "poems" sent in or as "letters," on the other hand, reveals their crucial epistolary function as well as their essential role and significance within their letter context.

In several instances, the enclosed or incorporated poem communicates part of the letter's message, in this way becoming an integral part of its "letter" context and assuming a function traditionally associated with epistolary rather than poetic discourse. This twofold discursive purpose is illuminated by juxtaposing Martha Nell Smith's and Lambert's comments: "When Dickinson sends a poem as a letter," Smith suggests, "what is most important is her transforming daily correspondence into a field for literature" (*Rowing* 106). But the reverse is also true: "Emily Dickinson saw poetry as a kind of communication designed to expand and make emotionally meaningful what may already have been said in prose" (Lambert 177). Sometimes Dickinson explicitly comments on this strategy of reassigning her letter's message to the incorporated or enclosed poem. In L250 to Samuel Bowles, for example, the poem "Title divine—is mine!" is followed by the lines, "Here's—what I had to 'tell you'— | You will tell no other?" And in L251, Dickinson explains, "Because I could not say it—I fixed it in the Verse." This message is followed by the poem "Through the strait pass of suffering" (J792/Fr187).

Any attempt to subdivide examples like the ones quoted above according to genre (to print the "poetry" and "prose" components of each letter in separate volumes, for example, or to discuss the poem without an awareness of its letter context) must necessarily result in a distortion of the "message." Without its complementary other half, both "prose" and "poem" remain incomplete.[23] Dickinson's letters and poems thus combine to form (intergeneric) dialogic utterances in a Bakhtinian sense: "an utterance is a link in the chain of speech communication, and it cannot be broken off from the preceding links that determine it both from within and from without, giving rise within it to unmediated responsive reactions and dialogic reverberations" (*Speech Genres* 94). To split a letter-cum-poem into its "prose" and "poetry" components would thus destroy the "dialogic reverberations" between the two genres and would constitute an interruption in the chain of speech communication. By distributing the epistolary application of her missives across their poetic and epistolary components, Dickinson thus ensures their connection, in this way highlighting the extent to which both "poem" and "letter" contribute to forming epistolary discourse. This also distinguishes Dickinson from the Bakhtinian definition of a (lyric) poet: "The poet is a poet insofar as he accepts the idea of a unitary and singular language and a unitary, monologically sealed-off utterance" (*Dialogic Imagination* 297). Dickinson's letters-cum-poems, however, are neither unitary nor monologically sealed off; rather, they initiate a dynamic, intergeneric dialogue.

This dialogue of genres, this mutual complementarity of "poems" and their "letter" context, also manifests itself in the fact that several poems without identifiable (external) referent for their pronouns[24] nonetheless acquire one potential referent from their letter context: the poem "How soft his Prison is—" (J1334/Fr1352), for example, does not specify a referent for the pronoun "his." In the context of L432, addressed to Elizabeth Holland, however, it can be interpreted as referring to Dickinson's deceased father. Similarly, the discussion of "Marian Evans" in L814 to Thomas Niles invites an identification of the female pronoun in the incorporated J1562/Fr1602 ("Her Losses make our Gains ashamed—") with George Eliot.[25]

A compounded version of such a dialogic interaction between a poem and its prose context is created by mailing a letter to a particular recipient and enclosing a poem containing a second-person-singular pronoun, a strategy that invites the addressee of the letter to identify herself/himself with the unnamed addressee of the poem: L235 to Samuel Bowles, for example, ends with the poem "My River runs to thee—" (J162/Fr219). L258 asks Susan Gilbert to identify herself with the addressee of the incorporated poem "Your—Riches— | taught me—poverty!" (J299/Fr418) by introducing the poem with the letter-salutation "Dear Sue."[26] In these instances the poem is linked to its prose context while it simultaneously acquires a degree of addressee specificity that is otherwise more characteristic of epistolary discourse.

This addressee specificity is most pronounced when a poem is directly addressed to a particular recipient. Several verses sent to Susan Gilbert, for example, contain her name: "To own a Susan of my own" (J1401/Fr1436 in L531); "Is it true, dear Sue?" (J218/Fr189 in L232).[27] One poem is dedicated to Kate Scott Turner Anthon: "When Katie walks, this simple pair accompany her side" (J222/Fr49 in L208). Sometimes a poem that already exists in a different version is adapted to the specific recipient of the letter. "But Susan is a Stranger yet—" (J1400/Fr1433C in L530), for example, is a variant of "But nature is a Stranger yet," the fifth and sixth stanza of the poem "What mystery pervades a well." The line "I could not drink it, Sue" (J818/Fr816A in L287) modifies "I could not drink it, Sweet" (J818/Fr816B). And "Sister of Ophir—" (J1366/Fr1462B in L585) also exists as "Brother of Ophir" and "Brother of Ingots."

Another type of addressee-specific poems in dialogue with their prose contexts are poems containing an event-specific, "occasional" reference to circumstances in the life of their respective recipients: "Could *I*—then—shut the door—" (J220/Fr188), addressed to Susan Gilbert in L239, is one example. Johnson, among others, has linked this poem to an increased tension between Dickinson and Susan Gilbert after Ned Gilbert's birth. It is sometimes placed in the context of a manuscript letter at the Houghton Library, marked "private," in Susan Gilbert's handwriting ("I have intended to write you Emily today, but the quiet has not been mine—I send you this, lest I should seem to have turned away from a kiss— — . . .").[28]

Given such "occasional," event-specific or addressee-specific readings of some of Dickinson's poems, there arises a crucial problem, which Margaret Dickie has referred to as "reprivatization" of the writer's poetry, and which Cristanne Miller has forcefully highlighted by concluding that "if the poems and letters must be seen as inseparable elements of the same intergeneric form (letter-poem, poem-as-letter), then historical context—if not biography outright—becomes the primary point of entry into the 'poem' " ("Whose Dickinson?" 248). Yet a closer examination of these seemingly event- or addressee-specific poems reveals that their "external" referent frequently changes according to its intratextual and intergeneric context. Some of Dickinson's "addressee-specific" poems, for example, were sent to two or more (different) recipients, and some of the above-mentioned "occasional" (event-specific) poems refer to substantially different occasions. Elizabeth Holland, for example, who received the poem "To see her is a Picture—" (J1568/Fr1597C), introduced by the sentence, "May I present your Portrait to your Sons in Law?" (L802), read this poem as a tribute to her friendship: "To see her is a Picture— | To hear her is a Tune— | To know her an Intemperance | As innocent as June— | To know her not— Affliction— | To own her for a Friend | A warmth as near as if the Sun | Were shining in your Hand" (J1568; Fr1597C). Yet the "same" poem (Fr1597D) was mailed to an unknown recipient, and introduced with the following words: "Dear friend, | I dream | of your little | Girl three successive | Nights—I hope | nothing affronts | her— | To see her | is a Picture— | To hear her is | a Tune— | To know her, a | disparagement of | every other Boon— | To know her | not, Affliction— | To own her for | a Friend | A warmth as near | as if the Sun | Were shining in | your Hand—" (Dickinson ms. 767–767a, Amherst; L809).[29] Sometimes, it is not only the poem's referent but its entire meaning that changes with its context. J1462/Fr1481A ("We knew not that we were to live") is a case in point. It is incorporated into L575, a congratulatory note written upon hearing of Higginson's engagement to his second wife, Mary Potter Thatcher. In L591 to Maria Whitney, however, the same poem (Fr1481B) commemorates the death of their mutual friend Samuel Bowles.[30]

This curious phenomenon of including the "same" poem in different contexts has been noted by several critics, most of whom agree that such a double mailing reduces the effects of occasionality and addressee specificity for the respective poem.[31] Cristanne Miller, while conceding that "in the context of any one mailing, a poem seems to be occasional, referring to particular events and the private relationship between writer and reader," continues to argue that many poems enclosed or incorporated in Dickinson's letters "were not conceived solely in the light of a single friendship" (*Emily Dickinson* 13). Rather, the double mailing of any one poem makes it "deceptively personal" (14), but nonetheless independent of its recipient. Miller concludes that Dickinson's letters are thus "private messages universalized by a double release from private circumstance" (15).[32] In this way, even the seemingly most "personal" or "private" poem continually subverts or at least ambiguates a narrowly autobiographical reading. At the same time, even the most "nonreferential" or "multi-referential" poem is endowed with at least a certain degree of referentiality through its incorporation within a specific epistolary context addressed to a specific correspondent.

Contemporary epistolary theory frequently describes the letter as an amorphous, often ambiguous genre characterized by several seemingly contradictory polarities. Janet Gurkin Altman, for example, discusses the epistolary genre in terms of privacy/publicity; portrait/mask; presence/absence; bridge/barrier; transparency/opacity; continuity/discontinuity; coherence/fragmentation; monologue/dialogue—apparent dichotomies that, according to Altman, are continually dismantled by the letter writer him/herself (*Epistolarity* 186). Focusing specifically on the intricate link between the letter as both a public *and* a private document, Ruth Perry further explains how it thus enables women to be "involved with the world while keeping it at a respectable arm's length" (69).[33] This seemingly paradoxical tension between a letter's "private" and "public" aspects is heightened even more by the ambivalent genre of the letter-poem, as Hank Lazer has pointed out: "The letter-poet is strangely egoless. Even though he writes to one person, his words, his letter, enter into a universal circulation" (245). In this way, Dickinson's own letter-poems and poem-letters thus become what Salska has aptly described as "unique creations in which the formality of a poem and the informality of a personal communication reflect on each other.

Poems become connected to the immediacy of the moment while letters participate in the impersonality of the finished artifact" ("Dickinson's Letters" 178). In other words, poems-as-letters partake of the properties of epistolary discourse while letters-as-poems assume poetic/literary qualities. Incorporating or including poems in letters, mailing poems as letters, as well as reducing epistolary qualities while increasing poetic properties in letters thus provide Dickinson with an effective strategy for fusing the "private" aspect of personal(ized) correspondence with the "public" aspect of circulating her poems among a larger—albeit strictly defined and controlled—audience.

Martha Nell Smith was the first to draw attention to Dickinson's poems mailed in or as letters as a form of "publication."[34] Drawing on the poet's own terminological distinction (L265 and L316), Smith argues that Dickinson preferred to "publish" (disseminate) her poems in manuscript form rather than "print" them (subject them to a translation into the print medium) because of the textual control this enabled her to exert.[35] Dickinson's "chirographic 'publication,'" according to Smith, was thus "a consciously designed alternative mode of textual reproduction and distribution" (*Rowing* 1–2) that allowed her to sidestep "editorial interference" (12) and to avoid the strictures imposed upon her calligraphic experiments by the typographical medium. Yet I maintain that—in addition to such strictly textual aspects—an additional reason for Dickinson's choice to "publish" her poems in an epistolary format may also lie in the sociocultural and political connotations of these two genres in a nineteenth-century context. Going beyond Smith's predominantly textual arguments, Agnieszka Salska has already highlighted the crucial importance of Dickinson's letters in terms of preparing an audience for her poetry: "Apart from the ordinary communicative function, . . . the central practical aspect of her letter writing" was to "let it be known in the competent and influential literary circles outside her immediate family and friends that she was seriously a poet. . . . Letters prepared and created an audience for her poetry" ("Dickinson's Letters" 168). In other words, letters thus afforded Dickinson with a means to approach and reach contemporary "influential literary circles" (including Higginson and Helen Hunt Jackson) directly yet "privately," that is, without subjecting herself to the official ("public") publication process.

Yet, in my opinion, Dickinson's letters accomplish even more than just fulfilling this "preparatory," subsidiary function as "publication vehicles" for her poetry. To circulate "poetry" within a "letter" framework, as well as to ascribe literary features to seemingly private letters while having poems partake of epistolary discourse, additionally challenges traditional preconceptions about generic properties that had been established by prescriptive nineteenth-century epistolary manuals.[36] More specifically, these strategies subvert the genre-political implications advanced in these manuals, including their hierarchically inflected differentiation between "women's letters" as a primarily nonliterary, private, socially useful mode of writing, and "poetry" as a stylistically more complex, "literary" genre predominantly within the purview of male (published) authors. By redefining her "letters" as "literature," Dickinson is able to transfer the letter from the sphere of (womanly) duty to the realm of (male-dominated) literary production. At the same time, by endowing her "poems" with epistolary properties, she is able to legitimize a genre primarily reserved for men (poetry) through the use of the (for women) socially acceptable epistolary format. By blurring generic boundaries in this way, Dickinson manages to keep the "publication" of her "literary" works (i.e., the dissemination of her poems and letter-poems) within the socially sanctioned confines of letter writing by circulating them *within or as integral parts of* her epistolary manuscripts. Dickinson's generic acts of transgression hence allow her to overcome what Stanton has called the "conflict between private and public" (14). Not quite public published documents ("literature") in the conventional sense, the mailed-out letters and letter-poems (especially in the form of double mailings) nonetheless challenge the boundaries of exclusively private missives and become—quite literally—a private form of publication, or a literary form of correspondence.[37] In this way, Dickinson's letter-poems and poem-letters partake of the (largely male-dominated) realm of literary publication under the guise of a (for women) socially acceptable epistolary frame. Yet it is this very challenge to traditional notions of generic purity and concomitant established generic hierarchies that has frequently been occluded by print editions of Dickinson's texts, a problem examined more fully in the following chapter.

They shut me up in Prose.

—EMILY DICKINSON

2

Editing Dickinson's Correspondence, 1894–1999

INTERESTINGLY ENOUGH, Dickinson's transgressive play with generic boundaries had already been noted by many of her first readers. One of the most frequently echoed nineteenth-century responses to the prose style of Dickinson's letters was an admiration for their "poetic quality." Reviewers almost unanimously agreed upon the close stylistic affinity between her poems and her correspondence.[1] As Grace Musser suggests in the *San Francisco Sunday Call* (September 20, 1896): "If Emily Dickinson had never written any verse, these letters would have stamped her a poet" (Buckingham, *Reception* 477, item 526). Similarly, a reviewer in the *Philadelphia Evening Telegraph* (December 5, 1894) observes that Dickinson's letters "add to the poet's production already published a thesaurus of verse of rare quality and permanent worth" (Buckingham, *Reception* 380, item 452). And W. F. Whetcho (*Boston Daily Advertiser*, November 23, 1894) agrees: "They show that her prose—and these letters are all the prose she is known to have written—is as full of the essential elements of poetry as is her verse" (Buckingham, *Reception* 380, item 421). Frequently, commentators even identify a discrepancy between the inherent poetic quality of Dickinson's letters and their typographical representation on the page: "There are many passages in these letters that are printed as stanzas of poetry. . . . But we have also many passages that are printed as prose which are as much verse as any of the parts printed as such" (Buckingham, *Reception* 427, item 490). This view was also shared by the *Critic* (February 16, 1895), which suggests that "not a few" of Dickinson's letters "are poems in everything but the conventional typographical arrangement in verses" (Buckingham, *Reception* 416, item 484).

Even prior to the emergence of a revisionist interest in Dickinson's manuscripts during the 1980s and 1990s, a number of twentieth-century critics had come to similar conclusions. Richard B. Sewall summarizes his response to Dickinson's letters in his 1974 biography, *The Life of Emily Dickinson:* "And in her letters as in her verses, she was a poet all the time" (751). Similarly, Brita Lindberg-Seyersted observes that in her correspondence, Dickinson "glides in and out of prose and verse" (20). Paul Ferlazzo discusses L868 as containing "nearly a perfect blending of prose and poetry" (134). And Thomas H. Johnson suggests in his 1955 introduction to her *Poems:* "Early in the 1860's, when Emily Dickinson seems to have first gained assurance of her destiny as a poet, the letters both in style and rhythm begin to take on qualities that are so nearly the quality of her poems as on occasion to leave the reader in doubt where the letter leaves off and the poem begins" (xv).

Although many reviewers and critics thus highlighted the "poetic" quality of Dickinson's letters and hence the close affinity between these two genres in her oeuvre, this critical observation was not translated into editorial action for almost an entire century. All of Dickinson's editors prior to the 1990s (and some even today) have attempted to draw a strict generic demarcation between the writer's "prose" and her "poems," arranging them with typographical distinctions according to genre, or even in separate volumes, and often, in fact, culling lines of poetry from her letters.[2] The question then arises: despite readers' observations and manuscript evidence to the contrary, how can this editorial insistence on an unambiguously clear distinction—and a not infrequent complete separation—between Dickinson's poetry and her letters be explained?

Jerome McGann has pointed out that each editorial act constitutes a sociohistorical process of reconstruction and, as such, has to take into account the audience's as well as the author's historical context: "To edit a text is to be situated in a historical relation to the work's transmissions, but it is also to be placed in an immediate relation to contemporary cultural and conceptual goals" (qtd. in *Textual Condition* 47). Thus the editor's task can be defined as a process of mediation between an author's text and its projected audience: "An author's work possesses autonomy only when it remains an unheard melody. As soon as it begins its passage to publication it undergoes a series of interventions which some textual critics see as a process of contamination, but which may equally well be seen as a process of training the poem [or, in this case, the letter] for its appearances in the world" (McGann, *Critique* 52). Though this training process is influenced by the materiality of the texts themselves (*Textual Condition* 8), it is the sociohistorical context of an edition, McGann argues, that ultimately determines its shape: "The rule of choice [for the editor] does not lie hidden in the documents. It lies hidden in the exigencies of the present and the future" (*Critique* 104).

One example for a conflict between sociohistorically determined "exigencies of the present and the future" and the materiality of Dickinson's manuscript documents can be found in some of the above-discussed nineteenth-century genre conceptions and their concomitant marginalization of women's letters as "minor"—especially in relation to other "conventional" literary genres. Nan Johnson summarizes the shift in generic hierarchies that took place in the course of the nineteenth century: "Early nineteenth-century theorists such as Jamieson and E. A. Ansley, who were heavily indebted to a Blairian theoretical system, reiterated Blair's categorical definition of epistolary writing as one of the leading divisions of literature. . . . Several later theorists, such as Quackenbos, David J. Hill, and John G. R. McElroy, treat the letter as a minor rather than major form of composition" (212). This devaluation of epistolary writing, combined with a general nineteenth-century dislike of genre "contaminations," as highlighted by Stedman's comments above, may in part explain Todd's (and Higginson's) privileging of Dickinson's poetry by editing three volumes of *Poems* first. Moreover, it may also have influenced Todd's decision to follow typographical conventions by distinguishing between "poems" and their "letter" context in the two subsequent volumes of *Letters.* Such editorial strategies ultimately served to highlight the "major" form of composition against the backdrop of the merely "subsidiary" letter context. In this way, Todd was preparing a nineteenth-century audience for Dickinson's unusual stylistic techniques and simultaneously adjusting Dickinson's texts to the generic expectations of their nineteenth-century readers—although, as the reviews above suggest, she may have been underestimating these readers.

Many of the post-Todd editions of Dickinson's correspondence—most of which contained hitherto unpublished letters—continue to regard her "epistolary prose" as subordinate or ancillary to her "poetry." For these editors, the primary value of Dickinson's letters consists in their biographical content. In contrast to Todd's, Martha Dickinson Bianchi's main aim in producing *The Life and Letters of Emily Dickinson,* for example, was not so much textual accuracy as the construction of a biographical narrative based on a chronological reorganization of "family letters hitherto withheld [from publication]" (*Life* n.p.). The fact that Bianchi, while adopting Todd's typographical distinction between "poetry" and "letters," nevertheless comes to a different conclusion as to the genre of specific passages, is most likely the result of neither editorial considerations nor her own textual studies.[3] Bianchi's sequel, *Emily Dickinson Face to Face,* has the same biographical emphasis. Summarizing her project, Bianchi explains: "Before her death the last of the Dickinsons should write a sympathetic sketch, recording for those interested in the personality of the poet, often found so elusive, and the unique background of her life as could only be possible to one who had a daily part in it" (*Face* xiv). Consequently, in editing the "very personal notes of a very personal family" (*Face* xxii), Bianchi is, again, more concerned with their content (and its biographical implications) than their genre (and its typographical representations).

Similarly, Millicent Todd Bingham's three volumes containing selected letters of Dickinson (some of them hitherto unpublished) all pursue narrative rather than strictly textual aims.[4] *Ancestors' Brocades* provides an account of the publication history of Dickinson's manuscripts based on Mabel Loomis Todd's diaries. Yet although Bingham intends to "provide accurate sources of information for future editors of Emily's poems" (viii) and therefore claims to reproduce selected letters "with all their imperfections even to lapses and colloquialisms" (*Ancestors' Brocades* viii), this, again, refers to the content rather than the textual form of Dickinson's manuscripts. Bingham's second book, *A Revelation*, is more specifically designed to "reveal" the contents of Todd's famous camphorwood chest, which had remained unopened for forty years and contained a collection of love letters, poems, and prose fragments written by Dickinson and possibly addressed to Judge Otis Lord.[5] In the context of constructing a love narrative, earlier editorial and typographical distinctions between Dickinson's "poems" and her "letters" are thus merely adopted rather than reconsidered or challenged.

Generally speaking, both Bianchi's and Bingham's editions organized Dickinson's letters chronologically, integrated them into a preconceived narrative/biographical framework, and frequently quoted only those parts of the letters which seemed "relevant" to their respective narrative constructs.[6] Typographically, they both clearly distinguished between Dickinson's "poetry" and her "prose." All these factors actively encouraged their readers to approach Dickinson's correspondence as autobiographical documents, to be regarded primarily as sources of information about the poet's life, and as ancillary vehicles for her poetry.

On the other hand, both Theodora Ward's collection of ninety-three letters entitled *Emily Dickinson's Letters to Dr. and Mrs. Josiah Gilbert Holland* and Johnson and Ward's still definitive three-volume variorum edition of *The Letters of Emily Dickinson* have aspired to textual accuracy, focused on producing, in Tanselle's words, "a witness to the past" (10). Ward was the first twentieth-century editor to have based her work on a detailed study of Dickinson's manuscripts; building on Ward's scholarship, Johnson and Ward's variorum edition has specifically aimed at completion and at a more accurate reproduction of Dickinson's idiosyncratic spelling and punctuation (in contrast to earlier "regularized" editions).[7] In this respect, Johnson and Ward's 1958 *Letters* constitutes a fundamental and significant advance over all earlier editions of Dickinson's correspondence.

It was not until critical interest in the textual aspects of Dickinson's work increased during the 1980s and 1990s that Johnson's editorial practices (specifically in relation to his 1955 edition of *Poems*) began to be subjected to severe critical scrutiny. In particular, a comparison between Dickinson's manuscript fascicle poems, reproduced in Ralph W. Franklin's facsimile edition *The Manuscript Books of Emily Dickinson*, and their representation in Johnson's print edition has induced several critics (including Jerome McGann, Martha Nell Smith, Ellen Louise Hart, Susan Howe, Marta Werner, Paul Crumbley, and others) to challenge Johnson's editorial practices as being inaccurate. These critics specifically emphasize the "graphocentric" (Smith, "Importance" 79), "scriptural" quality of Dickinson's texts that, in their opinion, has found inaccurate representation in Johnson's print editions: "[Franklin's] photographic reproductions reveal the importance of Dickinson's handwritten experimentations in punctuation, lineation, and calligraphic orthography" (Smith, "Importance" 75; cf. Hart and Smith, *Open Me* xxiii).

What has aroused the strongest critical objection is Johnson's method of organizing Dickinson's poems into quatrains consisting of alternating iambic tetrameter and trimeter lines (the traditional hymnal stanza format), and hence his ignoring of the actual physical line breaks in Dickinson's manuscripts. As Smith maintains: "[Dickinson] often broke her lines mid-syllable or in other unexpected places rather than according to the tetrameter, trimeter, dimeter conventions of the hymnal stanza and poetic quatrain" ("Importance" 76). Both Susan Howe and Ellen Louise Hart have likewise argued that Johnson's stanzaic organization has no basis in Dickinson's manuscripts but instead is the result of tacit editorial emendations of lineation, capitalization, and punctuation: "In order to form quatrains, Johnson regularly ignored Dickinson's line breaks and occasionally dropped capitalization beginning a new line if it interfered with his stanza format" (Hart, "Elizabeth" 68).

That these rearrangements on Johnson's part can have crucial implications for our understanding of Dickinson's generic experimentations was first noted by Jerome McGann. Highlighting the importance of respecting Dickinson's line breaks specifically in her poems incorporated in letters, McGann points out how Johnson's stanzaic arrangements can lead to a typographical misrepresentation of her correspondence: "Johnson's edition of the *Letters* assumes a sharp division between the formalities of verse and prose, so he prints the metrical prose margin to margin and the spatially disordered verse in 'correct' metrical lines. But a typographical translation of this extraordinary text of Dickinson's [L265] might just as well reverse Johnson's method in order to reveal what Johnson's translation overrides: the metrical subtext of the prose, and the prosy surface of the verse" ("Composition" 125–126). Analogous observations have led Hart to argue, more generally and more controversially, for the lineation of all of Dickinson's "poetry" and "prose":

> First, Dickinson did not visually separate prose and poetry in her letters. Her prose lines and the lines of a poem are similar in length, she did not consistently divide poetry from prose through spacing, and she did not vary margins. A standard prose format for the letters results in visual inaccuracies, such as Johnson's paragraphing: Dickinson did not use indentation to indicate paragraphs. Second, the relationship between poetry and prose is so complex in Dickinson's writing that lineating poetry but not prose sets up artificial genre distinctions. There are no easily drawn periods in Dickinson's writing, no distinct point where it is possible to say, 'Before this the genre of the letters is exclusively prose, and there is no need to lineate.' ("Elizabeth" 49)

This controversy over the most accurate representation of Dickinson's manuscripts finally led to the formation of the Dickinson Editing Collective in 1992. Its most prominent members, M. N. Smith, Hart, McGann, Howe, Werner, and Crumbley, are currently concentrating on reexamining and problematizing Johnson's and Franklin's print translations of Dickinson's calligraphy, punctuation, lineation, capitalization, and stanza format, as well as developing alternative forms of editing Dickinson's highly unstable texts. Acknowledging the fact that no single editorial method is appropriate for all scholarly and teaching purposes, the Editing Collective regards its (at times highly contested) suggestions as being, for the most part, complementary rather than competitive, and open to revision rather than carved in stone.[8]

The Collective's members have no doubt raised a number of crucial issues that will fundamentally change the ways in which we read Dickinson's texts, and though I share several of their concerns regarding manuscript representation in current print editions, I nevertheless also agree with some of the reservations voiced against their positions, believing that—particularly for a revised understanding of Dickinson's correspondence—some issues may need further qualification.

The most radical of the graphically oriented critics tend to reject all conventional print editions of Dickinson's texts, giving exclusive privilege to the writer's manuscripts in the forms in which they were left at her death (fascicles, sets, correspondences, and ungathered poems and drafts). This "scriptural" point of view is shared by McGann and Smith, in particular, who are profoundly skeptical of translating any manuscript documents—especially graphically experimental ones—into print format at all.[9] For this reason, Smith is currently coordinating the production of electronic photographic reproductions of Dickinson's manuscripts in the form of online hypermedia archives, the *Dickinson Electronic Archives*.[10]

Additionally, Smith and Hart have also argued for complementing this electronic facsimile edition with revisionist diplomatic print transcriptions, that is, "line for line print translations of poems and letters that attempt to represent the manuscripts as accurately as possible, with a detailed apparatus describing features that do not translate into print" (Hart, "Elizabeth" 72). Marta Werner's *Emily Dickinson's Open Folios*, a facsimile edition (with facing transcriptions) of forty late pencil drafts of poems and "scraps" associated with Judge Otis Lord (some of them previously unpublished), constitutes the first attempt to provide such diplomatic transcriptions.[11] Focusing on the visual aspects of Dickinson's manuscripts, Werner's *Open Folios* seeks to offer more accurate typographical representations of Dickinson's spaces between words; quotation marks, slanting dashes, lines, and erasures are inserted by hand.[12] Problems of Johnson's generic reclassification of fragments and drafts ("extrageneric events falling outside standard taxonomies" [*Open Folios* 45]) as "fair copy" letters receive special emphasis. Werner's *Open Folios* is complemented by her most recent project, entitled *Radical Scatters: Emily Dickinson's Late Fragments and Related Texts, 1870–1886*, a CD-ROM[13] that contains approximately one hundred of Dickinson's late scraps and fragments not collected in fascicles. Following her own editorial guidelines spelled out in *Open Folios*, specifically her emphasis on the visual, "scriptural" aspects of Dickinson's manuscripts, *Radical Scatters* enables access to these fragments in four formats: facsimile reproductions, diplomatic transcriptions, printed versions, and SGML-marked, searchable electronic texts.

Ellen Louise Hart and Martha Nell Smith's *Open Me Carefully*, an edition of selected writings by both Dickinson and Sue Gilbert that consists primarily of the former's "intimate letters" to her sister-in-law, is the most recent print continuation of this editorial direction and extends it for the first time to one of Dickinson's major correspondences.[14] In addition to its biographical focus, *Open Me Carefully* places particular emphasis on displaying the development of Dickinson's textual forms and poetic practices, including her unique generic experiments: "The letter-poem, a category that includes signed poems and letters with poems or with lines of poetry, will be seen here as a distinct and important Dickinson genre" (*Open Me* xxv). In this way, Hart and Smith's is also the first edition to arrange at least part of Dickinson's manuscripts not according to (possibly artificial) generic groups, but according to the audience for whom they were composed.

Although Hart and Smith's as well as Werner's editions thus translate into practice many of the revisionist editorial considerations that have recently been raised, they have also further heightened the controversy over the possible significance of Dickinson's manuscript lineation. Quite generally, critics continue to disagree as to whether Dickinson's line breaks constitute editorial substantials endowed with inherent signification, or whether they can be treated as editorial accidentals. Some textual critics have argued for an exact representation of Dickinson's lineation primarily for reasons of manuscript fidelity, while others go one step further in ascribing intentionality to the poet's visual strategies. Hart, for example, has adopted the latter position, insisting that "Dickinson used lineation to direct emphasis, create meaning, control pace, and guide her readers" ("Elizabeth" 50). Her description of Dickinson's line breaks as "visual strategies" (72) echoes an earlier observation made by Howe, who regards them as "visual intentionality" and concludes that "as a poet I cannot assert that Dickinson composed in stanzas and was careless about line breaks" ("Some Notes" 12).

"Line breaks and visual contrapuntal stresses," in Howe's opinion, "represent an athematic compositional intention" on Dickinson's part (*Birth-Mark* 139).[15]

It is this emphasis on intentionality, in particular, that critics like Ralph Franklin and Domhnall Mitchell tend to regard with a high degree of skepticism. Franklin, the most recent editor of Dickinson's *Poems,* has—in various discussions with Howe—explained that his reservations are "based on the assumption that a literary work is separable from its artifact, as Dickinson herself demonstrated as she moved her poems from one piece of paper to another" (*Poems* 1:27). And for this reason, even though in his own edition of *Poems* he "seeks to intrude minimally" in the physical arrangement of the manuscripts and "accept[s them] as their own standard" (1:27), Franklin nonetheless feels free to "again creat[e] a text that is not identical with any surviving document" (1:37). His deviations from surviving documents refer, in particular, to Dickinson's line breaks. While recording all genetic information and physical characteristics of the poetry manuscripts (including lineation) in the apparatus, Franklin does not regard line breaks as substantials: "Unconstrained by incidental characteristics of the artifact, this edition restores the lines, though also recording the turnovers. . . . [In certain cases] lineation has been arbitrarily established as in poems appearing as prose [in manuscript] but arranged as verse [in the print edition]" (1:36). This decision in favor of occasionally "arbitrary" rearrangements, according to Franklin, is justified by his conclusion that "available space ordinarily determined the physical line breaks in Dickinson's poems" (1:34). More specifically, "constraints such as the edges of the paper, the presence of a boss, stains or imperfections, or the overlap of envelope construction would redirect her pencil or pen. The shapes of her materials—odds and ends of wrapping paper, advertising flyers, notebook leaves, discarded stationery—gave physical contour to her poems as they went onto paper" (1:34).[16] Thus, as Mitchell summarizes, "Franklin does not believe that Dickinson's work sheets, drafts, and fair copies possess the detailed aesthetic significance attributed to them by later scholars, though his comments have often been interpreted as if they support such a view" ("Revising the Script" 706).

Franklin's skepticism is shared by Domhnall Mitchell, who extends this discussion to include Dickinson's letters. Examining word divisions in the writer's correspondence with Thomas Wentworth Higginson, Mitchell comes to the conclusion that "generally speaking, the material inscription of the letters that formed words and the words that formed lines in Dickinson's correspondence with Higginson were not an important concern for the poet" ("Revising the Script" 711). This observation leads Mitchell to ask: "If the letters were crafted with care (as they were) and yet feature nonsignificant word splitting, what does this mean for the significance of split words in the poems?" (712).[17]

The high degree of line-break accidentality that, according to Franklin and Mitchell, characterizes Dickinson's "poetry" as well as "prose" passages is also confirmed by my own examination of line breaks in "the same" poem incorporated into different letters (or, in one instance, into different drafts of "the same" letter [L976]). A reading of these manuscripts reveals that no version of any one poem incorporated or enclosed in a letter shows line breaks occurring at exactly the same positions as those in any other copy of the same poem. Franklin's comparisons of Dickinson's fascicle poem manuscripts with other manuscript copies of the same poem corroborate this observation: "There are many examples in which two or more copies of the same poem appear on papers of different shapes, yielding different line breaks for each" (*Poems* 1:34). This is especially true, according to Franklin, for poems that were sent to recipients in addition to being recorded in fascicles: "The former was typically on notepaper, the latter on stationery of larger size, yielding different configurations. Once line breaks began, it is not easy to find a manuscript of any poem in Dickinson's hand that exactly matches the physical lineation of the same poem in other copies" (1:35). This would indeed suggest (as Franklin concludes) that, for Dickinson, the question of lineation was *completely* insignificant.

Generally leaning toward this position himself, Mitchell, nonetheless, does not fully rule out the possibility of deliberateness in his discussion of the differences in lineation in two of the six extant manuscripts of J1068/Fr895 ("Further in Summer than the Birds"): "Either Dickinson was experimenting here, or she could afford to be casual because the changes were unimportant" ("Diplomacy" 48). Mitchell thus views Dickinson's line breaks as pointing "both/either to an innovative visual intelligence and/or to something approximating indifference to the material features of a poem's inscription" (51).

Though I tend to concur with Mitchell and Franklin that the specific line breaks in any given manuscript most likely held no intrinsic significance for Dickinson, I nonetheless argue that the visual features of a poem's inscription were not *completely* arbitrary either. Rather, in my view, Dickinson's manuscript pages—of letters in particular—do show an attempt to create justified left and right margins, a strategy that is visually supported in two different ways: if words cannot fill an entire line from left to right margin, Dickinson either tends to increase the space between words (so as to spread out the words evenly across the line) or she inserts dashes as visual "space fillers" at the end of a line or page (examples include L396, L630, L814, L865, L868). This strategy is necessary to distinguish lines within a paragraph from the last line of a paragraph. Since Dickinson does not use indentation to indicate the beginning of a new paragraph (she commonly only indents the first line of a letter after the salutation), subsequent new paragraphs are most frequently indicated by a shortened final line of the preceding paragraph.[18] Thus, in order to avoid "unintentional" indications of a paragraph break, Dickinson arranges all lines except the final line in each paragraph flush left and right. In this way, her line breaks and spaces between words, rather than "creat[ing] meaning" (Hart, "Elizabeth" 50), constituting a "compositional intention" (Howe, *Birth-Mark* 139), or being "part of rather than supplementary to the content of her encodings" (Werner, *Open Folios* 56), seem indeed to be dictated by the physical size and shape of the paper. Yet their complete accidentality seems contradicted by the ensuing visual effect, which is that of some kind of proportional spacing.

That Dickinson's deployment of blank space on the page may also acquire a crucial significance for distinguishing between "prose" and "poetry" passages has been suggested by Mitchell. Comparing the lineation of J1366/Fr1462C (incorporated within L677) to that of its surrounding "prose" context, Mitchell detects "*some* visual indication of a generic shift" ("Revising the Script" 715), thus directly refuting Hart's earlier contention that "Dickinson did not visually separate prose and poetry in her letters" ("Elizabeth" 49). Thus, building upon yet also modifying Franklin's position of line-break accidentality, Mitchell finally comes to the conclusion that "Dickinson's prose lineation is caused by a combination of arbitrary factors: the size of the page, for example, and the length of Dickinson's words as they are written on the page. Within the poem, however, *some* aspects of the lineation are deliberate, and we need to set up guidelines for knowing which" ("Revising the Script" 715). One of the "deliberate" aspects that Mitchell identifies in his discussion of J685/Fr500A (incorporated into L280) is an increased amount of open space surrounding words: "The sequence of open spaces not dictated by necessity tends to make the poem stand out more on the page. These spaces function almost as a typographical convention that signals the presence of a generic shift" (716). He therefore concludes that "the blurring of generic distinctions is accompanied by what might be construed as their continuing formal demarcation" (735 n. 20). However, as Mitchell himself emphasizes, this formal demarcation is by no means conclusive in each case. He cites J684/Fr499A and J685/Fr500A in L280 as examples that challenge any facile generic classification: "Dickinson gives no indication in her letter that she intended the first to be read *as poetry* or independent of the prose that surrounds it" (715).

Franklin has also tried to identify both internal and external kinds of evidence that would allow for such generic differentiations. He cites the existence of a fascicle copy as one "independent," external proof, since Dickinson only included "poems" in her fascicles (*Poems* 1:32). Capitalization, on the other hand, can be taken as an internal kind of evidence: "Sometimes there is no verification that she regarded a passage as poetry except for the way in which she wrote it. For poems, whether separate or incorporated into letters, she observed convention by capitalizing first words of lines" (*Poems* 1:32; see also Mitchell, "Revising the Script" 718). At the same time, however, Franklin, like Mitchell, has to concede that generic distinctions drawn along these lines may not always be conclusive. On the one hand, there are differences between early and late manuscripts: "The examples of her poetry incorporated into letters before 1858 are easily detected, since they were set apart and inscribed without turnovers. But certain passages in these letters suggest that poetry is not far away" (*Poems* 1:34). As for post-1858 materials, Franklin continues, "there is no definitive boundary between prose and poetry in Dickinson's letters. At times she may have surprised herself to find prose becoming verse" (1:32–34). In addition, the above-cited internal forms of evidence are likewise fraught with problems: certain lines "were often written as poetry in both letter and independent copy, though if the lines were few, they might join the rest as prose" (1:32). Both Franklin and Mitchell thus seem to come to the conclusion that sometimes it *is* possible to distinguish between letters and poems (especially in pre-1858 manuscripts), but not always, and not always with absolute certainty. In this way, they both seem to confirm rather than challenge the extent of Dickinson's generic borderblur.

Ultimately, however, this high degree of uncertainty raises a series of crucial questions: given Franklin's justified skepticism about conclusive genre demarcations in Dickinson's manuscripts, why does he nevertheless insist on conveying the impression in his print edition of *Poems* that clear distinctions can be drawn (by being very specific about what does and does not constitute a Dickinson poem)?[19] Moreover, even if we agree with Franklin and Mitchell as to the accidentality of Dickinson's line breaks in her manuscripts (i.e., even if we concur that line breaks are not "intended" to contribute to the meaning of any one poem or letter), does this "accidentality" on Dickinson's part (which cannot be equated with complete disregard for space in general, as we have seen) justify the specific large-scale rearrangements of her lines into tetrameters and trimeters, as practiced by both Johnson and, with changes recorded in the critical apparatus, Franklin? In other words, are we as editors allowed to modify what we have identified as accidentals to such an extent that we *create* signification (e.g., regular stanzaic arrangements) where there had been accidentality? And even if we acknowledge that in many cases (how many? how many are sufficient evidence?) it is possible to distinguish between the "poetry" and the "prose" part within a letter (due to a more generous spacing, say), would this justify a difference in indentation in print editions, if only "for clarity of presentation" (Franklin, *Poems* 1:36)? And what about ambivalent cases? And why—in spite of all prevailing critical doubts—do some editorial authorities still insist on the usefulness of maintaining such strict generic boundaries in the first place? For what purposes are we, quite generally, interested in a generic distinction that, in the past, has far too often implied hierarchical differentiation? A brief look at Johnson's and Franklin's editorial practices as they relate to Dickinson's correspondence manuscripts will clarify my point.[20]

I argue that Johnson's edition of *Poems* and his co-edited edition of *Letters* with Ward and, to a certain degree, also Franklin's revised edition of *Poems* in effect "create" (artificial) regularity where there had been accidentality, and hence produce misleading signification. It is particularly their systematic rearrangements of Dickinson's "poetry" lines into tetrameters and trimeters, as well as their indentation of what they have identified as "poetry" passages in contradistinction to "prose" lines, which tend to *create* specific impressions for their readers (the impression, for example, that Dickinson composed her poems in alternating tetrameter and trimeter lines, or that she clearly distinguished between the prose and poetry parts of her letters)—impressions that are, as we have seen, frequently contradicted by the manuscripts themselves. In other words, though the very accidentality of Dickinson's lines produces generically transgressive effects that often serve to "poeticize" epistolary features (such as signatures) or to "disguise" poetic features (such as end rhymes), Johnson's and Franklin's visual reorganization actually *reverses* these effects by "poeticizing" her poems and "epistolarizing" her letters. The extent to which their print editions (in different ways) thus tend to *establish* a high degree of generic purity where there had been generic fluidity, the extent to which they *obscure* Dickinson's fusion of poetic and epistolary discourses, and the extent to which this, in turn, has encouraged (and will still continue to encourage) the widespread assumption that Dickinson's letters are to be read as mere "vehicles" for her poetry can be illustrated by a closer look at some examples.

In addition to the specific forms of stanzaic reorganization that had been identified (and critiqued) before, Johnson's print editions also include additional elements that reinforce a strict generic differentiation between poetic and epistolary discourses and simultaneously privilege Dickinson's poems over her letters. Even though only some of these elements also recur in Franklin, his edition of *Poems* nonetheless manages to create many of the same effects—albeit by different means. On a very general level, Johnson and Ward's still definitive print edition of *Letters* significantly underrepresents the nature and extent of Dickinson's epistolary outreach. They tend to include a "poem" in this edition only if it has a "prose" context (see also Hart, "Elizabeth" 45). The critical apparatus of *Poems*, on the other hand, lists a large number of poems that can be ascertained to have been mailed to various correspondents.[21] Yet since no prose context exists or can be reconstructed for these poems, and since the letter that accompanied them (if any) can no longer be identified, they as a rule omit these poems from their edition of *Letters*.[22] This editorial strategy, however, disguises the fact that for Dickinson a "poem" frequently also became (i.e., was functionalized as) a "letter" (and vice versa), and thus it misrepresents the extent of poems mailed as letters within her oeuvre. In addition, as Hart has pointed out, Johnson was the first editor "to publish texts that previous editors called 'letters' as poems but not also as letters" ("Elizabeth" 45). This suggests that, although his edition of *Poems* includes a number of "new" texts and strives for a complete representation of Dickinson's *poetic* output, his edition of *Letters*, on the other hand, minimizes the quantity and falsifies the generic complexity of Dickinson's epistolary writings by omitting a large number of "poems-turned-letters."

Franklin has not (yet) published a revised edition of *Letters*, but many of his editorial decisions in *Poems* in effect resemble Johnson's in quantitatively reducing Dickinson's generic complexities. Franklin, for example, relegates everything that may be considered "generically ambivalent" to an appendix, including eight "prose" passages from Dickinson's early letters that "exhibit characteristics of verse without being so written" (*Poems* 3:1577; cf. Appendix 13).[23] As a result of their generic indeterminacy, these texts are excluded from his edition of *Poems*. FrA13–2 may serve as an illustrative example. Johnson had included this text in his edition of *Poems* as J2. Yet to justify this decision, he turned J2 into a seemingly freestanding "poem" by changing capitalization in one instance ("There," line 1), and destroying a syntactical unit to sever the "poetry" lines from their "prose" context.[24] Johnson acknowledges his editorial liberties in the apparatus for J2: "ED made no line division, and the text does not appear as verse. The line arrangement and capitalization of first letters in the lines are here arbitrarily established" (*Poems* 3). The fact that Johnson thus breaks up a textual manuscript unit in order to "create" a "poem" is indicative of both his general tendency to privilege "poems" (while marginalizing their "letter" context), as well as a New Critical inclination to represent a poem as a structurally unified, autonomous verbal artifact.[25]

Although Franklin adopts Johnson's line breaks for his own transcription of this poem (with manuscript line breaks noted in the critical apparatus), his editorial actions are far more faithful to both manuscript features and context. He neither breaks up syntactical units nor changes manuscript capitalizations to create a "freestanding" poem. Instead, he recontextualizes these lines within their original frame, that is, Dickinson's letter L58 to her brother, Austin. As a consequence, however, Franklin no longer regards this text as suitable for inclusion in his edition of *Poems*, relegating it instead to an Appendix entitled "Some Early Texts" (App. 13). Thus, while presenting his readers with a more accurate transcription of the entire text plus context, Franklin (like Johnson before him) nonetheless still strives to establish strict generic boundaries by separating "pure" poems from generically mixed or ambivalent ones.[26] His editorial decision to place this poem-letter in an appendix, moreover, symbolically signifies his devaluation and marginalization of generically transgressive texts, a hierarchical distinction that likewise contributes to a falsification of the quantity and generic complexity of Dickinson's actual epistolary and poetic output.

The most powerful feature of Johnson's edition of *Poems* that contributes substantially to producing misleading effects of "generic purity" is his tendency to reinforce poetic features typographically within texts he has classified as "poems." Kate Scott Turner Anthon's transcript of her copy of J222/ Fr49, for example, reads:

When Katie walks, this
simple pair accompany her
side, When Katie runs
unwearied they follow on the road,
When Katie kneels, their loving
hands still clasp her
pious knee—Ah! Katie!
Smile at Fortune, with *two*
so *knit to thee!* Emilie.
(Houghton MS Am 1118.5 [B126])

Johnson's transcript in *Poems* (J222), on the other hand, rearranges the lines in heptameters and hexameters, thus highlighting the triple anaphora ("When"), the triple incremental repetition in lines 1–3, as well as the "end" rhyme ("knee," "thee") and consonance ("side," "road") while omitting the signature:

When Katie walks, this simple pair accompany her side,
When Katie runs unwearied they follow on the road,
When Katie kneels, their loving hands still clasp her pious knee—
Ah! Katie! Smile at Fortune, with *two* so *knit to thee*!

Whereas the surviving manuscript's lineation thus obscures rather than emphasizes its poetic features by de-emphasizing one of the three anaphoras ("When Katie runs") and avoiding rhymes in end position, Johnson's reorganization draws additional emphasis to them. The poem's metrical "regularity" is another element that is particularly highlighted by Johnson's lineation. McGann has argued that in the context of Dickinson's poems, "it is exactly the loose 'prose' arrangement of the words on the page that allows the language to transcend the metronome" ("Composition" 127). Yet Johnson's rearrangement of these lines in heptameters and hexameters specifically reinforces the "poetic" features of J222 and at the same time suppresses its "prose" or "epistolary" properties—chief among them the signature "Emilie," which is relegated to the critical apparatus.[27] In the manuscript version, however, it follows the last line of the text, thus simultaneously also contributing to the internal rhymes established by "knee" and "thee" (that is, functioning as a signal for both poetic *and* epistolary discourse). In this way, Dickinson's own fusion of poetic and epistolary discourses is systematically reversed by redistributing generic features according to the principle of generic purity.

A similar effect is produced by Franklin's transcript of this poem (Fr49), which—except for one additional capitalization in line one—is identical to Johnson's version. Franklin justifies his "metricalized" lineation, and hence his classification of this text as "poem," with the following words: "The text, which in [Catherine Scott Turner Anthon's] transcript runs on like prose, may be presented as a quatrain" (*Poems* 1:99). In this way, Franklin's choice to "present" these lines as "quatrain" while likewise relegating the signature to the critical apparatus, again minimizes the epistolary aspects of this passage in favor of augmenting its poetic qualities. Thus, although the extant manuscript version of J222/Fr49 illustrates a blending of epistolary and poetic features, endowing the former with functions of the latter, Johnson's and Franklin's editions, on the other hand, both effectively undermine this generic borderblur by foregrounding "poetic" elements in "letters" and de-emphasizing the "epistolary" features of "poems."

Johnson's and Franklin's reinstitution of a strict generic boundary between poetic and epistolary discourses, their insistence on a text's generic classifiability, and their editorial discomfort with instances of generic ambivalence and borderblur accomplish more than just separating Dickinson's "poems" and "letters" on a textual level. These strategies simultaneously obscure the full extent of Dickinson's dialogue between poetic and epistolary discourses, together with the political implications this transgression of genre boundaries carries in a nineteenth-century context. Thus, by redefining Dickinson's letter-poems as "poems," and her poem-letters as "letters," Johnson's editorial practices have in the past at least partly contributed to a devaluation of Dickinson's letters, treating them as mere "vehicles" for the incorporated or enclosed "poems." To a certain degree, Franklin's edition of *Poems* is likely to perpetuate such readings. Both editions thus reveal the problems inherent not so much in *not* representing Dickinson's manuscripts (including line breaks) exactly as they are, but in representing them in ways that suggest that a clear differentiation between "poems" and "letters" is the best or most desirable way to do so. And it is for this reason that a revised edition of all of Dickinson's correspondence manuscripts, with specific emphasis on generically differentiating substantials (including, but not restricted to, end- or mid-position of rhyme words, positions or omission of salutation and signature, as well as position of markers of date or place), seems highly desirable for a better understanding of Dickinson's negotiations of nineteenth-century generic conventions as well as her (genre-political) acts of transgression. And since, as we have seen, Dickinson's line breaks, in particular, may display elements of *both* accidentality *and* deliberateness simultaneously, a revised edition of the poet's correspondence should, in my view, also foreground rather than obscure and distort this generic and textual instability by reproducing line breaks orthographically in *all* of her texts (poems as well as letters)—if only to give readers a chance to judge for themselves the degree of their (non)significance or accidentality in each instance.[28]

Franklin's monumental accomplishment—much like Johnson's earlier one—is significant for what it achieves as well as for the new questions it raises and the old ones it leaves unanswered. As Mitchell summarizes: "Each age constructs a new likeness of Dickinson's texts in the light of technological and ideological changes, but is also constricted by the still invisible limitations of the same ideologies and technologies" ("Diplomacy" 52). The largest challenge faced by Franklin as well as by any other editor—past or future—is the necessity to make decisions (and possibly finalize these decisions in print or any other format) on issues that scholars continue to debate. Within a few years, new ideologies, new technologies, new questions about intentionality may yield yet unanticipated answers. In such an intensely dynamic climate, it is impossible to dismiss Mitchell's warning that any features or effects we choose to identify in Dickinson's manuscripts today (especially radically experimental ones, such as generic borderblur) may not have been calculated ones at all: "It would be nice to believe that Dickinson intended such an effect, but it is impossible to say with any certainty that she did. . . . Almost any feature of Dickinson's manuscripts can be interpreted to suggest a proleptic concern with the semantic potential of the poem's visual properties—its line and word breaks as well as its punctuation. But such interpretations—however exciting—must remain conjectural" ("Revising the Script" 711). At the same time, we nonetheless have to ask—as does Mitchell—whether manuscript features contributing to specific effects "can be ignored when transcribing poems onto the page of a book or the screen of a computer? This is a difficult question, and the answer may depend on the intended audience and the kind of edition being prepared" (719). Yet, even more important, we also have to ask whether the current scholarly privileging of manuscripts is justified at all, a privileging that Mitchell has clear "misgivings" about: "Relying on the manuscripts alone might well represent the opposite extreme to depending solely on the print editions" ("Diplomacy" 50). That such an exclusive focus on the visual aspects of Dickinson's texts may indeed be one-sided was first emphasized by Cristanne Miller, who advances that, maybe, Dickinson's poetics were more strongly influenced by aural rhythms than by their visual representations on the page: "Dickinson may have given [a poem] various scriptural forms while maintaining the same metrical structure." Miller thus suggests that we "see these as multiple performances of a single production—each of which is instructive, as with the performance of any art, but none of which constitutes a separate production or poem" ("Whose Dickinson?" 248). As Mitchell confirms: "The presence of metrical patterns in the poem that operate irrespective of a line's material inscription suggest[s] that the way the poem is recorded cannot always be a reliable guide to any further textual transmission" ("Diplomacy" 53 n. 10).

Many of these doubts about privileging the visual aspects of Dickinson's manuscripts are prompted by the realization that "it is not at all clear . . . that Dickinson *intended* the printed versions of her works to reproduce all the details of her manuscripts" (Mitchell, "Revising the Script" 706). This is, of course, particularly true for printed versions of Dickinson's *correspondence*, which, we can almost be certain, Dickinson never "intended" to see in(to) print but rather—according to nineteenth-century conventions—expected to be burned after her death. Yet at the same time, we need to remember that her letters and those poems she mailed in / as letters were indeed specifically prepared for an audience. Moreover, Dickinson's intricate play with cutouts, stamps, and other features in several of her letters does indeed speak to the care she took in visually arranging her manuscripts (in addition to other organizational considerations that might have played a role). In this sense, I believe that a strong case can be made for looking toward Dickinson's "authorized" correspondence manuscripts in order to extrapolate her "final authorial intentions" concerning her letters, while not ignoring the fact that other, nonvisual principles of organization may have played an equally important role in her artistic productions.

Most important, however, we also need to recall that, as Shira Wolosky has reminded us, "the manuscripts represent one sort of context. They nevertheless by no means exhaust the networks of relationship that situate Dickinson's writing. Indeed, exclusive emphasis on the manuscript artifact may not disclose but may rather foreclose and enclose Dickinson's art" ("Manuscript Body" 89). Indeed, Dickinson's intergeneric dialogic exchange between "letters" and "poems" on the physical level of manuscripts is only one manifestation of a more general tendency toward dialogic polyvocality in her correspondence. Taking my departure from Dickinson's blurring of the textual boundaries between "letters" and "poems," in the following chapter I examine the extent to which analogously dialogic intersections of "fact" and "fiction," of "referentiality" and "nonreferentiality," of the "personal" and the "literary" manifest themselves in her correspondence. In other words, Dickinson's negotiation of nineteenth-century epistolary conventions, her blurring of the generic boundaries between epistolary and poetic discourses on a textual level can at the same time be interpreted as an interrogation of the discursive boundaries between the narrowly "personal" or "autobiographical" elements of everyday letters, and the more broadly "literary" or "imaginative" qualities of poetry. Much as Dickinson's letters resist a strictly generic editing, they also resist a strictly autobiographical interpretation. By freeing her letters from the generic constraints of autobiography or life writing proper, Dickinson can turn them into sites for imaginative renegotiations of multiple, discursively constructed subject positions, thus abolishing their speakers' "captivity" in the "closet" of nineteenth-century strictures of womanhood. To be "shut up in prose" by many of her editors thus becomes much more than a question of textual accuracy: it is a chastising of the poet's mind that prevents readers from appreciating some of the most central aspects of Dickinson's correspondence—the "abolition" of autobiographical "captivity," and hence the imaginative play with different roles and subject positions.

They shut me up in Prose—
As when a little Girl
They put me in the Closet—
Because they liked me 'still'—

Still! Could themself have peeped—
And seen my Brain—go round—
They might as wise have lodged a Bird
For Treason—in the Pound—

Himself has but to will
And easy as a Star
Abolish his Captivity—
And laugh—No more have I—
(J613/Fr445)

I am Eve, alias Mrs Adam.

I give you Good Night
with fictitious lips.

When I state myself,
as the Representative of the Verse—
it does not mean—me—
but a supposed person.

—EMILY DICKINSON

3

The "Female" World of Love and Duty

IN THEIR DISCUSSION of the autobiographical subject, both Felicity A. Nussbaum and Betty Bergland have advanced a model of subjectivity that emphasizes the subject's constructedness based on sociocultural discursive practices. According to Nussbaum, "individuals construct themselves as subjects through language, but individual subjects—rather than being the source of their own self-generated and self-expressive meaning—adopt positions available within the language at a given moment" (149). And Bergland agrees that any articulation of the self is inevitably shaped by the "historical conditions, material forces, and cultural discourses" prevailing at a given point in time: "a dynamic subject . . . changes over time, [and] is situated historically in the world and positioned in multiple discourses" (161, 134). Concurring with Paul Smith, Bergland thus concludes that "language cannot transparently *reveal* an essential and unified historical subject; rather, the speaking subject, historically situated and positioned in multiple and contradictory discourses, places the 'I' in the world in positions conceptually possible in language" (131). It is for this reason that Sidonie Smith, similarly, defines the subject of autobiographical writings as "a cultural and linguistic 'fiction' constituted through historical ideologies of selfhood" (45).[1]

The subject positions "conceptually possible in language" for New England's nineteenth-century upper-middle-class women, and the "historical ideologies of selfhood" that initially informed Dickinson's earliest epistolary self-representations, were predominantly influenced by the discursive systems of religion as well as domestic and family values. For women, these discourses tended to offer narrowly circumscribed, relational subject positions (daughter, wife, mother), based on what Barbara Welter has termed the ideal of "True Womanhood": "The attributes of True Womanhood . . . could be divided into four cardinal virtues—piety, purity, submissiveness and domesticity. Put them all together and they spelled mother, daughter, sister, wife—woman" (21).[2] To educate young women in these "four cardinal virtues," and to prepare them for their future roles as wives and mothers, became part of what Cott has referred to as "the philosophy of female education" in the nineteenth century. One way schools became instrumental in promoting these values of "true womanhood" was through advocating an ideology of female friendship. As Cott describes: "The philosophy of female education that triumphed by 1820 in New England inclined women to see their destiny as a shared one and to look to one another for similar sensibilities and moral support. By providing both convenient circumstances and a justifying ideology, academies promoted sisterhood among women. Even though most individuals spent only a few months at an academy at a time . . . the experience attuned them to female friendship with a force out of proportion to its duration" (177). One of the social functions of such female friendships formed at schools (and later often continued in letters) was for the women involved to assist each other in their transition from girlhood to womanhood.

FROM CONFESSION TO FICTION IN DICKINSON'S EARLY LETTERS

In many ways, Dickinson's earliest epistolary exchanges with Jane Humphrey, Emily Fowler, and Abiah Root are deeply rooted in this paradigm of sisterhood developed at school. Written during the late 1840s and the early 1850s, these letters illustrate the writer's negotiations of existing models of female friendship based on prevailing sociocultural and discursive configurations of womanhood.[3] In these letters, Dickinson frequently reflects on her own acquisition of such attributes as domesticity, submissiveness, and piety. Initially, she presents herself as making every effort to assume a woman's place as defined by her society. Describing her attempts to gain proficiency in such gendered tasks as cooking, sewing, or playing the piano, Dickinson strives to fulfill the role of the dutiful daughter—or at least to offer a flawless performance thereof: "I am now working a pair of slippers to adorn my father's feet" (L5); "After our return, Father wishing to hear the Piano, I like an obedient daughter, played & sang a few tunes, much to his apparent gratification" (L20); and also: "I am going to learn to make bread to-morrow. So you may imagine me with my sleeves rolled up, mixing flour, milk, salaratus, etc., with a deal of grace. I advise you if you don't know how to make the staff of life to learn with dispatch. I think I could keep house very comfortably if I knew how to cook. But as long as I don't, my knowledge of housekeeping is about of as much use as faith without works, which you know we are told is dead" (L8).

In addition to domestic chores, Dickinson is also preoccupied with spiritual questions.[4] In L10, addressed to Root and steeped in the rhetoric of conversion, she provides an extensive and orthodox meditation on the state of her soul: "I was almost persuaded to be a christian. I thought I never again could be thoughtless and worldly—and I can say that I never enjoyed such perfect peace and happiness as the short time in which I felt I had found my savior. . . . There is an aching void in my heart which I am convinced the world never can fill. . . . I hope the golden opportunity is not far hence when my heart will willingly yield itself to Christ, and that my sins will be all blotted out of the book of remembrance." Striving for "yielding herself up" to Christ, this letter illustrates, as Crumbley has noted, "how Dickinson struggled to adopt the socially acceptable, adult view of experience. This effort required that she silence all but the monologic voice attuned to Christian values and social expectation" (*Inflections* 74).

What emerges as a particularly striking feature of subsequent discussions of spiritual matters, however, is the close affinity between the acquisition of Christian virtues and the performance of domestic tasks. Emphasizing the compatibility of religious and domestic duties, Welter argues that "one reason religion was valued was that it did not take a woman away from her 'proper sphere,' her home" (22). Welter traces this compatibility to a shared value system: the dutiful daughter "was expected to help her mother in tasks recognized as 'female.' . . . These tasks were supposed to inculcate equally well-recognized feminine 'virtues' " (4). In other words, the performance of household tasks was considered to have a salutary influence on one's soul, an influence also noted by Dickinson: "Twin loaves of bread have just been born into the world under my auspices . . . the good I myself derive, the winning the spirit of patience the genial house-keeping influence stealing over my mind, and soul" (L36). In this way, religious and domestic duties become inseparable: to be a pious Christian is tantamount to being an obedient, dutiful daughter engaged in domestic activities, and vice versa. As Cott has emphasized, "ministers and pious women made every effort to conflate domestic values with religious values" (136).

Increasingly, however, Dickinson's letters reflect a more and more explicit resistance to the roles prescribed by the discourses of domesticity and orthodox Congregationalism: "I think of Dear Sarah & yourself as the only two out of our circle of five who have found a Saviour," she writes to Root, and goes on with, "I determined to devote my whole life to his service & desired that all might taste of the stream of living water from which I cooled my thirst." But instead, she regrets, "the world allured me & in an unguarded moment I listened to her syren voice . . . I feel that I am sailing upon the brink of an awful precipice, from which I cannot escape & over which I fear my tiny boat will soon glide if I do not receive help from above" (L11).[5]

This struggle with religious values is inextricably linked to Dickinson's ironization of a woman's domestic responsibilities: "The Sewing Society has commenced again . . . now all the poor will be helped—the cold warmed—the warm cooled—the hungry fed—the thirsty attended to—the ragged clothed—and this suffering—tumbled down world will be helped to it's feet again—which will be quite pleasant to all" (L30). Dickinson admits that she doesn't attend these meetings, "which must puzzle the public exceedingly. I am already set down as one of those brands almost consumed—and my hardheartedness gets me many prayers" (L30). In particular, Dickinson satirizes what Barbara Welter has called the "morally uplifting" aspects of housework (33):

> . . . mind the house—and the food—*sweep* if the spirits were low—nothing like exercise to strengthen—and invigorate—and help away such foolishness—work makes one strong, and cheerful—and as for society what neighborhood so full as my own? The halt—the lame—and the blind—the old—the infirm—the bed-ridden—and superannuated—the ugly, and disagreeable—the perfectly hateful to me—all *these* to see—and be seen by—an opportunity rare for cultivating meekness—and patience—and submission—and for turning my back to this very sinful, and wicked world. Somehow or other I incline to other things[.] (L30)[6]

This inclination to "other things" is caused by the realization that domesticity and marriage turn into what Crumbley refers to as "sites of imprisonment, prisons which entrap unwitting women in limiting, domestic identities" ("Art's" 79).

Such a renunciation of traditional domestic duties, however, is discursively and sociopolitically tantamount to a renunciation of Christian virtues; that is, a rejection of the traditional female role in society is consequently equated with "wickedness" and "sin." It is for this reason that all letters in which Dickinson emphasizes her inclination to "other things" simultaneously also dwell on her "wickedness" and express a strong awareness of her deviance (L30, L31). Most of all, however, it is this resistance to domestic and Christian virtues that ultimately threatens Dickinson's relationships with her Amherst friends. Cott draws attention to the importance of shared religious convictions as the basis for female friendships: "Intense attachments between women were often rooted in shared or similar experiences of conversion to Christianity. More inclusive than the female academy in its social range, the church was even more instrumental, overall, in shaping female friendships" (179). Whereas becoming a Christian can thus lead, according to Cott, to "becoming a member of a voluntary community not only in a psychological but in a literal sense," a resistance to conversion, on the other hand, may threaten one's membership in such a community (142).[7]

For Dickinson, membership in the community of her Amherst friends became increasingly more difficult. The writer's resistance to piety and her concomitant rejection of the culturally prescribed ideal of "true womanhood" gradually excluded her from the world of her socially more conservative peers. Frequently, she experienced a growing sense of isolation from her female friends: "Christ is calling everyone here, all my companions have answered, even my darling Vinnie believes she loves, and trusts him, and I am standing alone in rebellion, and growing very careless" (L35). Interestingly enough, however, what Dickinson regrets most is not her own unregenerate state, but the resulting estrangement from her friends: "The bad ones slink away, and are sorrowful—not at their wicked lives—but at this strange time, great change. *I* am one of the lingering *bad* ones, and so do *I* slink away" (L36).[8] What Dickinson longs for is a continuation of her friendships, irrespective of ideological differences: "My own dear Abiah, For so I will still call you, though while I do it, even now I tremble at my strange audacity . . . but I love you better than ever notwithstanding the link which bound us in that golden chain is sadly dimmed" (L26). Yet her efforts to maintain possession of her friends ("My own") do not succeed: "How lonely this world is growing," she observes in 1850 (L35). Thus Dickinson finally comes to terms with the fact that her friends are adopting the role of "woman," while she herself resists this transformation: "I see but little of Abby," she informed Abiah Root later during the same year, "she cannot come to see me, and I walk so far not often, and perhaps it's all right and best. Our lots fall in different places; mayhap we might disagree. We take different views of life, our thoughts would not dwell together as they used to when we were young—how long ago that seems! She is more of a woman than I am, for I love so to be a child—Abby is holier than me—she does more good in her lifetime than ever I shall in mine" (L39).[9]

It is at this point that Dickinson's letters themselves begin to change substantially, moving more and more away from the typical nineteenth-century epistolary discourse as outlined in letter-writing manuals. Whereas some of her earlier correspondences were written in the tradition of the letter as confession, offering the disclosure of secrets to a confidante, for example, Dickinson now stops sharing her most intimate thoughts: "I will try not to say any more—my rebellious thoughts are many, and the friend I love and trust in has much *now* to forgive" (L39).[10] The revelation of emotions and emotionally charged issues, in particular, is carefully monitored: "How very sad it is to have a confiding nature, one's hopes and feelings are quite at the mercy of all who come along; and how very desirable to be a *stolid* individual, whose hopes and aspirations are safe in one's waistcoat pocket, and *that* a pocket indeed, and one not to be picked!" (L69).

Rather than sites for self-disclosures to an intimate friend, Dickinson's letters gradually become spaces for rhetorical performances, for entertaining an audience, and, ultimately, for controlled acts of self-representation *deliberately* tailored toward a specific recipient. The letter-writing act itself is consequently redefined as a creative, literary task dependent on imagination and inspiration: "I have now sit down to write you a long, long, letter," she tells Root. "My writing apparatus is upon a stand before me, and all things are ready. I have no flowers before me as you had to inspire you. But then you know I can imagine myself inspired by them and perhaps that will do as well" (L7). In her earlier letters, Dickinson had regarded epistolary exchanges as a means to bridge the distance created by the addressee's physical absence, and had therefore insisted on "telling all the news": "I will try to make it [my letter] communicate as much information as possible" (L9). Now, however, a mere chronicling of events, "communicating information," becomes an inferior epistolary task, to be avoided by Dickinson as much as possible: "I'm telling all the news, Austin, for I think you will like to hear it. You know it's quite a sacrifice for *me* to tell what's going on" (L141). What Dickinson prefers is to concentrate on the more "poetical" topics that allow for a display of rhetoricity and descriptive detail: "Vinnie will tell you all the news, so I will take a little place to describe a thunder shower which occurred yesterday afternoon" (L89).

Entertaining her audience now becomes Dickinson's major purpose in writing letters. The essential ingredient of a good letter, according to her—and the quality she most admires in other people's correspondences—is wit. Dickinson specifically accentuates this rhetorical feature in her own letters, asking Root: "Haven't I given a ludicrous account of going home sick from a boarding-school?" (L23). Her most elaborately humorous story, again addressed to Root, is an extended account of catching a cold, personified as a "dear creature" who torments his victim (L31). This episode concludes with the remarks: "but this is a wicked story. . . . Now my dear friend, let me tell you that these last thoughts are fictions—vain imaginations to lead astray foolish young women. They are flowers of speech, they both *make*, and *tell* deliberate falsehoods, avoid them as the snake, and turn aside as from the *Bottle* snake, and I dont *think* you will be harmed" (L31). By emphasizing the "wickedness" of her story and the corruptive influence of these "deliberate falsehoods," Dickinson self-ironically maps out Root's "orthodox" response, which echoes the Puritan rejection of "fiction" as dangerous lies. Yet although she exhorts her friend to "avoid them as the snake," she describes herself as being irresistibly drawn to this cunning serpent that is able to beguile others through the power of words. Already in 1846 she declared to her friend Abiah Root: "I have lately come to the conclusion that I am Eve, alias Mrs Adam. You know there is no account of her death in the Bible, and why am not I Eve?" (L9). Margaret Homans explains the implications of Dickinson's identification with Eve:

> Eve's words are secondary and stray from the truth. Because she learns Adam's language rather than inventing it with him . . . , she can learn another as well, and she learns Satan's. Satan teaches her to doubt the literal truth of the language that God and Adam share. . . . It is Eve's discovery that both God and Satan are fictive speakers, and that no discourse is literally true. Adam becomes the traditional symbol for literal language in which words are synonymous with meaning, but Eve is the first to question that synonymity. . . . When she [Dickinson] talks about wickedness, then, in the context of fiction or of religion, what she fears is not the conventional notion of sin, but rather the figurativeness of language that allows even the most sincere speech to be a fiction among other fictions. (171)

Dickinson alias Eve thus casts herself in the role of a creator of fiction, a user of and beguiler through figurative language whose texts become a "fiction among other fictions." In contrast to Homans, however, I submit that in her correspondence, Dickinson, rather than "fearing" this fictional potential of figurative language, explores and exploits it to create her own textually enacted epistolary personae. As Betsy Erkkila has summarized: "Recognizing at once the power of language and its essential fictiveness, [Dickinson] realizes first in her letters to women and later in her poems that it is on the level of language that she can resist subjection to the systems of masculine power—religious, social, and linguistic—by questioning and destabilizing its terms" (*Wicked Sisters* 24). Yet, as we shall see below, it is primarily in her letters to *men* that Dickinson destabilizes male-dominated discursive systems by adopting double voices that enable her to negotiate between socially permissible and impermissible spaces, and thus to critique prevailing sociocultural constructions of womanhood. In her letters to women, these critiques assume more subtle forms. Throughout all of her letters, however, the guise of Eve, with its potential for writing figuratively, allows Dickinson to construct multiple epistolary personae that eventually enable her to rewrite and orchestrate all of her relationships on her own discursive terms.

Yet the effectiveness and persuasiveness of such textual gestures of self-fashioning and self-performance depend largely on an otherwise drastically reduced amount of direct social interaction. Indeed, after gradually omitting any intimate disclosures from her letters to Root, Humphrey, and Fowler, Dickinson eventually breaks off any personal contact with her friends altogether: "When some pleasant friend invites me to pass a week with her, I look at my father and mother and Vinnie, . . . and I say no—no, cant leave them" (L86). It is not incidental that the end of Dickinson's interaction with each of her Amherst friends coincides with their adoption of the ultimate role expressive of the ideal of "true womanhood": that of wife. Johnson has pointed out this correlation, noting that Dickinson's correspondence with Jane Humphrey "was abruptly terminated by Jane's marriage" (*Letters* 946), and that the author's final extant letter to Abiah Root was written in 1854, the year of the latter's marriage.[11] Similarly, Dickinson's epistolary exchange with Emily Fowler comes to a standstill one year after her marriage, in 1854.[12]

Emily Fowler is the only one of her three friends with whom Dickinson had explicitly discussed the subject of marriage, indicating that for her, friendship and marriage are incompatible: "I know I cant have you always—some day a 'brave dragoon' will be stealing you away and I will have farther to go to discover you *at all*" (L40). Fowler's adoption of a wife's role, according to Dickinson, ultimately excludes her from girlhood friendships: "and must we stay alone . . . and you do not come back again, . . . I knew you would go away, for I know the roses are gathered, but I guessed not yet . . . 'I can go to her, but she cannot come back to me'" (L146). The theme of departure, finality, and, metaphorically, death is further underlined by the following quotation from a hymn, incorporated at the end of the same letter: "So fades a summer cloud away, / So smiles the gale when storms are o'er / So gently shuts the eye of day, / So dies a wave along the shore." And the concluding line, "Will you write me sometime?" is as indicative of the end of their friendship as the statement in Dickinson's subsequent letter: "I would tell you about the spring if I thought it might persuade you even now to return" (L161).[13]

That Root's, Humphrey's, and Fowler's marriages prompted Dickinson to end her friendship with them is highly unusual. In her analysis of nineteenth-century female epistolary friendships, Carroll Smith-Rosenberg has found that "marriage altered neither the frequency of their correspondence nor their desire to be together" ("Female World" 4). On the contrary, Smith-Rosenberg notes, "these eighteenth- and nineteenth-century friendships lasted with undiminished, indeed often increased, intensity throughout the women's lives" (26). Yet it was Dickinson's resistance to the value systems these female friendships were based on which eventually led to their termination.

Although Dickinson finally breaks off her exchanges with her earliest Amherst friends, these letters nevertheless fulfilled a crucial function in the development of her epistolary strategies. Prompted by the gradual estrangement from these women to reduce the confessional aspects of her letters, Dickinson begins to turn them into fictional sites that enable her to playfully enact multiple roles and to develop carefully crafted and controlled self-articulations specifically tailored toward her respective addressees. In this way, Dickinson transforms her letters into tools that allow her to reconstruct relationships on her own discursive terms by problematizing a referential link between the writer's physical self and her epistolary personae, in other words, between the personal and the fictional, the referential and the nonreferential, the factual and the constructivist. Especially Dickinson's post-1850s epistolary self-conceptualizations and self-representations can best be understood in terms of such a blurring of factual needs and linguistic constructions or "fictions" (rather than simply the unmediated "confessions" of an essentialist self). In a July 1862 letter to Thomas Wentworth Higginson, Dickinson explicitly emphasizes the aesthetic distance between her "self" and its textual representations: "When I state myself, as the Representative of the Verse—it does not mean—me—but a supposed person" (L268). Most discussions of Dickinson's poetic "personae" have taken their departure from here.[14] Yet I contend that this statement can profitably be extended to include Dickinson's letters as well as her poems. Even though each of Dickinson's correspondences, taken by itself, seemingly chronicles a personal relationship (and has often been read as such), all of her later epistolary exchanges are to some extent also carefully constructed textual performances.[15] These elements of performativity and self-fashioning (often modeled on fictional discourses) are particularly striking in Dickinson's textual transformation of the emotionally charged relationship with her sister-in-law, Sue Gilbert.

SUSAN HUNTINGTON GILBERT DICKINSON

Starting at a time when her friendships with Jane Humphrey, Abiah Root, and Emily Fowler were gradually coming to an end, Dickinson's friendship with Sue Gilbert constitutes an important stage in the writer's development of textual strategies to sustain an often intense and highly complex relationship.[16] The question of how to describe the exact nature of this relationship has received much critical attention. Several scholars, including Juhasz and Sewall, reject a strictly lesbian interpretation: "However much some feminist critics want to dwell upon Dickinson's homoerotic impulses toward Sue," Juhasz argues, "I would maintain that she did not conceive of enacting them in anything like a literal or physical way, which is what gave her the security to express those feelings" ("Reading" 178). Sewall concurs: "Sue emerges as someone with whom, at a safe distance, she [Dickinson] could at least play at wit and love" (*Life* 199). Erkkila, on the other hand, regards Dickinson's relationship with Sue as a love relationship while leaving the question of physical contact open: "Dickinson's love for Sue was a form of saying *No* to the masculine and heterosexual orders of Church and State in order to say *Yes* to herself" (*Wicked Sisters* 31). Irrespective of the exact nature of Dickinson's homoeroticism, Erkkila argues, it is the significance of this female bond which needs to be emphasized: "Despite the efforts of the

Dickinson family and later critics to erase and write over the erotic traces of this relationship, it was Dickinson's intense, passionate, and sometimes troubled love relationship with Sue and not her love relationship with the Master . . . that was the central and enduring relationship of her life" (41).

Questioning the traditional assumption that Victorian friendships among women were necessarily nonsexual (*Rowing* 24) and challenging the view that the Dickinson-Sue relationship was nonphysical (25), Martha Nell Smith argues for an acknowledgment of Dickinson's lesbian passions: "To characterize these passionate letters to Sue as conventional manifestations of female love and ritual seems naive, for time and again Dickinson inscribes the self-consciousness evident when she apologizes for writing 'all these *ugly things*'" (162–163). Specifically, Smith provides intriguing evidence of (sometimes partly recoverable) deletions in Dickinson's manuscript letters addressed to Austin Dickinson, which suggest that either Dickinson's brother or Todd or both had attempted to erase Sue's name: "Noting that the deletions do not begin to occur until the fall of 1851, when Emily begins to write Sue passionately (see L56, L57), and keeping in mind that the passages deleted all refer to Sue, examining the altered letters to Austin in context of the letters Dickinson was writing to Susan Gilbert at the same time substantiates the conclusion that the expurgations clearly seek to expunge the record of Dickinson's affection for this woman" (20–21). This emphasis on the eroticism as well as the "emotional, spiritual, and physical communion" between Dickinson and Sue (Hart and Smith, *Open Me* 63) is further highlighted in Smith's most recent projects, including her edition (together with Ellen Louise Hart) of "Dickinson's intimate letters" to Sue, entitled *Open Me Carefully*.

In "The Female World of Love and Ritual," alluded to by Smith, Carroll Smith-Rosenberg has attempted to define the nature and significance of female friendships for middle-class North American women in the mid–nineteenth century: "An abundance of manuscript evidence suggests that eighteenth- and nineteenth-century women routinely formed emotional ties with other women. Such deeply felt, same-sex friendships were casually accepted in American society. . . . These relationships ranged from the supportive love of sisters, through the enthusiasms of adolescent girls, to sensual avowals of love by mature women" ("Female World" 1–2). According to Smith-Rosenberg, these friendships were frequently conducted and supplemented by letters: "Nineteenth- and twentieth-century readers concur about one matter: nineteenth-century women wrote love letters to one another" (*Disorderly Conduct* 35–36). Answering her own question "But did the word 'love' connote to these women, as it does to us, the recognition of sexual desire?" (35–36), Smith-Rosenberg concludes that the unselfconsciousness of these letters makes a lesbian interpretation doubtful (36). Emphasizing the social constructedness of sexual behavior, Smith-Rosenberg also challenges the two-tiered twentieth-century view of love: "The twentieth-century tendency to view human love and sexuality within a dichotomized universe of deviance and normality, genitality and platonic love, is alien to the emotions and attitudes of the nineteenth century and fundamentally distorts the nature of these women's emotional interaction" (Smith-Rosenberg, "Female World" 8; see also *Disorderly Conduct* 58–59). Citing the example of Sarah Butler Wistar and Jeannie Field Musgrove, Smith-Rosenberg suggests that their love appears as "both sensual and platonic" to twentieth-century minds (*Disorderly Conduct* 55): "There is every indication that these four women [Wistar, Musgrove, "Molly," and "Helena"], their husbands and families—all eminently respectable and socially conservative—considered such love both socially acceptable and fully compatible with heterosexual marriage. Emotionally and cognitively, their heterosocial and their homosocial worlds were complementary" (59).

Although the exact physical nature of the relationship between Dickinson and Sue Gilbert will probably always have to remain conjectural, I believe that Dickinson's rhetorical strategies of self-fashioning utilized in her epistolary (re)constructions of this friendship can at least hint at a possible interpretation. In many respects, Dickinson's letters do indeed conform to Smith-Rosenberg's description of nineteenth-century expressions of love among women, but they display at least one crucial difference: for Dickinson, her love for Sue is *not* compatible with Sue's later (heterosexual) marriage to Dickinson's brother, Austin. In fact, it is specifically Sue's marriage that eventually precipitates an intense crisis—which, in turn, provokes compensatory (rhetorical) strategies in Dickinson's letters and letter-poems. Prior to Sue's marriage, both Dickinson and Sue enjoy frequent social interactions, modeled, indeed, on what Smith-Rosenberg has termed the "female world of love and ritual." During this stage, Dickinson considers her letters as a substitute, albeit a vastly insufficient one, for the absent person, written to maintain contact across a spatial distance. Whenever fictional roles are appropriated at this point, they present an ideal version of female friendship based on mutual love. It is not until Sue gets married that the writer's letters to her assume a substantially different function.

Sue became engaged to Dickinson's brother, Austin, in November 1853 and was married in 1856, at which time she moved into the Evergreens next door to the Homestead. She had also joined the church in August 1850, in this way occupying the two most important roles (wife and church member) according to the "ideology of true womanhood." Commenting on both Sue's profession of faith and her marriage, Erkkila argues that "Dickinson experiences her loss of Sue to both religion and marriage as a kind of death in which Sue's life is 'yielded up' to the masculine and heterosexual orders of man and God" (*Wicked Sisters* 35). Erkkila focuses on the negative rather than the transformative aspects of these developments by claiming that "this loss of the female to the law of the fathers is a central and almost obsessively recurrent motif in Dickinson's letters and later in her poems" (36). Although this certainly holds true for Dickinson's earlier friendships, I argue that, with Sue, these two events now become the transformative stimulus for Dickinson to reconceptualize and rewrite a friendship discursively on her own terms. After Sue's marriage, Dickinson begins to translate their relationship onto a predominantly textual level that enables her to counterbalance actual realities. Renouncing the horizontal model of female (noncarnal) love and friendship (based on mutuality) that dominates her early letters to Sue, Dickinson instead appropriates the hierarchical and male-identified discourse of courtly love to redefine both Sue's and her own role discursively. In doing so, she replaces the actual person Sue Gilbert with an idealized yet perpetually inaccessible textual construct that, by virtue of its unavailability (due to marriage), guarantees the epistolary continuation of what had started as a passionate love relationship.

Consisting almost exclusively of declarations of love combined with expressions of yearning for the other's presence, Dickinson's earliest letters to Sue (her "*billets doux*") highlight the intensity of her emotions: "The precious billet, Susie, I am wearing the paper out, reading it over and over"

(L74).[17] Yet love letters, however precious, cannot be an adequate substitute for physical presence: "How vain it seems to *write*, when one knows how to feel—how much more near and dear to sit beside you, talk with you, hear the tones of your voice" (L73). The same dissatisfaction with letters is echoed in L96 and L85: "I *disdain* this pen, and wait for a *warmer* language" (L96); "When you come home, darling, I shant have your letters, shall I, but I shall have *yourself*, which is more" (L85).[18] To replace language with physical contact is the ultimate desire: Dickinson wants to "steal a kiss from the sister" (L38); she asks Sue, "*please* be corporal" (L70); and she longs to "have you in my arms" (L70): "If you were here—and Oh that you were, my Susie, we need not talk at all, our eyes would whisper for us, and your hand fast in mine, we would not ask for language" (L94).[19]

Yet Sue seems not to have responded emphatically enough to Dickinson's effusions; she needs to be reminded of what to write: "just write me every week *one line*, and let it be, 'Emily, I love you,' and I will be satisfied" (L74). Whenever her friend does not answer quickly enough, Dickinson urges her: "Why dont you write me, Darling? Did I in that quick letter say anything which grieved you, or made it hard for you to take your usual pen and trace affection for your bad, sad Emilie? Then Susie, you must forgive me before you sleep tonight, for I will not shut my eyes until you have kissed my cheek, and told me you would love me" (L103).[20]

Dickinson's repeated exhortations to get proof of Sue's love suggest that, at this early stage in their friendship, she had begun to envision Sue as a partner in a permanent love relationship enduring even after death: "If this life holds not another meeting for us, remember also, Susie, that it had no *parting* more, wherever that hour finds us, for which we have hoped so long, we shall not be separated, neither death, nor the grave can part us, so that we only *love*" (L93). To better highlight their (mutual) roles, Dickinson turns to fictional models to explain her concept of love. Hart and Smith ascribe to this use of characters from novels or plays a " 'masking' function, implying that Susan and Emily related their secrets through the personalities of literary and biblical characters with whom they were both familiar" (*Open Me* xviii). I would add that they also have a (re)constructivist function, spelling out (or possibly prescribing) the respective roles that Dickinson wants both herself and her addressee to occupy. Drawing on the depiction of female love and friendship in several popular sentimental novels, Dickinson outlines the exact parameters of their relationship. In L38, for example, Sue is associated with Alice Archer, a character in Longfellow's *Kavanagh;* Sue's room is referred to as "your little 'Columbarium [which] is lined with warmth and softness'" (L38). And Dickinson continues to make the analogy more explicit: "There is no 'silence' there—so you differ from bonnie 'Alice'" (L38). The importance of Alice Archer and Cecilia Vaughan's friendship as an analogue for Dickinson's friendship with Sue has also been noted by Richard Sewall. He quotes a passage in Dickinson's copy of this novel which has been marked by two hands and which, according to Sewall, came "so close to what Emily felt for Sue as, it would seem, to have been unmistakable, at least to Emily: 'They sat together in school; they walked together after school; they told each other their manifold secrets; they wrote long and impassioned letters to each other in the evening; in a word, they were in love with each other'" (qtd. in *Life* 683).

A second source is Ik Marvel's [Donald G. Mitchell's] fictional essays: "perhaps we would have a 'Reverie' after the form of 'Ik Marvel,'" Dickinson writes to Sue, "indeed I do not know why it would'nt be just as charming as of that lonely Bachelor, smoking his cigar—and it would be far more profitable as 'Marvel' *only* marvelled, and you and I would *try* to make a little destiny to have for our own" (L56). Reading Marvel, Dickinson deliberately blurs the boundaries between fact and fiction; she translates the "art" of his essays into "life" ("I would *try* to make a little destiny to have for our own"), while "life" is simultaneously interpreted through "art": "Dont you hope he [Marvel] will live as long as you and I do—and keep on having dreams and writing them to us; . . . We will be willing to die Susie—when such as *he* have gone, for there will be none to interpret these lives of our's" (L56). Longfellow and Marvel thus constitute two early examples of Dickinson's attempts to employ texts in order to map out the roles for both Sue and herself discursively. In her later letters, this strategy is explored to its fullest.

One of the factors that had contributed to Dickinson's gradual estrangement from her Amherst friends was their conversion to Christianity and their concomitant subscription to domestic values. When Sue joins the church, however, this event is discursively redefined. Dickinson replaces the orthodox Christian church with the church of love: "The bells are ringing,

Susie, . . . and the people who love God, are expecting to go to meeting; dont *you* go Susie, not to *their* meeting, but come with me this morning to the church within our hearts, where the bells are always ringing, and the preacher whose name is Love—shall intercede there for us!" (L77). By defining both herself as well as Sue as members of the same "church of love," Dickinson discursively annihilates any ideological differences that her own resistance to professing membership in the orthodox Christian church might have created. While Dickinson can thus remain uncommitted as to her own relationship to the Christian God, her redefinition of Sue as an angel ("while you are taken from me, I class you with the *angels* [L77]), and eventually as a Christ figure (" 'two or three' are gathered in your name, loving, and speaking of you—and will you be there in the midst of them?" [L77]) enables her to worship Sue *as* Christ, thus turning love—or more particularly her love for Sue—into an alternative form of religion.

In L88, the transformation is complete: Sue replaces God, and thus worshiping Sue—rather than constituting a sacrilege—becomes tantamount to worshiping the Christian deity: "when I was gone to meeting . . . I could not find a *chink* to put the worthy pastor; when he said 'Our Heavenly Father,' I said 'Oh Darling Sue'; when he read the 100th Psalm, I kept saying your precious letter all over to myself, and Susie, when they sang . . . I made up words and kept singing how I loved you" (L88). The fact that Sue has replaced God, that Sue is situated at the center of Dickinson's religion of love, finally allows the latter to separate religious from domestic duties and align them with love duties instead: "The dishes may wait dear Susie—and the uncleared table stand, *them* I have always with me, but you, I have 'not always' " (L73). In this way, Dickinson resolves the conflict encountered in her relationships with Root, Humphrey, and Fowler. Instead of occupying the narrowly circumscribed subject positions offered to women by religious discourse, Dickinson appropriates religious discourse to create her own subject positions as lover and worshiper of Sue as God.

Even more so than Sue's conversion, her potential marriage also threatens the continuation of their friendship. Dickinson's earlier fears of losing Fowler to a "brave dragoon" (L40) are echoed and inverted in a letter to Sue: "I have thought today of what would become of me when the 'bold Dragon' shall bear you both away, to live in his high mountain—and leave me here alone; and I could have wept bitterly over the only *fancy* of ever being so lone" (L70). In 1852, a year before Sue's official engagement, Dickinson explains her profound ambivalence about the state of wifehood:

> You and I have been strangely silent upon this subject, Susie, we have often touched upon it, and as quickly fled away, as children shut their eyes when the sun is too bright for them. I have always hoped to know if you had no dear fancy, illumining all your life, no one of whom you murmured in the faithful ear of night—and at whose side in fancy, you walked the livelong day; and when you come home, Susie, we must speak of these things. How dull our lives must seem to the bride, and the plighted maiden, whose days are fed with gold, and who gathers pearls every evening; but to the *wife*, Susie, sometimes the *wife forgotten*, our lives perhaps seem dearer than all others in the world. (L93)

Dickinson's choice of simile ("as children shut their eyes") echoes her earlier attempts to prevent both herself and her addressees from growing up and becoming "women." In the following letter to Sue, Dickinson's desire to return to childhood assumes even greater urgency: "That you and I in *hand* as we e'en *do* in heart, might ramble away as children, among the woods and fields, and forget these many years, and these sorrowing cares, and each become a child again—I would it were so, Susie, and when I look around me and find myself alone, I sigh for you again" (L94); and again in L96: "Oh Susie, my child." Motivated by her fears that Sue will complete the transition to woman- and wifehood while leaving herself back "alone," Dickinson increasingly attempts to reconfigure Sue in the role of child, particularly in letters written shortly before Sue's marriage: "There has not been a day, Child, that I've not thought of you" (L172); "dear Child" (L177); "Dear Children—Mattie—Sue" (L178); "my Children" (L178). L173, written in 1854, illustrates the culmination of this crisis. Dickinson's perspective is that of the child:

> Sue—you can go or stay—There is but one alternative—We differ often lately, and this must be the last. . . . It is the lingering emblem of the Heaven I once dreamed, and though if this is taken, I shall remain alone, and though

in that last day, the Jesus Christ you love, remark he does not know me—there is a darker spirit will not disown it's child. Few have been given me, and if I love them so, that for *idolatry*, they are removed from me—I simply murmur *gone*, and the billow dies away into the boundless blue. . . . We have walked very pleasantly—Perhaps this is the point at which our paths diverge—then pass on singing Sue, and up the distant hill I journey on.

This letter has played a key role in almost all discussions of Dickinson's relationship to Sue, with most critics using it to prove the occurrence of an actual estrangement between the two women.[21] Although a solution to this question on external grounds may never be established with certainty, a possible answer can be found by reading L173 in dialogic interaction with its concluding poem. The poem incorporated at the end of the letter stands in antithetical juxtaposition to the missive's opening:

I have a Bird in spring
Which for myself doth sing—
The spring decoys.
And as the summer nears—
And as the Rose appears,
Robin is gone.

Yet do I not repine
Knowing that Bird of mine
Though flown—
Learneth beyond the sea
Melody new for me
And will return. . . .

In a serener Bright,
In a more golden light
I see
Each little doubt and fear,
Each little discord here
Removed.

Then will I not repine,
Knowing that Bird of mine
Though flown
Shall in a distant tree
Bright melody for me
Return. (L173)

In contrast to the poem that, with its images of finality and death, marked the end of Dickinson's friendship with Fowler ("So fades a summer cloud away," L146), this poem emphasizes change and growth ("Learneth," "Melody new"). Moreover, whereas Fowler's marriage, in Dickinson's eyes, precluded her return ("she cannot come back to me," L146), Sue will return "In a serener Bright, | In a more golden light." Although Sue will have changed, the poem implies, and though their relationship will consequently have to undergo changes as well, Sue's eventual "return" is nonetheless considered a certainty (emphasized by the double repetition and the end position of "return").

The interim changes, however, are quite substantial. The "Robin's" temporary absence is experienced as fraught with intense pain; "doubt" and "fear" prevail. Yet the nature and intensity of these tensions are at the same time also indicative of the importance of this relationship for Dickinson. To alleviate the pain caused by Sue's "absence" (through marriage), Dickinson repeatedly attempts to claim discursive possession of her sister-in-law in poems that have been specifically personalized for her:

> One Sister have I in our house, | And one, a hedge away. | There's only one recorded, | But both belong to me. || One came the road that I came— | And wore my last year's gown— | The other, as a bird her nest, | Builded our hearts among. || She did not sing as we did— | It was a different tune— | Herself to her a music | As Bumble bee of June. || Today is far from Childhood— | But up and down the hills | I held her hand the tighter— | Which shortened all the miles— || And still her hum | The years among, | Deceives the Butterfly; | Still in her Eye | The Violets lie | Mouldered this many May. || I split the dew— | But took the morn— I chose this single star | From out the wide night's numbers— | Sue—forevermore! (J14/Fr 5A, 1858)

This poem outlines the tensions Dickinson encounters in her newly redefined relationship with Sue: emphasizing attempts to "own" her sister-in-law ("both belong to me," "I held her hand the tighter") in spite of the fact that, as Austin's wife, she "belongs" to him, Dickinson nevertheless also accents Sue's distance through difference ("She did not sing as we did"). Ultimately, the dark undertones ("Deceives the Butterfly," "Mouldered") reflect Dickinson's ambivalence about their changed relationship. Despite closer ties through marriage, Sue has, if anything, become even more remote: "But Susan is a Stranger yet— | The Ones who cite her most | Have never scaled her Haunted House | Nor compromised her Ghost— || To pity those who know her not | Is helped by the regret | That those who know her know her less | The nearer her they get" (J1400/Fr1433C, 1877).[22]

As this late poem illustrates, Dickinson's sense of distance and alienation from Sue, her experience of the sister-in-law's closeness as the lover's absence, does not seem to have lessened substantially over time. The most profound difficulties, however, manifest themselves in texts written during the mid-1860s. For this period, even Hart and Smith, who generally emphasize the enduring intimacy between the two women, note "the strain of profound differences of opinion" (*Open Me* 65).[23] In 1861, for example, Dickinson is concerned with ways to assure herself of Sue's love: "You love me—you are sure— | I shall not fear mistake— | I shall not *cheated* wake— | Some grinning morn— | To find the Sunrise left — | And Orchards—unbereft— | And Dollie[24]—gone! || I need not start—you're sure— | That night will never be— | When frightened—home to Thee I run— | To find the windows dark— | And no more Dollie—mark— | Quite none? || Be sure you're sure—you know— | I'll bear it better now— | If you'll just tell me so— | Than when—a little dull Balm grown— | Over this pain of mine— You sting—again!" (J156/Fr218A, 1861). In J673/Fr285A, Dickinson further elaborates on the pain stemming from her own (a "child's") love for Sue. Introduced by the lines "*Excuse* me—Dollie—" (qtd. in Franklin, *Poems* 1:303, and Johnson, *Poems* 520), the poem reads: "The Love a Child[25] can show—below— | Is but a Filament—I know— | Of that Diviner— Thing— | That faints upon the face of Noon— | And smites the Tinder in the Sun— | And hinders—Gabriel's—Wing! || 'Tis This—in Music—hints—and sways— | And far abroad—on Summer Days— | Distils—uncertain—pain— | 'Tis

This— afflicts us in the East— | And tints the Transit in the West— | With Harrowing —Iodine! || 'Tis This—invites—appals—endows— | Flits—glimmers— proves—dissolves— | Returns—suggests—convicts—enchants— | Then—flings in Paradise!" (J673/Fr285A, 1862).[26]

One of the strategies Dickinson employs to ensure Sue's eventual "return" and thus a continuation of their love relationship—despite Sue's married status—is to reconstruct it on an idealized, fictional level.[27] Even though her sister-in-law came to live next door, Dickinson communicates with her in writing on a regular basis by sending poems and letters over to the Evergreens.[28] In addition to possibly inviting Sue's (literary) criticism—an argument advanced by Hart and Smith (*Open Me* 147)—these missives also directly comment on and negotiate their relationship. Juhasz draws attention to the creative and revisionist potential inherent in such a predominantly textual (as opposed to exclusively social) interaction: "But if Dickinson had wanted to perpetuate her particular relationship with Sue, a relationship which in real life would certainly have had to alter as Sue moved from best friend to sister-in-law, and if Dickinson had wanted to perpetuate as well her role as writer of love letters, then the letters themselves had to continue, for they were what constituted the alternative reality of which I speak and not the social association between the two women *per se*" ("Reading" 182). In this way, a regular exchange of letters and letter-poems allowed Dickinson to take more immediate discursive control, that is, to construct and tailor their relationship to her own needs.

One discursive strategy to deal with Sue's inaccessibility is to elevate her position. Whereas distance and alienation might threaten a friendship based on mutuality and reciprocity, they can readily be dealt with in a superior being.[29] Thus, after Sue's marriage, Dickinson's role ascriptions to both her sister-in-law and herself gradually change from the horizontal model of nineteenth-century female love and friendship based on equality and mutuality to the vertical model of courtly love and unfulfilled passion based on a power hierarchy.[30] In this constellation, Dickinson represents herself as the suffering, rejected male lover/poet, while Sue is cast in the role of the idealized, quasi-divine female beloved, perpetually out of reach. The real-life figure Sue is magnified into a larger-than-life construct: "I must wait a few Days before seeing you—You are too momentous. But remember it is idolatry, not indifference" (L581). With such words, Sue is transformed into an idol, constructed specifically for purposes of worship rather than actual social interaction: "Susan's Idolator keeps a Shrine for Susan" (L325). Sue's power becomes so overwhelming that Dickinson loses her own independent identity, her "proper" name; she becomes "Susan's Idolator" (L325), and "Susan's Emily" (L333). Whereas Dickinson thus regards herself as Sue's property, this transfer of ownership is not reciprocal: the former friend has been lost to Dickinson, and the divine idol is out of reach: "To lose what we never owned might seem an eccentric Bereavement but Presumption has it's Affliction as actually as Claim" (L429). Yet, paradoxically, Dickinson ultimately considers this transformation of Sue as gain ("Of so divine a Loss | We enter but the Gain" [L364/], as it allows for the continuation of their relationship, albeit on different terms. Sue's association with an inaccessible divinity is also emphasized in several poems sent to her: "Content of fading | Is enough for me— | Fade I unto Divinity— || And Dying—Lifetime— | Ample as the Eye— | Her least attention raise on me" (J682/Fr888A, 1864). The distance between Sue Gilbert and Dickinson is explained (and excused) due to the former's "superiority," her "ascension" to "too remote a Hight": "The Soul's Superior instants | Occur to Her—alone— | When friend—and Earth's occasion | Have infinite withdrawn— || Or She—Herself—ascended | To too remote a Hight | For lower Recognition | Than Her Omnipotent" (J306/Fr630A, 1863).[31]

Sue's elevated, idealized, divine status is also mirrored in Dickinson's choice of literary roles ascribed to her sister-in-law. Shakespeare's *Antony and Cleopatra* has been noted as a central literary model for the writer's relationship with Sue.[32] In L430, Dickinson first associates herself with Antony, while addressing Sue metonymically as "Egypt": "'Egypt—thou knew'st.'" The full context of this quotation is supplied by Johnson: "'Egypt, thou knew'st too well, / My heart was to thy rudder tied by the strings, / And thou shouldst tow me after. O'er my spirit / Thy full supremacy thou knew'st, and that / Thy beck might from the bidding of the gods / Command me'" (qtd. in *Letters* 533).[33] Farr comments on this letter: "What Dickinson means here is that Sue has revealed to her the same depth of selfishness, the same craze for power, that Antony discovers in the queen" (*Passion* 172). Yet the above-quoted passage additionally reflects Dickinson's construction of Sue's "full supremacy" over herself; while Sue had replaced God in earlier letters, her power now *surpasses* that of the gods.[34] As Farr has summarized: "She [Dickinson] came to use the play as an emblem for the domination of one person by another" (" 'Engulfing' " 232).

Moreover, the play also becomes an emblem for Dickinson's own unfulfilled passion. As Finnerty observes: "Antony and Othello are coded representatives of proscribed female jealousy and extreme passion. By identifying with them, Dickinson extends safely through association the prescribed limits of acceptable femininity" (68). And Dickinson herself admits: "Susan's Calls are like Antony's Supper—'And pays his Heart for what his Eyes eat, only—' " (L854). Bennett reads this letter as an explanation of Dickinson's vision of love: "Dickinson identified with Antony, . . . she longed for a 'Supper' (a vision of love) she could eat with her eyes only" ("Orient" 112). I maintain, however, that these lines more likely express Antony's/Dickinson's dissatisfaction with the "Supper" that can be provided by Cleopatra/Sue. Like Antony, she longed for more. Dickinson had already explored a similar idea much earlier. The following poem was, according to Johnson, sent to her sister-in-law in 1864: "The luxury to apprehend | The luxury 'twould be | To look at Thee a single time | An Epicure of Me | In whatsoever Presence Makes | Till for a further food | I scarcely recollect to starve | So first am I supplied— | The luxury to meditate | The luxury it was | To banquet on thy Countenance | A Sumptuousness bestows | On plainer Days, | Whose Table, far | As Certainty—can see— | Is laden with a single Crumb— | The Consciousness of Thee" (J815/Fr819B). Here, Dickinson is twice removed from Sue. Rather than "eating with her eyes only," she can merely "meditate" upon the significance of having seen and sensuously enjoyed Sue in the past ("The luxury it was | To banquet on thy Countenance"), and "apprehend" the pleasure of seeing her again in the future ("The luxury 'twould be | To look at Thee a single time"). In the present, however, she is reduced to starve on "a single Crumb": the memory/knowledge of Sue's existence.[35]

Although Dickinson's appropriation of *Antony and Cleopatra* has been variously recognized, I suggest that another, equally important key to reading the Dickinson-Sue correspondence can be found in L393. This note provides a multilayered explication of Dickinson's own fictionalized love for her sister-in-law and exemplifies her strategy of ensuring a continuation of their (textually redefined) relationship. It proposes an idealization of Sue as the divine beloved in the tradition of courtly love, which then serves as a discursively predefined justification of her inaccessibility while it allows Dickinson to occupy the role of "singer," pouring out an incessant stream of love poems and letters.

In L393, Dickinson identifies with three male writers of love letters and sonnets: "We remind her we love her—Unimportant fact, though Dante did'nt think so, nor Swift, nor Mirabeau." Several compelling similarities between Dante's, Swift's, and Mirabeau's and Dickinson's amatory writings suggest why the latter would have selected these three as intertexts to remind Sue of her own love for her. Like Dickinson's epistolary exchanges, some of these love letters are highly literary, all are in part fictionalized, some are written in letter format, some in a mixture of poetry and prose (Dante), and all three of them evoke the image of a suffering poet-lover separated from his beloved due to external circumstances. Like Dickinson's love for Sue, Dante's love for Beatrice, expressed in his *Divina Commedia* and *Vita Nuova;* Swift's series of intimate love letters to Esther Johnson collected in his *Journal to Stella;* and Mirabeau's love letters to Marie-Thérèse de Ruffey, written from prison (*Lettres écrites du donjon de Vincennes*) are characterized by passionate yet unfulfilled longing, often enforced by physical distance or by the partner's married status, and reduced to predominantly textual (rather than physical) expression.[36] Like divine Beatrice, who is married to somebody else, and like Marie-Thérèse de Ruffey, who is "imprisoned" in a convent, Sue also remains perpetually inaccessible for Dickinson. Moreover, the fictional quality inherent in all of their names parallels the degree to which Sue has similarly been transformed, fictionalized, and idealized in Dickinson's letters: although inspired by an actual woman, Dickinson's "Sue," like Swift's "Stella," Dante's "Beatrice," and Mirabeau's "Mimi," constitutes a construct of an idealized object of love, removed from the realities of daily interaction.[37] In his *Atlantic Monthly* discussion of *The New Life of Dante,* Charles Eliot Norton has commented on the ways in which such an idealization enabled Dante to "ignore" Beatrice's married status: she "married sometime previous to 1287, and . . . no notice of it is taken by Dante in what he has written concerning her. That the fact of her marriage changed in no degree the feeling with which Dante regarded her is plain. . . . To the marriage of true souls there was no impediment, and he would admit none, in her being the wife of another" (33).

Yet even though both Dante and Dickinson fully exploit this motif of the beloved's elevation, they nonetheless differ in one crucial aspect. In the course of the *New Life*, Dante's love is transformed from desire, or *cupiditas* (i.e., the love for another human being), into *caritas*, or the spiritual love for God, while Beatrice is simultaneously transformed from the object of desire into the agent of Dante's spiritual salvation. Dickinson, on the other hand, as we have seen, literally displaces "God," replacing him with "Sue," thus transforming Sue herself into a spiritualized object of desire or, alternatively, an eroticized divinity. The two collapse into one. In either case, however, this elevation of the beloved serves a crucial purpose. Whereas any relationship between equals depends on reciprocity and frequent exchanges, a relationship with a divine, God-like creature entails—by definition—a more indirect interaction from a distance. And it is in this context that, despite an enforced or a perceived separation of the lovers and thus a restricted enactment of their relationship, the lover-poet-letter-writer achieves a textual sublimation of pain in the act of writing, in the textual celebration of an idealized/idolized woman. As Dante explains in his *New Life*, when asked by women friends, "To what end dost thou love this lady, since thou canst not support her presence?" (36), he responds: "my lord Love, thanks be to him, has placed all my bliss in that which cannot fail me. . . . In those words which speak my lady's praise" (36). Yet he continues: "Not that to tell her praise in full I think, / But to discourse that I may ease my mind." Similarly, Dickinson's letters and letter-poems to Sue thus constitute a textual exploration and celebration of their love, which allows for an "easing of the mind," a transcendence of the pain and distance that, according to Dickinson, Sue's married status had caused. In this way, by actively appropriating and translating amatory pain into textual productivity, by removing her relationship with Sue from the horizontal realm of female friendship and mapping it onto the vertical model of courtly love, Dickinson can maintain their friendship even *without* Sue's active or publicly sanctioned participation. Whereas Dickinson's earlier friendships with Root, Humphrey, and Fowler had depended on a mutual sharing of religious and domestic concerns, the discourse of courtly love functions despite—or rather because of—an absence of reciprocity. Dickinson is able to justify and deal with Sue's inaccessibility textually and can thus ensure a continuation of their relationship merely on the basis of *her own* incessant stream of love letters and poems. In fact, the more remote, the more divine her beloved becomes, the more inspired becomes the supplicant lover: "Still—Clad in your Mail of ices— | Thigh of Granite—and thew—of Steel— | Heedless—alike—of pomp—or parting | Ah, Teneriffe! | I'm kneeling—still—" (J666/Fr752, 1863). In this way, Dickinson's "Robin" has indeed returned "In a more golden light," albeit on a "distant tree" (L173).

Whereas Dickinson's friendship with Sue has thus been redefined in terms of a highly artificial literary discourse, the author's way of ensuring a continuation of her relationship with Elizabeth Holland takes a different turn. With the latter friend, Dickinson hyperbolically inhabits the discourse of "true womanhood," almost to the exclusion of other, more subversive voices.

ELIZABETH HOLLAND

With the exception of Sue Gilbert, Elizabeth Holland became Dickinson's closest female friend; their correspondence, begun in 1853 and continuing until the writer's death in 1886, chronicles one of Dickinson's most enduring epistolary relationships. Dickinson's friendship with Holland has often been interpreted as being particularly open, confiding, and intimate. Most recently, this view has been voiced by Stephanie Tingley: "Dickinson's letters to Elizabeth Holland demonstrate that she overcame much of her natural reticence and took unusual risks with this correspondent. Daring to think aloud, she confides her joys, worries, doubts, and disappointments more freely in this epistolary friendship than she does with most other correspondents" ("Holland Letters" 182). According to Tingley, Holland thus became for Dickinson the "ideal friend," as outlined in Emerson's essay "Friendship": "A friend is a person with whom I may be sincere. Before him [or her, in this case] I may think aloud" (qtd. in "Holland Letters" 182). With her emphasis on "confiding," "free," and "sincere," Tingley interprets Dickinson's self-articulations in her letters to Holland as being highly unmediated.

A reading of Dickinson's letters and poems mailed to this friend in the context of other correspondences, however, reveals the extent to which the writer's self-fashionings are carefully monitored poses displaying a calculated effect. In contrast to her increasingly critical and ambivalent letters to Root, Fowler, and Humphrey, and in contrast to her gender-transgressive fictionalized poses in her correspondence with Sue Gilbert, Dickinson presents herself in her letters and poems to Holland as inhabiting culturally sanctioned subject positions for women so completely (even tailoring her transgressive sense of humor toward the sensibilities of her friend) that possible gender-role ambivalences are largely erased from this epistolary exchange. It is by constructing both her own as well as Holland's personae on the basis of permissible subject positions that Dickinson strives to avoid the conflicts encountered in her friendships with Root, Humphrey, and Fowler. Offering to share with Holland (wife and mother of two) the cultural values of "true womanhood" almost to perfection thus becomes Dickinson's predominant strategy of sustaining their epistolary relationship.

Topics discussed with Holland focus mainly on areas traditionally gendered female within the discourse of "true womanhood": nature, flowers, Dickinson's garden, family affairs, and household duties. Dickinson frequently portrays herself as performing—otherwise unloved—tasks: "Vinnie and I talked of you as we sewed, this afternoon" (L133). The same discursive fields are echoed in Dickinson's poems mailed to Holland, almost all of which serve to reinforce rather than undermine Dickinson's docile feminine voice.[38] J824/Fr796 constitutes a particularly interesting example, as it specifically foregrounds domestic imagery in the copy mailed to Holland while erasing it from Higginson's version. The beginning of Holland's copy of this poem reads: "The Wind begun to knead the Grass— | As Women do a Dough— | He flung a Hand full at the Plain— | A Hand full at the Sky" (J824/Fr796A). In Higginson's variant, however, we encounter a more forceful metaphor: "The Wind begun to rock the Grass | With threatening Tunes and low— | He threw a Menace at the Earth— | A Menace at the Sky" (J824, second version; Fr796D). The subsequent four stanzas of the two versions show only minor differences in punctuation, spelling, or tense, with one additional semantic variation: in Holland's copy, line 10 features a verb traditionally associated with female conversation: "The Thunders gossiped low." For Higginson, this line was changed to "The Thunder hurried slow."

Tingley argues that in her correspondence to Holland, "Dickinson creates a self-confident, authoritative persona, a poet who . . . feels free to articulate her fervent hopes for immortality and posthumous fame" and therefore "shares many of her poetic aspirations and inspirations with Elizabeth Holland" ("Holland Letters" 184, 183). Yet in contrast to her letters to Austin Dickinson and Thomas Wentworth Higginson (discussed below), Dickinson's professional objectives as a poet are here repeatedly fused with the (traditionally female-gendered) tasks of consolation and nurturing. As Dickinson explains: "Perhaps you laugh at me! Perhaps the whole United States are laughing at me too! *I* can't stop for that! *My* business is to love. . . . '*My* business is to *sing*'" (L269). Rather than merely an end in itself or a means to achieve "immortality" and "fame," "to sing" becomes syntactically, and thus conceptually, equated with "to love." I thus partly disagree with Tingley, who reads this letter primarily as an indication of Dickinson's "career-mindedness": "In contrast to Elizabeth, the family-oriented mother bird," Tingley claims, "the poet describes herself as a single-minded career woman, as a solitary songbird rather than a nesting bird comfortably surrounded by her nestlings" ("Holland Letters" 192). Yet rather than exclusively emphasizing a (public) poetic career, this letter serves to link the "business" of "singing" with the socially sanctioned one of "loving" and nurturing.

Moreover, only seven years Holland's junior, Dickinson also repeatedly presents herself as the young child to her friend Holland, as the dependent one who is afraid, inexperienced, and in constant need of comfort, guidance, and protection.[39] However, in contrast to Dickinson's letters to Sue, in which her yearning for a return to childhood was equated with the (utopian) yearning for a return to their premarital state of intimacy, love, and mutual affection, Dickinson's childhood poses in her letters to Holland are couched in language of excess and exaggeration, which occasionally creates an ironic effect: "for I am but a simple child" (L182); "You know we're children still, and children fear the dark" (L207); "Thanking you tenderly as a child" (L370); "Three is a scant Assembly, but Love makes 'One to carry—' as the Children say—That is all of my Learning that I recall" (L542).[40] In keeping with this childlike pose (yet in marked contrast to Dickinson's correspondence with her brother, Austin, for example), Dickinson also claims to occupy an inferior, dependent role within her family: "Will you please to help me?" she asks Holland; "I guess I have done wrong—I don't know certainly, but Austin tells me so, and he is older than I, and knows more of ordinances. When Vinnie is here—I ask her; if she says I sin, I say, 'Father, I have sinned'—If she sanctions me, I am not afraid, but Vinnie is gone now, and to my sweet elder sister, in the younger's absence, something guides my feet" (L202). The subtle ironic humor inherent in this self-belittling pose is only thrown into full relief once we encounter her domineeringly patronizing pose as the "elder"(!) sister of her brother, Austin (L22)—a pose that, of course, remains cunningly hidden from Holland.

Dickinson's imagery suggests that it is spiritual guidance, in particular, that she seeks from Holland: "The minister to-day, not our own minister, preached about death and judgment, and what would become of those, meaning Austin and me, who behaved improperly—and somehow the sermon scared me, and father and Vinnie looked very solemn as if the whole was true, and I would not for worlds have them know that it troubled me, but I longed to come to you, and tell you all about it, and learn how to be better" (L175).[41] In contrast to her correspondence with Higginson, with whom—despite his former position as minister—she hardly ever discusses spiritual issues, Dickinson continually raises her religious scruples with Holland, always indicating that religion is one of her predominant concerns: "Austin and I were talking the other Night about the Extension of Consciousness, after Death and Mother told Vinnie, afterward, she thought it was 'very improper.' She forgets that we are past 'Correction in Righteousness—' " (L650). Such earnest concern is occasionally combined with spirited self-irony and (potentially subversive) humor: "When a Child and fleeing from Sacrament I could hear the Clergyman saying 'All who loved the Lord Jesus Christ—were asked to remain—' My flight kept time to the Words" (L412). Crumbley has emphasized this humorous, playful aspect of Dickinson's letters to Holland, arguing that it "draw[s] readers into the tensions that inform her poetic self" (*Inflections* 67). Yet these (humorously masked) tensions are never allowed to dominate these letters to the same degree that they had dominated her correspondences with Root, Humphrey, and Fowler. Sharing her religious struggles with her friend, Dickinson nonetheless always emphasizes her need of Holland as spiritual guide and protector: "Thank you for the protecting words—The petit Shepherd would find us but a startled Flock, not an unloving one—" (L794).[42] Unlike Sue, who becomes an inaccessible, awe-inspiring Jehovah-like figure to be worshiped from afar, Holland represents the comfort and support found in Christ: "It was sweet to touch the familiar Hand that so long had led us—'Though thou walk through the Valley of the Shadow of Death, I will be with thee,' you have taught us was no exaggeration" (L820).

Juhasz has argued that comfort—rather than conflict—is what Dickinson experiences with *all* of her female correspondents ("Reading" 189). Yet in light of Dickinson's highly tension-ridden relationship with Sue Gilbert, I would argue that Juhasz's argument is more specifically true for the poet's epistolary friendship with Holland. Without signs of any potential conflict between these two women (i.e., resolving possible gender-specific role conflicts through humor or negotiating them in other correspondences), and hence without repeating the problems encountered in her friendships with Root, Humphrey, and Fowler, Dickinson manages to maintain a nonconflictual, often humorously playful mother-daughter, advisor-advisee relationship with Holland. According to Smith-Rosenberg, it was mother-daughter relationships, in particular, that were typically conflict-free: "Expressions of hostility which we would today consider routine on the part of both mothers and daughters seem to have been uncommon indeed" ("Female World" 15). Smith-Rosenberg continues to suggest that "it is possible that taboos against female aggression and hostility were sufficiently strong to repress even that between mothers and their adolescent daughters" (17). She refutes this taboo hypothesis, however, by arguing that the letters she has examined "seem so alive and the interest of daughters in their mothers' affairs so vital and genuine that it is difficult to interpret their closeness exclusively in terms of repression and denial" (17). In this sense, Dickinson's epistolary friendship with Elizabeth Holland thus closely resembles Smith-Rosenberg's description of nineteenth-century mother-daughter relationships.

Even though occasionally denominating her as "sister," Dickinson nonetheless depicts Holland as the ideal mother-nurturer, able to provide a motherly sense of warmth and security, throughout her correspondence. She is consistently associated with summer, sun, warmth, comfort, and safety.[43] Dickinson cherishes her "little sunny Acts (L619); her "sunny heroism" (L723); and her "sunny face" (L732); but, most specifically, her protection: "We [Vinnie and I] talk of you together, then diverge on life, then hide in you again, as a safe fold" (L208). Dickinson's type-casting of Holland as a representative of the feminine values of motherhood, domesticity, and piety also manifests itself discursively in the description of her friend as the Victorian "angel in the house."[44] She calls her Dr. Holland's "Angel Wife" (L687), and upon the birth of her second grandchild, Holland is depicted in terms of Christian iconography: "So Madonna and Daughter were incomplete, and Madonna and Son, must supersede!" (L977). In addition, almost everything relating to Holland is "little" and "childlike": "As 'little Mrs Holland,' then, I think I love you most, and trust that tiny lady will dwell below" (L185); in keeping with Grace Greenwood's definition of the "feminine genius" as a "perpetual childhood" (qtd. in Welter 29), she becomes the "Doctor's 'Child Wife' " (L487).[45]

That Holland, in very concrete terms, may have assumed the role of Dickinson's surrogate mother was first pointed out by Sewall (*Life* 601). And indeed, some letters suggest that Dickinson's own mother failed to fulfill this function. To Higginson, Dickinson confides in 1874: "I always ran Home to Awe when a child, if anything befell me. He was an awful Mother, but I liked him better than none" (L405). The only other two instances where Dickinson speaks openly about her mother's "absence" occur in letters to Holland. In L391, Dickinson suggests that her sister Vinnie "has no Father and Mother but me and I have no Parents but her." And in L792 (written in 1882, the year of her mother's death), Dickinson explains: "We were never intimate Mother and Children while she was our Mother—but Mines in the same Ground meet by tunneling and when she became our Child, the Affection came." Smith-Rosenberg has pointed out that it was not uncommon for young women to look upon friends as surrogate mothers: "Older girls in boarding school 'adopted' younger ones, who called them 'Mother.' Dear friends might indeed continue this pattern of adoption and mothering throughout their lives: one woman might routinely assume the nurturing role of pseudomother, the other the dependency role of daughter" ("Female World" 19). In this sense, Dickinson may thus have filled the perceived "absence" of her own mother by fashioning Holland as a kind of protective, caring substitute mother. Yet in order not to threaten the continuation of this relationship by imparting too many of her religious scruples or too much of her otherwise critical attitude toward the "ideal of true womanhood," Dickinson hyperbolically stylizes herself in the role of perpetually dependent, ignorant child-daughter. Apart from occasional humorous deflections suggestive of a certain distance between Dickinson's epistolary self-constructions and her opinions voiced elsewhere, and apart from a potential impression of excess and exaggeration, this correspondence can thus be described as Dickinson's most monological (i.e., her least double-voiced) one.

IN many ways, Dickinson's correspondences with her female friends thus chronicle the writer's transition from composing largely "confessional" or autobiographical letters (in the sense advocated by epistolary manuals) to producing carefully constructed and controlled acts of self-(re)presentation and self-fashioning. Since nineteenth-century friendships among women were frequently dependent on a shared acceptance of socially sanctioned yet narrowly circumscribed female subject positions—in particular those of church member, obedient daughter/sister, mother, and wife—Dickinson's resistance to adopting such predefined and limiting roles initiates a breakdown of her early friendships. This problem is circumvented in Dickinson's subsequent relationships by two strategies: she utilizes her letters as the primary form of social interaction (i.e., she translates her friendships onto a predominantly textual or literary level), which then enables her to exercise a high degree of control by turning her letters into spaces for developing carefully crafted articulations of discursively constructed roles for both herself and her respective addressees.

In her correspondence with Elizabeth Holland, Dickinson draws on the discursive basis of nineteenth-century friendships among women, the ideology of "true womanhood," to create her textual self-representations. These letters feature the writer's hyperbolic appropriation of the role of perpetual child-woman while stylizing Holland as the surrogate "mother," a strategy that allows her to circumvent any challenges to the continuation of their friendship by largely obscuring possible gender-role ambivalences on her part. In order to ensure the continuation of her friendship with Sue Gilbert, on the other hand, Dickinson removes this relationship from the socio-culturally circumscribed realities of interpersonal interaction and transports it to the discursive realm of courtly love: Sue is idealized as the perpetually inaccessible female beloved, while Dickinson inhabits the role of the continuously pining and adoring male lover/poet. In Dickinson's letters to both Holland and Sue Gilbert, it is thus the desire to maintain emotional bonds, despite (often considerable) ideological differences, that initiates these epistolary strategies of discursive self-fashioning. At the same time, Dickinson also significantly expands the traditional function of women's letters as advocated by epistolary manuals: they ultimately not only serve her to *maintain* friendships but also enable her to orchestrate and control them on her own (discursive) terms.

In several respects, Dickinson's correspondences with Elizabeth Holland, Sue Gilbert, and her early female friends are thus instrumental in initiating a crucial borderblur between "factual" sociocultural circumstances and "fictional" epistolary responses, between the referential and the nonreferential, between the personal and the literary realm. To that effect, both letters and poems are employed in complementary ways as fictional spaces for rethinking and renegotiating women's sociocultural roles. It is in her correspondences with male friends and relatives, on the other hand, that epistolary and poetic voices are more and more frequently placed in dialogic juxtaposition—a strategy primarily utilized to negotiate gendered power relations. Although issues of power had inevitably yet indirectly manifested themselves in Dickinson's epistolary exchanges with Holland and Sue Gilbert, negotiations of power relations move to center stage in Dickinson's correspondences with male friends and relatives—with one crucial difference: in her letters and poems to Holland and Sue Gilbert, it is Dickinson who seems to willingly and unambiguously occupy the inferior position (dependent child-daughter and supplicant courtly lover-poet, respectively). In this way, she exerts power primarily indirectly through discursively orchestrating these relationships. Her correspondences with male friends, on the other hand, feature often highly ambivalent yet explicit claims to superiority. In her "Master" letters, these self-affirmative claims are almost completely overpowered by self-abnegating poses, but it is in the dialogue between the self-confident voice of the poet and the submissive voice of the pupil emerging from her letters to Higginson that Dickinson most effectively challenges preconceived notions of gendered power relations. Yet it is the ambivalent dialogic juxtaposition of the rebellious and apologetic daughter/sister in her exchanges with her brother, Austin, that prepares the way for these strategies of self-empowerment.

equivocal to the end—

who are you?

—ADRIENNE RICH

I must be Rhinoceros

Or Mouse

At once—for Thee

—EMILY DICKINSON

4

The "Male" World of Power and Poetry

AUSTIN DICKINSON

MOST OF DICKINSON'S letters to her brother, Austin, are contemporaneous with her letters to Fowler, Humphrey, and Root.[1] In many respects, they are thus related to her earliest attempts to challenge and negotiate socially prescribed roles for women, especially the relational ones of daughter and sister. In this familial context, they also acquire special significance in comparison to her epistolary exchanges with her "mother surrogate" Elizabeth Holland. Yet in contrast to the harmonious (monologic) tone of the latter correspondence, Dickinson's letters to Austin consistently depict family relations in terms of highly conflictual (dialogic) power relations. From the outset, as soon as Austin's absence from home allows Dickinson to (re)negotiate their relationship on a predominantly textual basis, she competes with her firstborn brother for the primary position within their family, thus challenging her ascribed role as submissive daughter and younger, intellectually inferior sister. These attacks on prevailing power relations acquire two specific forms: she redefines the traditionally female-gendered role of sister-nurturer as a position of strength and superiority, and she appropriates the traditionally male-gendered role of intellectual poet. Both usurpations, however, are repeatedly undercut by humor, which mitigates the severity of her transgressions even more pronouncedly than it did in her letters to Holland.

Drawing on literary analogies, Dickinson initially fashions herself in the seemingly nontransgressive role of sister-nurturer. Yet by specifically highlighting a nurturer's required attributes, such as strength, experience, and a superior capacity for handling pain and affliction, Dickinson is able to subtly tip the relational power balance. This becomes clear in the fictional roles she ascribes to both her brother and herself. In L62, she contemplates: "and then I thought of 'Hepzibah' how sorrowful *she* was, and how she longed to sleep, because the grave was peaceful, yet for affection's sake, and for the sake of 'Clifford' she wearied on. . . . I dont mean that you are *him*, or that Hepzibah's *me* except in a relative sense, only I was reminded" (L62). Dickinson identifies herself with Hepzibah, the stronger and more competent sister in Hawthorne's *House of the Seven Gables*, who takes care of her troubled brother, Clifford. "In a relative sense," then, Dickinson regards the relationship between herself and her brother as analogous to the one between Hepzibah and Clifford. This gives her confidence enough to consider herself, although one year Austin's junior, his "older" sister: "I am pining for a Valentine. . . . Probably, Mary, Abby & Viny have received scores of them from the infatuated wights in the neighborhood while your *highly accomplished & gifted elder sister* is entirely overlooked" (L22).

Several additional letters echo this pose of an "older," more experienced sister patronizing her younger, less competent brother who thus comes to depend on her care and advice: "Take care of your lungs, Austin—take that just as I told you, and pretty soon you'll be well" (L145); "I would'nt sit up late, if I were you, or study much evenings" (L156); "I feel so anxious about you that I cannot rest until I have written to you and given you some advice" (L57). In L66, Dickinson proposes to suffer for her brother (much like

Hepzibah), as she claims to be more accustomed to dealing with pain: "May I change places, Austin? *I* dont care how sharp the pain is, not if it dart like arrows, or pierce bone and bone like the envenomed barb, I should be twice, *thrice* happy to bear it in your place. Dont try to teach school at all, until you get thoroughly well! The committee will excuse you . . . ; tell them if they dont I will tell the Mayor of them and get them all turned out!" Even though undercut by hyperbolic humor, Dickinson's announcement to take the necessary steps to dismiss his school's committee is apt to illustrate the kind of strength that even a female nurturer may develop when determined to help someone she cares about.

That such a high degree of acquired strength and its concomitant self-confidence may potentially also be directed against the very object of care is only a logical consequence. In this sense, Dickinson occasionally also imagines herself to be Austin's equal in both strength *and* gender, capable of defeating him: "The next time you a'nt going to write me I'd thank you to let me know—this kind of *protracted* insult is what no man can bear—fight with me like a man—let me have a fair shot, and you are 'caput mortuum' et 'cap a pie,' and that ends the business!" (L49). In this letter, the appropriation of power is combined with gender crossing. What Dickinson challenges her brother to do is fight with her like an equal; she is confident about having "a fair shot."

If Dickinson's attempts at becoming her brother's *elder* sister or his *male* equal were still playful and facetious, she enters into a more serious competition in another arena. She is at her most rivalrous—yet simultaneously at her most ambivalent—in the context of intellectual and writerly achievements. It is in these areas that her negotiations between socially sanctioned and socially transgressive (female) roles become most pronounced, challenging established familial power relations not only vis-à-vis her brother but also vis-à-vis her father. Subtly mocking her father's ignorance in literary matters, for example, she completely abolishes the role of dutiful daughter and adopts a "son's" position, comparing her stance to that of her brother: "Father was very severe to me; he thought I'd been trifling with you, so he gave me quite a trimming about 'Uncle Tom' and 'Charles Dickens' and these 'modern Literati' who he says are *nothing*, compared to past generations, who flourished when *he was a boy*. Then he said there were 'somebody's *rev-*

e-ries,' he did'nt know whose they were, that he thought were very ridiculous, so I'm quite in disgrace at present, but I think of that 'pinnacle' on which you always mount, when anybody insults you, and that's quite a comfort to me" (L113). Fully self-confident owing to her superior knowledge of contemporary literature, Dickinson, rather than submitting to her father's authority, mocks his ignorance, considers herself wronged and insulted, and, like her brother, proudly withdraws to a lofty "pinnacle." Further acts of resistance on Dickinson's part include a satirizing of her father's severe temperament: "Let me add as I go along, that father's frame of mind is *as usual* the *happiest*, developing itself in constant acts of regard, and *epithets of tenderness!*" (L79).[2] L141 displays a gratified feeling of intellectual superiority at having outwitted her father: "I said so all the while, and tho' I was disappointed, yet I could'nt help smiling a little, to think that I guessed right. I told Father I *knew* you w'd vote somehow in Cambridge, for you always did what you wanted to . . . whether 'twas against the law or not, but he would'nt believe me, so when he was mistaken, I *was* a little gratified" (L141). Like Austin, Dickinson describes herself as fighting against rather than submitting to her father's authority: "Father's real life and *mine* sometimes come into collision, but as yet, escape unhurt!" (L65).[3] Rather than being the submissive and dutiful daughter, Dickinson thus emulates Austin in his struggle against paternal dominance—particularly on the intellectual plane.

With regard to her father, Dickinson thus equates her own role within the family to that of her brother, that is, to that of a "son," but she simultaneously also claims intellectual superiority over Austin. As soon as he has left home, Dickinson is no longer willing to tolerate his intellectual condescension: "I suppose I am a fool—you always said I was one, and yet I have some feelings that seem sensible to me, and I have desires to see you now that you are gone which are really quite intelligent. Dont take too much encouragement, but really I have the hope of becoming before you come quite an *accountable being*! Why not an 'eleventh hour' in the life of the *mind* as well as such an one in the life of the *soul*—greyhaired sinners are saved—simple maids may be *wise*, who knoweth?" (L44). Her profoundly ambivalent stance toward power manifests itself in the fact that the harshness of her transgression is carefully mitigated by her humorous tone as well as by her display of genuine love and affection for Austin. While demonstratively emphasizing her own capacity for reason and intelligence, Dickinson nonetheless associates her intelligence with the desire to see her brother, which in turn renders any protestations on his part impossible and her self-assurance less aggressive.

In addition, there also ensues a highly ambivalently charged writerly competition between Dickinson and Austin. The degree of wit in their respective letters, in particular, constitutes a mark of epistolary excellence. At times, Dickinson acknowledges and even admires her brother's stylistic superiority: "I have just finished reading your letter which was brought in since church. . . . I like it grandly—very—because it is so long, and also it's *so* funny—we have all been laughing till the old house rung again at your delineations of men, women, and things. I feel quite like retiring, in presence of one so grand, and casting my small lot among small birds, and fishes" (L45). Yet a few lines later, she qualifies her seemingly unstinting praise, suggesting that Austin may be overdoing it: "Your letters are richest treats, send them always just such warm days—they are worth a score of fans, and many refrigerators—the only 'diffikilty' they are so very *queer*, and *laughing* such hot weather is *anything* but *amusing*. A little more earnest, and a little less of jest until we are out of August, and then you may joke as freely as the Father of Rogues himself, and we will banish care, and daily die a laughing!" (L45). Though Austin's highly developed sense of humor is a "rich treat," Dickinson nonetheless subtly hints at its occasional inappropriateness to the situation ("a little less of jest until we are out of August"). And rather than regard Austin's letters as a cheerful means to alleviate everyday cares and concerns, Dickinson also emphasizes that it is *the reader* of his letters *himself/herself* who has to "banish care" in order to be able to appreciate his missive fully. Yet this critique so imperceptibly merges with praise and admiration that it would be hard for Dickinson's brother to raise any serious objections.

In another highly competitive but ambivalent pose, Dickinson strives to become her brother's "equal" by developing a sophisticated epistolary style:

> You say you dont comprehend me, you want a simpler style. *Gratitude* indeed for all my fine philosophy! I strove to be exalted thinking I might reach *you* and while I pant and struggle and climb the nearest cloud, you walk out very leisurely in your slippers from Empyrean, and without the

> *slightest* notice request me to get down! As *simple* as you please, the *simplest* sort of simple—I'll be a little ninny—a little pussy catty, a little Red Riding Hood, I'll wear a Bee in my Bonnet, and a Rose bud in my hair, and what remains to do you shall be told hereafter. (L45)

On the one hand, Dickinson again seems to concede her brother's writerly superiority, emphasizing the effort it takes her to reach his level ("I strove to be exalted thinking I might reach *you*"). She promises to withdraw, to adopt a "simpler style" by turning herself into hyperbolically female-gendered personae. Yet on the other hand the exaggerated theatricality of Dickinson's surrender simultaneously suggests that she has no intention of adopting these roles. As Stephanie Tingley has pointed out: "Her comments to her brother, complete with the list of acceptable female voices and roles, show her simultaneous awareness of and resistance to such stereotypical personae" ("Letter" 7). Juhasz has argued that this resistance particularly manifests itself in the fact that "the whole supposed capitulation is written in the very style that he [Austin] has censured" ("Reading" 177). Thus, Juhasz continues, "not only does Dickinson criticize Austin (while appearing not to), but she does so in and on his own terms, wit and linguistic flair" (177). In this way, critique and surrender again blend equivocally.

Even more explicit, however, is L110, in which Dickinson declares that she has no intention of yielding, of returning to the "simple" style of "little ninnies," but rather competes with Austin for a place on Helicon, the mountain sacred to the muses: "And Austin is a Poet, Austin writes a psalm. Out of the way, Pegasus, Olympus enough 'to him,' and just say to those 'nine muses' that we have done with them! Raised a living muse ourselves, worth the whole nine of them. Up, off, tramp! Now Brother Pegasus, I'll tell you what it is—I've been in the habit *myself* of writing some few things, and it rather appears to me that you're getting away my patent, so you'd better be somewhat careful, or I'll call the police!" In this letter, Dickinson circumscribes her brother's role in precise terms: by virtue of his gender, Austin has privileged access to Olympus, which, as the residence of the supreme gods, stands for public power and imperial supremacy.[4] Yet at the same time, he should also be content with this sphere of influence ("Olympus enough 'to him' "). Dickinson herself decides not to compete for an occupancy of Olympus (a position in public life); her goal instead is the conquest of Mt. Helicon. Yet it is important to note that, rather than merely occupying Helicon and thus adopting the role of the (traditionally female-gendered) "muse," Dickinson displaces the nine resident muses ("we have done with them"), and appropriates for herself the role of creator by raising her own "living muse." In this way, rather than becoming a "sister" of the muses, Dickinson usurps a place as an equal at the side of "Brother Pegasus." In other words, Dickinson is prepared to grant her brother his dominant role(s) in public and social life, yet in the field of poetic creativity, she strives to abandon the role of "sister" and instead appropriates that of creator. Literature, the realm of the mind (which had explicitly been gendered male by most epistolary manuals), is the field in which Dickinson fully discards the strictures of nineteenth-century womanhood.

Although this passage in L110 constitutes Dickinson's most explicit challenge to her culture's gender-inscribed roles, she nonetheless undercuts her bold voice once again immediately afterward: "Well Austin, if you've stumbled through these two pages of folly, without losing your hat or getting lost in the mud, I will try to be sensible, as suddenly as I can, before you are quite disgusted" (L110). In these lines, her self-confidence as poet-creator, her textual attempts at erasing gender-based differences between herself and Austin, and her efforts to appropriate the space and concomitant power of Pegasus's "Brother," are—for Austin's sake—reconfigured as "folly," foolish absurdity, a reversal of the social order that has to be restored immediately. To maintain her brother's goodwill and reassure him of her expedient return to socially sanctioned gender roles, Dickinson ends with the declaration, "I will try to be sensible, as suddenly as I can."

Yet the self-confident voice of the poet erupts again. Even though Dickinson does not aspire to compete with her brother for a public career, she nevertheless critiques his political opinions. Interestingly enough, here for the first time she uses the form of poetry (the voice of the poet-creator) for this kind of criticism. At a time of "keen political rivalry between Edward Dickinson, a 'straight' Whig, and Ithamar Francis Conkey, a 'republican' Whig" (Johnson and Ward, *Letters* 381), Dickinson sends her brother the following letter-poem: "Austin— | Father said | Frank Conkey—touched | you— | A Burdock— | clawed my Gown— | Not *Burdock's*—blame— | But *mine*— | Who went too near | The Burdock's *Den*— || A *Bog*—affronts my shoe— | What *else* have Bogs—*to do*— | The only Trade they *know*— | The *splashing Men!* | Ah, *pity—then*! || 'Tis *Minnows can despise!* | The *Elephant's*—calm eyes | Look *further on!* | Emily—" (Dickinson ms. 626, Amherst; L240). Blaming Austin for venturing too near the wrong political candidate, Dickinson exhorts him to change his political opinion. And, interestingly enough, assured of her power as a poet, this letter-poem now constitutes an unequivocal claim to superiority—no longer in need of any disclaimers.[5]

These poems and letters highlight both Dickinson's determination to establish her superiority as a poet and her simultaneous ambivalence about usurping a dominant, socially and gender-transgressive familial position vis-à-vis her brother and her father. Dickinson's appropriation of the role of the more experienced "elder" sister Hepzibah, her textual competition with Austin on equal terms, their shared resistance to paternal authority, and, finally, her rejection of the role of "sister" and "muse," all highlight her attempts to break out of the strictures of womanhood and the discursive positions of submissive and dutiful daughter and sister. Yet at the same time Dickinson regularly undercuts any self-ascriptions of superiority, status, or power and thus deflates her brother's potentially aggressive responses by the same techniques she had, to some degree, already employed in her letters to Holland: a playfully disarming sense of humor and an adoption of hyperbolically female-gendered poses. In exaggerated gestures of submission, she returns to the realm of domestic trifles: "I shall never write any more grand letters to you, but all the *little* things, and the things called *trifles*, and the crickets upon the hearth, you will be sure to hear" (L114). Yet in contrast to her Holland correspondence, this hyperbolically feminized voice of (gender) conformity is here repeatedly joined to a powerfully subversive countervoice: the voice of the poet-creator. This double-voicedness undermines any sense of a monological homogeneity of subject positions. A similarly double-voiced discourse, reflective of Dickinson's profound ambivalence about gendered forms of power and dominance, can also be found in her correspondence with Thomas Wentworth Higginson.

THOMAS WENTWORTH HIGGINSON

As Dickinson's second most frequently addressed correspondent, Thomas Wentworth Higginson occupies a pivotal place in any analysis of the writer's epistolary strategies. Dickinson's association with the nationally reputed abolitionist, orator, writer, critic, editor, women's rights advocate, and man of letters has played a central role in almost all biographical and critical studies to date. During the early stages of Dickinson criticism, Higginson had frequently been portrayed as the obtuse critic who failed to recognize and promote the literary "genius." As Tilden G. Edelstein has summarized: "Her association with Higginson, for these male scholars and literary critics, was viewed as a disaster. Portrayed as a critical barbarian, he became the repugnant representative for the narrow literary taste of Dickinson's contemporaries" ("Emily Dickinson" 38). With its careful distinction between Higginson's achievements as a social reformer and his failures as a literary critic, Ferlazzo's view of Higginson is representative of most critics' voices of this era: "Higginson was a well-known and prolific writer, a leading spokesman of liberal New England social reform and a cultivated literary conservatism. . . . Higginson was not a great literary critic; he was merely a representative one of mid-nineteenth-century America. He was subject to the same values, ambitions, and prejudices of the average lot. . . . If he had not attracted something in Emily Dickinson which caused her to begin a lifelong correspondence with him, he might not now have very much literary immortality" (135). "The scholarship of the 1960's, however," Edelstein continues, "revealed new tolerance of Higginson" ("Emily Dickinson" 38). Critics such as Edelstein himself, Anna Mary Wells, Benjamin Lease, and, more recently, Susan Howe and Nancy Johnston have all demonstrated to what extent "the role of Colonel Thomas Wentworth Higginson in his relations with Emily Dickinson has been consistently misrepresented and he himself maligned" (Wells, "Soul's Society" 221). More recently, Higginson's importance has been displaced (by Martha Nell Smith, among others) in the context of a feminist emphasis on the significance of Dickinson's female friendships. Though I agree with Smith's insistence on viewing Sue Gilbert, in particular, as Dickinson's most important personal friend, I concentrate here on demonstrating that it is the writer's literary friendship with Higginson that is most consistently negotiated on an exclusively discursive level.

In her correspondence with Higginson, Dickinson's orchestrations of dialogic interplays between multiple, antithetical voices reach their most sophisticated form. On the one hand, she repeatedly attempts to translate their relationship onto an exclusively textual level by directing her "preceptor's" gaze away from her physical self. Evading a personal meeting with her "preceptor" for eight years, refusing to send him a photograph of herself, and reducing her "proper" name to gender-ambivalent forms of signatures, Dickinson endeavors to delimit her identity to that of poet and writer, stripping it of any sociocultural gender ascriptions. She invites Higginson to see her as "the mind alone without corporeal friend" (L330). At the same time, however—like in her correspondence with Austin—she also adopts highly gendered, often hyperbolically female poses in both letters and poems that deflate these self-confident voices in order to produce a carefully balanced effect.[6] Yet even more so than in her epistolary exchanges with Austin, the "prose" parts of her letters tend to reinforce Dickinson's gender and power ambivalence, while the "poems" more frequently acquire a subversive function. At the same time, their dialogic juxtaposition suggests that in her negotiations between various gendered subject positions, Dickinson tries to render the power of her voice as "poet" less aggressive by undercutting it with the submissive voice of scholar/pupil or daughter.[7]

That Dickinson initially (especially in her very first letter) aimed at a complete severance between her textually constructed and her bodily inscribed voices is explained in one of her early missives to Higginson: "A Letter always feels to me like immortality because it is the mind alone without corporeal friend. Indebted in our talk to attitude and accent, there seems a spectral power in thought that walks alone" (L330).[8] Whereas specific geographical, sociocultural, or gendered features ("attitude and accent") are inevitably inscribed in one's bodily voice ("talk"), Dickinson suggests that the imaginative power of "the mind alone" is unencumbered by any form of (biological or cultural) determinism and thus free to create nonexisting ("spectral"), revisionist "thought[s]"/realities disentangled from prevailing sociocultural configurations. In other words, Dickinson assumes that a letter's disembodied voices are no longer tied to a subject's specific sociocultural location and its spatiotemporal coordinates ("immortality"), and are thus able to replace the single bodily inscribed voice by a multiplicity of (textually invented) voices of the pen. As Dickinson explains, again in a letter to Higginson: "a Pen has so many inflections and a Voice but one" (L470).[9] In this way Dickinson challenges what Bergland has called the "easy relationship between discourse and the speaking subject, particularly the notion that *experience* produces *voice*—that, for example, *being a woman* means speaking in *a woman's voice*"(qtd. in Gilmore 10).

Dickinson uses two complementary strategies to signal to Higginson that for her, "being a woman" does not necessarily mean "speaking in a woman's voice": she reduces her interaction with him to an exclusively textual environment, and within this textual environment, she attempts to erase any traces of her culturally constructed, gendered body. Her most striking gesture is to delay a face-to-face encounter with her preceptor for almost eight years. Higginson must have suggested the possibility of an actual meeting as early as four months after receiving Dickinson's first letter. At this time, Dickinson politely but firmly manages to settle the issue: "You told me in one letter, you could not come to see me, 'now,' and I made no answer, not because I had none, but did not think myself the price that you should come so far—I do not ask so large a pleasure, lest you might deny me—" (L271). Prompted by the prospect of war, however, she does express a desire to see Higginson in early 1863 and becomes even more willing to meet him after he has been wounded (L290).[10] Yet no meeting ensues, and the issue is picked up again by Higginson in 1866. At this time, Dickinson hesitates to visit him in Boston but invites him to Amherst instead: "I should be glad to see you, but think it an apparitional pleasure—not to be fulfilled. I am uncertain of Boston. . . . Is it more far to Amherst? You would find a minute Host but a spacious Welcome" (L316). Relying on her father's authority to decline a second invitation to Boston, she finally consents to a meeting in Amherst: "I must omit Boston. Father prefers so. He likes me to travel with him but objects that I visit. Might I entrust you, as my Guest to the Amherst Inn?" (L319).[11] In L330, she repeats her invitation: "You speak kindly of seeing me. Could it please your convenience to come so far as Amherst I should be very glad, but I do not cross my Father's ground to any House or town." The actual meeting, however, did not take place until more than a year later, on August 16, 1870—more than eight years after she had first contacted him.[12]

During these years, Higginson repeatedly expressed his dissatisfaction with Dickinson's withdrawal and self-mystification: "I have the greatest desire to see you, always feeling that perhaps if I could once take you by the hand I might be something to you; but till then you only enshroud yourself in this fiery mist & I cannot reach you . . . I think if I could once see you & know that you are real, I might fare better. It brought you nearer e[ven] to know that you had an actual [?] uncle" (L330a). Crumbley has pointed out that it is in particular a "stable sense of self" that Higginson missed: "however enigmatic the self's outward expression, it exists ultimately as a kernel of reality housed in a specific locale" ("Art's" 78). Summarizing his relationship with Dickinson thirty years later in the *Atlantic Monthly*, Higginson draws attention to its unusual quality: "Perhaps in time I could have got beyond that somewhat overstrained relation which not my will, but her needs, had forced upon us. Certainly I should have been most glad to bring it down to the level of simple truth and every-day comradeship" (qtd. in Johnson and Ward, *Letters* 476).

A further example of Dickinson's attempts to define her relationship with Higginson on her own terms and, therefore, to sever any direct link between her physical self and her epistolary personae is the writer's refusal to send Higginson her photograph. Upon his request for a likeness, Dickinson draws a verbal portrait instead: "Could you believe me—without? I had no portrait now, but am small, like the Wren, and my Hair is bold, like the Chestnut Bur—and my eyes, like the Sherry in the Glass, that the Guest leaves—Would this do just as well?" (L268). Jonathan Morse explains that Dickinson's resistance to have herself photographed or to send out photographs was indeed unusual: "When Thomas Wentworth Higginson asked Dickinson for a photograph of herself, he was making a gesture expected by the etiquette of the era: offering his correspondent an opportunity to place herself on display in his photograph album. Used to facilitate conversation in the parlor, albums like Higginson's were typically filled with small, mass-produced photographic keepsakes known as *cartes de visite*" (61). Barthes has emphasized the inherent referentiality of any photographic representation:

"A specific photograph, in effect, is never distinguished from its referent (from what it represents), or at least it is not *immediately* or *generally* distinguished from its referent . . . the Photograph always carries its referent with itself" (*Camera* 5). Dickinson's verbal portrait, on the other hand, undercuts any direct referentiality. Rather, it directs Higginson's gaze to (and only to) the features she wants him to see while controlling the way he perceives them.[13] I thus disagree with Juhasz's interpretation of Dickinson's refusal to send a photograph of herself to Higginson as a gesture of humility; Juhasz has argued that "remaining an anonymous author would be best, because then she would never have to attribute any significance to herself" ("Reading" 183). Rather than wanting to remain "anonymous," Dickinson resists being fixed in one unalterable and narrowly gendered identity.

Moreover, Dickinson also dislikes "Molds," as she explains to Higginson, because of their inadequacy to represent a subject-in-process: "I noticed the Quick wore off those things, in a few days" (L268).[14] In her discussion of daguerreotype photography, Judith Farr has drawn attention to its often "devitalizing" effects: "It was well known that daguerreotypes not only failed to suggest the vital personality but frequently so depressed the sitter in the process that she or he looked 'half-dead' " (*Passion* 21). In other words, a daguerreotype photograph is outdated after a few days because it cannot capture change but rather "kills" and thus objectifies its subject by artificially arresting it within fixed spatiotemporal coordinates: "The Photograph represents the very subtle moment," Barthes points out, "when, to tell the truth, I am neither subject nor object but a subject who feels he is becoming an object: I then experience a micro-version of death" (*Camera* 12). Therefore, Barthes continues, " 'myself' never coincides with my image; for it is the image which is heavy, motionless, stubborn (which is why society sustains it), and 'myself' which is light, divided, dispersed" (12). In this way, Dickinson's refusal to send Higginson a photograph of herself also foregrounds her self-presentation as a "dispersed," "divided," "double-voiced" subject ("small" yet "bold"), while preventing Higginson from reading her letters as the unmediated expression of a unified, stable, referential self.[15]

The most interesting example of Dickinson's attempts to erase gendered inscriptions from her letters manifests itself in her play with signatures. During her entire epistolary relationship with Higginson, Dickinson uses her first name on only one occasion (discussed below); in every other instance, she instead adopts an ungendered relational identity ("Your Scholar," Your Friend"), appropriates her father's signature ("E. Dickinson"), signs "Dickinson," "D," or omits a signature altogether (replacing it by a dash).[16] That Dickinson deliberately claims to usurp the role of "father" through the appropriation of her father's signature is revealed by its contextual use. L894, addressed to Higginson, but referring to his daughter Margaret, concludes with the lines: "It would please me that she take her first Walk in Literature with one so often guided on that great route by her Father— | E Dickinson—." Thus Dickinson, guided by Margaret's father (Higginson) now wishes to assume his role as "father" (signified through her father's signature) as a literary guide in the life of Margaret.[17]

The only time Dickinson includes her first name as part of her signature is in her introductory letter to Higginson (L260). In this case, I contend, it constituted an essential piece of information, required by Higginson—whom she wanted to respond to her inquiry—to be able to identify correctly the letter writer. That an omission of her first name might, indeed, have led to possible confusions is revealed by Dickinson's comment to Samuel Bowles: "please address to my full name, as the little note was detained and opened, the name [Dickinson] being so frequent in town, though not an Emily but myself" (L724). Once Dickinson has ensured, however, that Higginson will be able to direct his response to the correct address, she never again includes her first name as part of her signature.

Yet even in L260, the revelation of her (gendered) identity is delayed. The letter itself is unsigned, but, as Johnson and Ward have described, "in place of a signature, ED enclosed a card (in its own envelope) on which she wrote her name" (*Letters* 403).[18] Frequently, this gesture has been interpreted as a strategy of reticence, as the poet's shying away from publicity. When Higginson himself reflected on Dickinson's first letter to him almost thirty years later, his metaphors suggest such a reading: "she had written her name on a card and put it under the shelter of a smaller envelope inclosed in the larger; and even this name was written—as if the shy writer wished to recede as far as possible from view—in pencil, not in ink" ("Emily Dickinson's Letters" 185). Most subsequent critics tacitly adopt this interpretation. Ruth Miller and Suzanne Juhasz, for example, are representative in viewing Dickinson's refusal to sign her first letter as a gesture of humility: "She, on the other hand, is so insignificant that she does not describe herself at all and does not even sign her name; rather, she encloses it, on a card, in a separate envelope" (Juhasz, "Reading" 183).[19] Yet in the context of Dickinson's carefully crafted signatures in her correspondence with Higginson, another interpretation suggests itself. What Dickinson wanted to conceal (or rather delay to reveal—until Higginson had read her letter as well as the enclosed poems) was her gendered identity (and any potential sociocultural associations ascribed to it). That Higginson's response to her poems could possibly be influenced by the writer's gender manifests itself in a letter written by one of Dickinson's admired contemporaneous authors: "after writing to her publisher that she was 'neither man nor woman,' [Charlotte Brontë] went on to say, 'I come before you as an author only. It is the sole standard by which you have a right to judge me—the sole ground on which I accept your judgment' " (qtd. in Heilbrun 110–111).[20] In an attempt to come before Higginson "as an author only," in her very first letter Dickinson thus searched for a way to prevent a prejudged, gender-biased reading of her letter and poems.[21]

In order to be able to enter into a professional literary dialogue with Higginson, to encourage him to treat her as an "author only," it was essential for Dickinson to break down any gender-specific preconceptions. Reluctant to occupy the role of female "poetess" (like some of Higginson's literary protégées), Dickinson thus becomes "E. Dickinson," "Dickinson," or just "D," but more frequently, she becomes Higginson's "friend" and "scholar."[22] Moreover, Dickinson frequently refers to herself metonymically as "Mind" ("The Mind is so near itself—it cannot see, distinctly" [L260]), and she defines her age by the number of poems she has written: "You asked how old I was? I made no verse—but one or two—until this winter—Sir" (L261).[23]

On the one hand, these strategies reflect Dickinson's attempts to prevent any facile association between her self/her gender, and her epistolary forms of representation. On the other hand, however, Dickinson's language, particular aspects of her style (such as excessive apologies and self-denigratory gestures), her hidden corporeality, as well as the specific epistolary personae emerging from her letters—often hyperbolically gendered female—seem to undermine these very efforts. Although she urged Higginson to see "the mind alone, without corporeal friend," Dickinson simultaneously also refers to her texts as "corporeal"—they become identified/identical with her body.[24] This manifests itself in the poet's recurrent use of "surgery" imagery. Higginson's editorial criticism of her poems is experienced as a physical violation of her body: "Thank you for the surgery—it was not so painful as I supposed" (L261); in the following letter, the metaphor is continued: "Perhaps the Balm, seemed better, because you bled me, first" (L265). Dickinson's textually constructed voices, rather than being de-corporealized, thus metonymically represent her body: "Will you tell me my fault, frankly as to yourself, for I had rather wince, than die. Men do not call the surgeon, to commend—the Bone, but to set it, Sir, and fracture within, is more critical" (L268).

This apparent contradiction is indicative of a more general equivocation on Dickinson's part as to the roles she adopts in her correspondence with Higginson. The tension between her attempts to sever any link between epistolary subject positions and physical self on the one hand, and the constant intrusion of bodily metaphors into her texts on the other, reflects the writer's efforts to negotiate between degendered and gendered voices. Dickinson's epistolary personae evolving in her correspondence with Higginson are thus principally "dispersed" or dialogic ones, engaged in balancing her self-ascribed gender-neutral role as "author only" with her socially constructed identity as "woman."[25] This process of negotiation—echoing a strategy already employed in her letters to Austin—frequently manifests itself in dialogic reverberations between multiple epistolary voices. Dickinson speaks alternately as a woman/pupil and as a poet, in this way juxtaposing self-denigration (submissiveness) and self-affirmation (confidence in her work).[26] I argue that this carefully crafted balance of power appropriation and voluntary disempowerment is, in part, motivated by Dickinson's attempts to secure Higginson's continued interest in her work and thus a continuation of their (professional) friendship. Aware that Higginson has acted as a literary mentor for several female poets and writers, Dickinson's ambivalent self-presentation is influenced by her efforts to depict herself *simultaneously* as worthy of his professional attention and as in need of his instruction; she aims at drawing the self-portrait of a writer good enough to merit Higginson's advice, yet unschooled enough to be in need of his tutorship.

With the exception of Ruth Miller's study, earlier discussions of Dickinson's relationship to Higginson primarily focused on her "letters" while treating the enclosed "poems" as works of art, separate from the letter context, and submitted to a literary critic for analysis, or, as John Stuart Mann has suggested, as "not for communication but simply as gifts, art objects to be cherished by their lucky recipients" ("Motives" 3). Such a concentration on the "letters" alone, however, overemphasizes one side of Dickinson's carefully balanced self-presentation: her humility. Many critics were thus primarily concerned with determining whether Dickinson's expressions of humility were genuine or ironic in tone. The first to emphasize that Dickinson's self-denigrations could not be taken at face value was her brother, Austin. In an October 18, 1891, diary entry, Mabel Loomis Todd writes: "Those [letters] to Mr. Higginson are not of a private nature, and as to the 'innocent' and 'confiding' nature of them, Austin smiles. He says Emily definitely posed in those letters; he knows her thoroughly, through and through, as no one else ever did" (qtd. in Bingham, *Ancestors' Brocades* 166–167). Bingham herself, however, disagrees: "If she [Dickinson] had wanted to indulge in pleasantries, or to assume a facetious pose, does it seem likely that she would have chosen to do so before Colonel Higginson, the literary stranger to whom she had turned for advice?" (*Ancestors' Brocades* 167). One of the critics who, agreeing with Bingham, reads Dickinson's letters to Higginson literally is Lambert: "In her first encounter with Higginson," he argues, "she portrays herself finally as a shy, dependent virgin whose letter and poetic offerings are a moral risk" (67). Most critics, however, have come to agree that these letters cannot always be taken literally. Ruth Miller summarizes many of the current positions thus: "The characterization of herself as a new poet is a pose; her humility is a pretense"; and adds, "Too much disservice has been done the poet by critics who have taken the mask for real" (64, 69). Miller also emphasizes that "Emily Dickinson requires no counsel from Higginson. . . . She seeks no guidance. She introduces herself and hopes for welcome" (61). Yet though most interpretations tend to read Dickinson's "humility" as "pretense," I maintain that the situation is more complex. A contextual reading of Dickinson's letters in conjunction with all poems enclosed within those letters reveals how each gesture of self-denigration is carefully counterbalanced by a gesture of self-affirmation.

Thus, for a better understanding of Dickinson's epistolary relationship with Higginson, it is essential to abandon the strict generic distinction between "letters" (as message) and "poems" (as literature) and listen to their intertextual dialogic exchange.

In order to emphasize her need of Higginson's instruction, Dickinson downplays her education at Mt. Holyoke, one of the most prestigious nineteenth-century female seminaries in New England: "I went to school—but in your manner of the phrase—had no education" (L261). This self-confessed ignorance remains a constant theme throughout her entire correspondence: "An ignorance, not of Customs . . . Myself the only Kangaroo among the Beauty, Sir, if you please, it afflicts me, and I thought that instruction would take it away" (L268).[27] Assuring Higginson that he is, indeed, the only one who can provide the needed instruction ("I have none to ask," L260), she rules out both her parents and her earlier friends as possible "tutors": "Mother does not care for thought—and Father, too busy with his Briefs—to notice what we do—He buys me many Books—but begs me not to read them—because he fears they joggle the Mind" (L261). In addition, two of her earlier tutors, among them Ben Newton, can no longer be approached for help: "I had a friend, who taught me Immortality—but venturing too near, himself—he never returned—Soon after, my Tutor, died . . . Then I found one more—but he was not contented I be his scholar—so he left the Land" (L261).[28]

In accordance with her self-ascribed role of "scholar" (i.e., pupil), Dickinson also promises her "preceptor" submissiveness and obedience, qualities that induced Barbara Antonina Clarke Mossberg to describe Higginson's relationship to Dickinson as that of father to daughter: "Preceptor, I shall bring you—Obedience—the Blossom from my Garden, and every gratitude I know" (L268). This obedience includes, Dickinson claims, an unquestioning acceptance of Higginson's literary advice: "I shall observe your precept—though I dont understand it, always" (L271).[29] Her textual docility also informs the self-confessed selection of her readings: eschewing Whitman because she "was told that he was disgraceful," Dickinson concentrates on "Miss Prescott's 'Circumstance'" (L260), no doubt aware that Harriet Prescott Spofford had been one of Higginson's first literary protégées.

This seemingly clear-cut self-fashioning as submissive, obedient pupil, however, is constantly subverted by Dickinson's voice of the poet. Asking Higginson to be her guide, she nonetheless clearly delimits his "guidance" to the realm of literary criticism. Possibly because of its gendered connotations, she expresses her (not entirely genuine, as we have seen in her Holland correspondence) indifference to religion—despite Higginson's former career as a clergyman: "They [her parents and siblings] are religious—except me—and address an Eclipse, every morning—whom they call their 'Father' " (L261).[30] And despite affirmations to the contrary, Dickinson also shrewdly reserves for herself the right to decide to what extent she will eventually accept Higginson's literary advice. In L676, she remarks: "Thank you for the advice—I shall implicitly follow it" (L676). L265 is even more explicit: "If I might bring you what I do—not so frequent to trouble you—and ask you if I told it clear—'twould be control, to me—The Sailor cannot see the North—but knows the Needle can." Embedded in a compliment for Higginson, Dickinson's use of the compass metaphor illustrates the degree of "control" she allows him to exert over her poetry: as "preceptor," he will point out the "right" direction (the "accepted" way of writing poetry), yet it will be up to the "Sailor" to steer the boat.[31]

In another sense, the term *control* also delimits the *kind* of instruction and advice that Dickinson is willing to accept from Higginson. She speaks in no uncertain terms about the *power* of her poetic voice: "I had no Monarch in my life, and cannot rule myself, and when I try to organize—my little Force explodes—and leaves me bare and charred" (L271).[32] What her poetry lacks, therefore, is "organization," something that she was convinced Higginson would be able to supply. Juhasz has suggested that two of the four poems enclosed in Dickinson's first letter to Higginson are among her more irregular ones (J319/Fr304 and J320/Fr282), an indication that "she has to show her work to be in need of exactly what Higginson might have to offer, discipline" ("Reading" 184).[33]

That the issue at stake is indeed "discipline" or "control" is illustrated in L271. Dickinson introduces her poems enclosed in this letter by asking, "Are these more orderly?"—a question she returns to again in the accompanying poem J326/Fr381A, "I cannot dance upon my Toes." On the surface, J326/

Fr381A seemingly echoes the same thoughts that had already been expressed in several of Dickinson's earlier letters: she is concerned about a lack of formal "order," "rule," and "organization" in her poems:

I cannot dance upon my Toes—
No Man instructed me—
But oftentimes, among my mind,
A Glee possesseth me,

That had I Ballet knowledge—
Would put itself abroad
In Pirouette to blanch a Troupe—
Or lay a Prima, Mad,

And though I had no Gown of Gauze—
No Ringlet, to my Hair,
Nor hopped to Audiences—like Birds,
One Claw upon the Air,

Nor tossed my shape in Eider Balls,
Nor rolled on wheels of snow
Till I was out of sight, in sound,
The House encore me so—

Nor any know I know the Art
I mention—easy—Here—
Nor any Placard boast me—
It's full as Opera— (J326/Fr381A)

The ballet metaphor, with its emphasis on accurate "foot" work and strictly regularized and disciplined patterns of steps, strongly suggests an analogy to formalistic, metrically regular poetry. Dickinson again emphasizes her ignorance of the technical aspects of "dance" due to her lack of "instruction": without formal training, she has never learned to "dance" properly, to write prosodically "correct" poetry. She even implies that, with such knowledge, she might consider publication ("Would put itself abroad"). Yet the final stanza completely reverses Dickinson's seeming apology for her awkward poetic form. "Nor any know I know the Art | I mention—easy—Here" is the confident self-affirmation of a poet who strongly believes in her work. And the concluding line provides Higginson with a key to understanding her poems: Dickinson wants him to realize that hers is a generically different art form. Rather than belonging to the formalized environment of measured/ "metered" steps ("ballet"), her poetry is characterized by the power of her voice(s): "It's full as Opera." Ruth Miller has observed that "Higginson understood the quality of poetry to reside in its craftsmanship; Emily Dickinson believed it resided in the subject matter" (96). According to this poem, I would add, it primarily resides in the power of Dickinson's voice(s).

This self-confident voice of the poet regularly erupts in Dickinson's correspondence with Higginson—predominantly in her enclosed poems—thus constantly offsetting her self-denigrating pupil pose. The fourth poem enclosed in her first letter constitutes another example. J216/Fr124 ("Safe in their Alabaster Chambers") had been published, albeit anonymously, under the title "The Sleeping" in the *Springfield Daily Republican* of March 1, 1862, only six weeks before Dickinson initiated her correspondence with Higginson. Aware that Higginson, as a reader of the *Springfield*, might remember this particular poem, Dickinson signs it separately, using her "poet's" signature "E. Dickinson."[34] By thus including a published poem (and clearly claiming ownership of the anonymous publication), Dickinson uses her first letter to Higginson to display some of her credentials, proving her worthiness of his professional attention. Dickinson also makes a point of emphasizing to Higginson that she has indeed had several opportunities to publish her work but has *chosen* not to do so: "Two Editors of Journals came to my Father's House, this winter—and asked me for my Mind—and when I asked them 'Why,' they said I was penurious—and they, would use it for the World" (L261). Interestingly enough, however, this statement (in the poet's voice) is immediately afterward undercut by the pupil's voice, which adds a reference to her own self-perceived "smallness" and insignificance: "I could not weigh myself—Myself—My size felt small—to me" (L261).

The same duality of voices manifests itself in almost all of the early letters to Higginson. In L265, for example, pride in earlier praise for her poetry is juxtaposed with an emphasis on the special significance of praise coming from Higginson. Juhasz speaks in this case of a "seesaw motion" between pride and obsequiousness ("Materiality" 433), whereas Crumbley characterizes it as "shifting voices that constitute the continuum between the child and the Queen" (*Inflections* 80): "Your letter gave no Drunkenness, because I tasted Rum before . . . yet I have had few pleasures so deep as your opinion, and if I tried to thank you, my tears would block my tongue. . . . Your second letter surprised me, and for a moment, swung—I had not supposed it. Your first—gave no dishonor, because the True—are not ashamed—I thanked you for your justice—but could not drop the Bells whose jingling cooled my Tramp—Perhaps the Balm, seemed better, because you bled me, first" (L265). Throughout this letter, Dickinson emphasizes her own faith in her poetic vocation: "My dying Tutor told me that he would like to live till I had been a poet . . . If fame belonged to me, I could not escape her—if she did not, the longest day would pass me on the chase" (L265). These statements of self-affirmation, however, are then regularly undercut by references to her "smallness": "I have a little shape—it would not crowd your Desk—nor make much Racket as the Mouse, that dents your Galleries" (L265).

The constructedness of Dickinson's epistolary poses in her letters to Higginson is further underlined by the fact that Higginson himself felt ambivalent about occupying the subject position that she had outlined for him. Reflecting on his correspondence with the writer in 1890, he observes that Dickinson was "always persistently keeping up this attitude of 'scholar,' and assuming on my part a preceptorship which it is almost needless to say did not exist" ("Letters" 193). Rather than claiming the superior authority of "preceptor" that Dickinson had invested him with, Higginson, in fact, frequently displays an effort to please Dickinson: "Sometimes I take out your letters & verses, dear friend, and when I feel their strange power, it is not strange that I find it hard to write & that long months pass. . . . I should like to hear from you very often, but feel always timid lest what I *write* should be badly aimed & miss that fine edge of thought which you bear. It would be so easy, I fear, to miss you. Still, you see, I try" (L330a). As Anna Mary Wells has argued: "He [Higginson] always wrote Miss Dickinson as if she were not merely his intellectual equal but his superior" ("Soul's Society" 226). Higginson concludes the same letter by assuring Dickinson: "Write & tell me something in prose or verse, & I will be less fastidious in future & willing to write clumsy things, rather than none. Ever your friend" (L330a).[35]

Dickinson, however, adamantly resists Higginson's attempts to dismantle this carefully crafted power imbalance.[36] In reaction to L330a, for example, she elevates him even further: "You were not aware that you saved my life" (L330). And when Higginson confesses to having difficulties understanding her letters and poems, Dickinson responds: "You say 'Beyond your knowledge.' You would not jest with me, because I believe you—but Preceptor—you cannot mean it? All men say 'What' to me, but I thought it a fashion" (L271). In her response, Dickinson thus immediately undermines the authority her superior style might grant her by reaffirming Higginson's dominant position as "Preceptor," and by replacing her voice of the poet by that of the "little Girl": "When much in the Woods as a little Girl, I was told that the Snake would bite me" (L271).

It is in order to maintain a power-differentiated hierarchy, I suggest, that Dickinson consistently repeats her pleas for instruction throughout her letters to Higginson: "But, will you be my Preceptor, Mr Higginson?" (L265); "Would you have time to be the 'friend' you should think I need?" (L265); "Would you instruct me now?" (L314); "If I still entreat you to teach me, are you much displeased?" (L316); "Bringing still my 'plea for Culture,' Would it teach me now?" (L323); "Would you but guide Dickinson" (L368); "Could you teach me now?" (L396); "Will you instruct me then no more" (L396); "Would you but guide Your Scholar" (L459); "Since you cease to teach me, how could I improve? Your pupil" (L513); "You can scarcely estimate the opinion to one utterly guideless . . . Your Scholar" (L676).

One of the reasons Dickinson insists on maintaining her "pupil's" voice, and thus continually disempowers her own position in relation to Higginson, is explained by J1210/Fr1275C, enclosed in L381. In L261, Dickinson had asked Higginson, "I would like to learn—could you tell me how to grow?" J1210/Fr1275C returns to this question:

The Sea said 'Come' to the Brook—
The Brook said 'Let me grow'—
The Sea said 'Then you will be a Sea—
I want a Brook—Come now'!

The Sea said 'Go' to the Sea—
The Sea said 'I am he
You cherished'—'Learned Waters—
Wisdom is stale—to Me.'

ı illustrates Dickinson's acute awareness of socially constructed gendered) forms of dominance and submission. The pupil is that once she has "grown" from a "brook" into a "sea" herself, once she has "outgrown" her instructor, the sea/Higginson will no longer be interested in a continuation of their friendship/his mentorship. In other words, Dickinson fears that *only* as long as Higginson is convinced he has something to teach her will he maintain this epistolary relationship; as soon as she has become his "equal," however, as soon as she has left the traditionally female pose of submission and has become "masculinized" ("I am *he* | You cherished"; emphasis added), Higginson will dismiss her.[37] Dickinson's constant self-fashioning as "pupil," her systematic subversion of her (degendered) poet voice is thus ultimately an attempt to ensure a continuation of her relationship with Higginson by curbing and circumscribing her own power, by pretending to remain less knowledgeable than her preceptor. Ferlazzo has argued that "Dickinson's correspondence with Higginson begins at this point to look like something of a charade. She would play the inquiring scholar asking for the instructions she had no intention of using, and he was to play the pretended preceptor who presented the lessons that would not be learned" (140).[38] Yet it is more than just "a charade." In Dickinson's opinion, her relationship with Higginson depends on the maintenance of the socially sanctioned model of relationship between a (male) mentor and his (female) protégée, and thus on the maintenance of a gender-inscribed hierarchy of power and authority. And one way of ensuring the preservation of this hierarchy is to balance the (degendered) voice of the poet (the "author only") with the highly gendered voice of the submissive pupil/protégée.

It is in Dickinson's arguably most famous correspondence with an as yet still unidentified recipient referred to as "Master" that this intensely ambivalent circumscription of her own power receives its most poignant expression.

"MASTER"

In contrast to the carefully maintained balance between a poet's self-affirmation and a (female) pupil's self-denigration in Dickinson's epistolary exchanges with Higginson, the scales frequently tip toward the pole of complete self-abasement in her so-called Master letters.[39] One of Dickinson's most self-humbling and intensely gendered poses occurs in the second of these letters,[40] written about 1861: "Oh, did I offend it— . . . Daisy—Daisy—offend it—who bends her smaller life to his . . . who only asks—a task— . . . something to do for love of it—some little way she cannot guess to make that master glad" (L248).[41] Throughout this letter, Dickinson emphasizes her "smallness" and insignificance, referring to herself as "Daisy," an ignorant female "child": "Daisy—who never flinched thro' that awful parting . . . who would have sheltered him in her childish bosom (Heart)—only it was'nt big eno' for a Guest so large—*this* Daisy—grieve her Lord—and yet it (she) often blundered . . . Daisy . . . knows all that—but must she go unpardoned—teach her, preceptor grace—teach her majesty—Slow (Dull) at patrician things—Even the wren upon her nest learns (knows) more than Daisy dares" (L248). To please her "Master," she is willing to give up her "self" completely, to be subsumed by him, and to become her "Master's" "best little girl": "Master—open your life wide, and take me in forever, I will never be tired—I will never be noisy when you want to be still. I will be . . . your best little girl—nobody else will see me, but you—but that is enough—I shall not want any more" (L248).

Both Judith Farr and Adalaide Morris have commented on Dickinson's use of the "Daisy" role. Farr roots it firmly within Victorian traditions, emphasizing its representation of the "acceptable Victorian feminine qualities of demure dependency and weakness" (*Passion* 195). Morris, dwelling on the aspects of dependency and tropism between "Daisy" and "sun" (108), argues that "the Master letters and poems offer the spectacle of a self willing itself to be an inessential other" (106). Morris thus views "Daisy" as someone who completely abandons her own independent identity and becomes invisible to anyone but her "Master" in order to please him. Yet in my opinion this focus on self-effacement captures only one side of this role. The double-voiced ambivalence of Dickinson's "Daisy" pose is suggested by the word's etymology. In its Old English form "daegesege," as well as Middle English "dayesye," "Daisy" signifies "the day's eye," that is, the sun itself. In this way, "Daisy" can thus stand for both the demurely insignificant little flower/girl *dependent* on the sun and the most powerful ruler of the sky itself.

This ambivalence, this wavering between a powerful and a disempowered

"Daisy," is more clearly reflected in Dickinson's third "Master" letter. Here, "Daisy" adopts a more reproachful tone: "One drop more from the gash that stains your Daisy's bosom—then would you *believe?*" (L233); "I dont know what you can do for it—thank you—Master—but if I had the Beard on my cheek—like you—and you—had Daisy's petals—and you cared so for me—what would become of you?" (L233); "you know what a leech is, dont you—and . . . Daisy's arm is small" (L233). Interspersed between references to smallness and gestures of submission and self-humbling, there emerges a metaphoric reversal of dependencies: while earlier it was "Daisy" who turned toward the "sun" for survival, she now is the one to provide the "arm" for the "leech's" parasitic (and potentially destructive) sustenance.

Yet it is not only the "leech" that might overtax his host. "Daisy" also hints at her own destructive powers; the fragile "Daisy" suddenly turns into a forceful volcano: "You say I do not tell you all—Daisy confessed—and denied not. Vesuvius dont talk—Etna dont— . . . one of them said a syllable—a thousand years ago, and Pompeii heard it, and hid forever" (L233). Even though in her "Master" letters, Dickinson never explicitly employs her "poet's" voice to negotiate power relations, this association of explosive destructiveness with "speaking" ("syllable") highlights "voice" as the source of the speaker's volcanic power. In a sense, then, these lines recall the description of (poetic) voice that Dickinson had utilized in a poem addressed to Higginson: "It's full as Opera" (J326/Fr381A). Yet though "Opera" impresses through vocal power governed and reigned in by a musical frame, a volcanic voice has lost this element of control: even a single syllable can potentially be lethal. In many respects, Dickinson's wavering between positions of dominance and submission, between gestures of empowerment and voluntary disempowerment in her "Master" letters recalls similar ambiguities and equivocations in her correspondences with Higginson and Austin Dickinson. Yet there is one crucial difference: here, any sense of proportion, any sense of control, has been lost. Strategies of both humiliating self-denigration and destructive self-empowerment are at their most painful extremes.

THE subject positions occupied in letters to her male correspondents Austin Dickinson, Thomas Wentworth Higginson, and "Master" reveal Dickinson's profound ambivalence about gendered forms of status, power, and authority. *Equivocality,* to use Adrienne Rich's term utilized in her dedicatory poem ("I am in Danger—Sir"), is a hallmark of each of these epistolary exchanges. In each case, Dickinson's letters become "double-voiced," featuring dialogic juxtapositions of voices of dominance and submission, of conflict and conformity. Frequently (but not always) Dickinson adopts the voice of the poet (in both "poems" and "letters") to express superiority and authority (literary and otherwise), while she employs humor (Austin) in addition to inhabiting culturally sanctioned, hyperbolically female-gendered poses (little girl, protégée, Daisy) to undercut this authority and signal submission and obedience (Austin, Higginson, "Master"). Although in none of her correspondences does Dickinson discard sociocultural gender-role restrictions completely, she nonetheless appropriates them for her own purposes and interrogates them consistently, with critiques ranging from a careful balance (Higginson) to a highly subtle and indirect form of revolt ("Master").

As in her correspondences with female friends, Dickinson's main reason for such careful negotiations seems to have been her interest in taking control of the respective relationships by carefully monitoring her own acts of self-representation. Yet while her letters to female friends had primarily been characterized by a blurring of the boundaries between the personal/referential and the literary/nonreferential in order to mask gender-specific ideological differences, her letters to male friends are more specifically characterized by a dialogic interaction between authoritative ("poetic") and nonauthoritative voices in order to negotiate gender-specific power relations. Whereas her epistolary exchanges with female friends can thus be said to be dominated by relationships of (passionate) love and (female) duty, her letters to her male friends focus more consistently on relationships of (literary) power and authority. It is the voice of the poet, of the "author only," that acquires special significance. Yet ultimately it can be argued for all of Dickinson's epistolary exchanges that although seemingly "personal" and "intimate," her letters to Sue Gilbert, Elizabeth Holland, Austin Dickinson, Thomas Wentworth Higginson, and "Master" illustrate different ways in which textually constructed voices appropriate, usurp, critique, and negotiate between different subject positions in order to orchestrate specific relationships. At times, Dickinson inhabits or subverts strongly gender-inscribed roles, questioning culturally determined gender dynamics and interrogating the possibilities for female-female as well as male-female relationships in nineteenth-century New England. At other times, she ascribes fictional roles to both herself and her respective addressees, thus manipulating them into a precisely circumscribed behavior. And at still other times she playfully exploits the textual, revisionist possibilities that an appropriation of Eve's figurative language offers. In this way, rather than speaking "in her own personal voice" (Turco, *Woman of Letters* 1), Dickinson, to use Sidonie Smith's expression, "fractures the narrated 'I' into multiple speaking postures," postures that "privileg[e] a presence, or identity, that does not exist outside language" (Sidonie Smith 47, 5). As Finnerty argues in his discussion of J738/Fr736: "The speaker will take on any identity and therefore is without an essential identity"; additionally, "The ability of the speaker to move from one role to another disputes not only the notion of stable gender identity but also the nature of opposites"; the speaker's identity is thus lost "beyond the actualization or performance of an assigned role" (70). Dickinson thus repeatedly emerges as both powerful and powerless; she is "Rhinoceros | Or Mouse | At once" (J738/Fr736).

The five examples discussed above have illustrated the extent to which Dickinson's epistolary selves—rather than presenting unmediated, self-revelatory chronicles of real-life experiences from the perspective of a unified "self"—become discursive constructs created for and addressed to a specific audience. Even though they were inevitably prompted by individual needs or circumstances, they constitute textual performances enacted in response to specific sociocultural constructions of womanhood, thus effectively blurring the boundaries between "fact" and "fiction." The performative aspect of these epistolary self-articulations manifests itself most clearly, however, when reading them contextually, as simultaneous enactments of different, often contradictory roles. In any one of the above-discussed examples, Dickinson textually inhabits or negotiates between a limited number of "personae," but the multiplicity of her epistolary voices is highlighted by the simultaneous articulation and occupation of these diverse subject positions. Dickinson thus plays the role of both dependent child (Holland, "Master") and rebellious daughter (Austin Dickinson); she describes herself as Austin's obedient sister in her letters to Holland, while challenging his authority within the family in her correspondence with Austin himself. In addition, comments on Dickinson's religious stance—of critical importance in her earliest Amherst friendships—are carefully monitored, ranging from deep concern (Holland) to studied disinterest (Higginson) to a discursive redefinition of "God" and the concept of "worship" (Sue Gilbert). Moreover, Dickinson's self-articulation as a poet becomes a female-gendered act of nurturing and consolation in her letters to Holland, while it is modeled on the traditions of courtly love and male sonneteers in her expressions of unfulfilled passion to Sue; yet it also produces the degendered voice of power and self-confidence, of an "author only" in her letters to Higginson, only to turn into an uncontrollably destructive, "volcanic" force in her "Master" letters. Such a high degree of textual self-fashioning and performativity illustrates how Dickinson's multiple "supposed persons" ultimately challenge the reader's search for a stable, referential, "autobiographical" self in her correspondences.

Yet it is not only the stability of the speaker's self but also the stability, referentiality, and autobiographical authenticity of her addressees that Dickinson challenges. Most critics agree that the author's letters are carefully tailored to her respective audiences: "Emily Dickinson was audience-conscious," Higgins points out; "she carefully adapted each correspondence to her estimate of the reader's capacities" (5). Ferlazzo agrees: "Another aspect of her art reveals how conscious she always was of her audience, trying to send to her correspondents what best fitted their minds and needs" (127). Similarly, Wider emphasizes: "A flexible form that could be shaped to suit every occasion, the letter provided Dickinson with a way of establishing common ground between herself and her correspondents" (19). Bakhtin confirms this importance of the addressee in epistolary writing: "A characteristic feature of the letter is an acute awareness of the interlocutor, the addressee to whom it is directed. The letter, like a rejoinder in a dialogue, is addressed to a specific person, and it takes into account the other's possible reactions, the other's possible reply" (*Problems* 205).

On the surface, Dickinson's way of adapting her letters/her voices to her respective addressees thus seems to fulfill one essential requirement of epistolary discourse in general that was also stipulated by nineteenth-century epistolary handbooks: "always adapt your style to the subject, and likewise to the capacity of your hearers or readers" (McCabe 36). According to letter-writing manuals, the purpose of this addressee specificity, in addition to facilitating communication, was to please one's respective recipient. Bilworth, for example, explains that "when you write merely out of compliment, it is done more to please your correspondent than yourself; and therefore you should endeavour to hit his taste" (Introduction, *Complete Letter Writer* n.p.). Drawing a link to the *female* letter writer's duties, in particular, Ruth Perry thus summarizes: "Letters were the perfect vehicle for women's highly developed art of pleasing, for in writing letters it is possible to tailor a self on paper to suit the expectations and desires of the audience" (69).

Yet for Dickinson, epistolary performativity is more than just a (female-gendered) need to please. Rather than merely "tailor[ing] a self on paper to suit the expectations and desires of the audience" (Perry 69), Dickinson's discursive strategies of self-fashioning often simultaneously also ascribe specific roles to her addressees, thus manipulating them into playing a prescribed part. In this way, Dickinson uses textually constructed roles to tailor her *addressees* to suit her *own* expectations. As a result, the genre of the private letter is turned into a radical tool of control, manifesting itself in Dickinson's reconstructions and redefinitions of her respective addressees' roles, such as the casting of Sue Gilbert as the divine, perpetually inaccessible object of courtly love; Elizabeth Holland's functionalization as "surrogate mother"; or Higginson's construction as "preceptor." Though it is impossible to ascertain whether Holland or Sue accepted their respective role ascriptions, we do know that Higginson, at least later, publicly refuted his prescribed role.

In addition to the above-sketched personae and role ascriptions that tend to orchestrate and reorganize entire relationships (or at least substantial parts thereof), Dickinson also utilizes these strategies on a smaller scale. Very often, such individual, "occasional" role ascriptions acquire a playful quality and are designed to coax her respective addressee to exhibit a specific response in a specific situation.[42] In L282, for example, Dickinson, fearing she has offended Higginson, apologizes with the following words: "I know not what to deem myself—Yesterday 'Your Scholar'—but might I be the one you tonight, forgave, 'tis a Better Honor—Mine is but just the Thief's Request—Please, Sir, Hear 'Barabbas'—." By appropriating first the role of Thief, and then that of Barabbas, Dickinson explicitly maps out Higginson's response: by implication, he is expected to become "Christ," graciously forgiving the Thief. Simultaneously, Higginson is also cast in the role of Pilate, who will release the condemned Barabbas in spite of the latter's manifest guilt. Dickinson thereby assures herself of double forgiveness, even in the face of guilt. Similarly, an apology to Samuel Bowles concludes with the line "Good night, God will forgive me—Will you please to *try?*" (L223), thus rendering it virtually impossible for Bowles *not* to try.

Yet it is not only biblical characters that Dickinson appropriates for her role plays and role ascriptions; she also draws on a wide variety of mythological, historical, literary, and real-life characters. To Samuel Bowles, for example, she writes: "I fear I am your little friend no more, but Mrs Jim Crow" (L223); "Pray forgive me now: Respect little Bob o'Lincoln again!" (L223); "This is all that I have to say—Kinsmen need say nothing—but 'Swiveller' may be sure of the 'Marchioness' " (L241). In L256, again to Samuel Bowles, Dickinson uses her brother's name as a "cover" throughout: "Will you be kind to *Austin*—again? . . . Austin is disappointed—He expected to see you—today—He is sure you wont go to Sea—without first speaking to Him. I presume if Emily and Vinnie knew of his writing—they would entreat Him to ask you—not—" (L256). A letter to Sue Gilbert is signed "Yours till death—*Judah*" (L97). Thanking Cornelia Peck Sweetser for a pitcher ("The Pitcher shall be an emblem—"), Dickinson uses a signature that recalls jar-offering "Rebecca" (L836). L981, addressed to Sarah Tuckerman, concludes with the lines "Accept a loving Caw from a nameless friend, 'Selah.' " One letter to Higginson is signed "Your Gnome" (L280). A brief note to Ned Dickinson reads: "Phoebus—'I'll take the Reins.' Phaeton" (L642). A role adopted twice occurs in a note accompanying a gift for her nephew Ned: in an attempt to conceal her identity as giver of the gift, Dickinson writes: "Omit to return Box—Omit to know you received Box—'Brooks of Sheffield' " (L204).[43] In two letters, Dickinson identifies with the painter Thomas Cole. L34 is signed "C." and L214 reads: "My 'position'! Cole. P.S. Lest you misapprehend, the unfortunate insect upon the left is Myself, while the Reptile upon the *right* is my more immediate friends, and connections. As ever, Cole." In L604 Dickinson adopts the perspective and name of Ned's two horses, "Dick" and "Jim," to sign a poem that, according to Martha

Dickinson Bianchi, explains why his horses had run away with him (*Face to Face* 251). To her brother, Austin, she sends a note signed "Samuel Nash—" (L954).[44]

In most of these instances, as critics have repeatedly pointed out, Dickinson's choice of personae and aliases is based on her respective addressee's (literary) background and interests. Taking into account her correspondents' familiarity with the literary, biblical, or mythological provenance and context of respective roles, each of Dickinson's fictional "names" usually functions—as has been noted by Farr and others—as a self-explanatory shorthand notation or "code" explicating a specific situation by analogy without the need for elaborate contextualizations. In Eberwein's words: "A stylistic trait of the letters that Dickinson carefully nurtured in preparation for her poetry was play on literary and scriptural allusions—yet another device for establishing a privileged relationship with the particular reader who would appreciate their personal resonance and also a means of enlarging trivial circumstances to adumbrate her haunting themes of fragility, loss, death, and immortality" (49).[45]

What most critics tend to overlook, however, is the subversive potential inherent in Dickinson's chosen fictional roles.[46] Although her adoption of epistolary aliases initially constitutes a predominantly playful strategy, many of Dickinson's personae can also be interpreted as challenges to prevailing social constructions of womanhood and their concomitant power relations. It is striking to note, for example, that—in contrast to the hyperbolically female-gendered poses designed to produce a calculated effect of submission—almost all of the personae are male. In addition to the above-quoted signatures "*Judah,*" "Phaeton," "Brooks of Sheffield," "Cole," and "Samuel Nash," as well as the earlier role of "Antony," Dickinson at times also refers to *herself* as a man: "Ned tells that the Clock purrs and the Kitten ticks. He inherits his Uncle Emily's ardor for the lie" (L315). And to Ned himself she writes, "Mother told me when I was a Boy, that I must 'turn over a new Leaf' " (L571). Such a frequent appropriation of male roles can be read as a critique of the narrowly circumscribed range of socially and discursively available roles for women. By this method, Dickinson can subvert existing gender relations not only by speaking in a poet's voice (as in her letters to Austin and Higginson) but also by appropriating a multiplicity of other male voices. L107, for example, provides an array of male fictional and historical identities: "Why, dear Susie, it must'nt scare you if I loom up from Hindoostan, or drop from an Appenine, or peer at you suddenly from the hollow of a tree, calling myself King Charles, Sancho Panza, or Herod, King of the Jews—I suppose it is all the same" (L107). All these roles are invariably associated with power (King Charles, Herod), with art and artists (Cole, Phaeton),[47] with the publishing industry (Nash), or with adventure and shrewdness (Sancho Panza). By thus emphasizing the male-dominated areas of public life, politics, and art, Dickinson's epistolary roles constitute an attempt to reconfigure and rewrite her own (a woman's) position(s) within society. Focusing on Dickinson's male personae in her poems, Cristanne Miller has argued that "she is ambivalent about identifying with women" (*Grammar* 166).[48] A similar claim, I suggest, can be made for Dickinson's use of male personae in her letters.[49]

Dickinson's adoption of a wide variety of epistolary voices or "supposed persons," functionalized in order to interrogate various gender-inscribed and power-differentiated subject positions within different correspondences, is, however, only one specific form of a larger range of discursive criticism that manifests itself within her letters. In addition to addressee-specific negotiations of concrete relationships by *adopting* specific authoritative and nonauthoritative (fictional, biblical, literary) roles, voices, and personae, Dickinson also *critiques* the gendered and power-differentiated inscriptions in the very voices she appropriates. This critique manifests itself primarily in the ways she assimilates or otherwise frames direct quotations within her letters. The high degree of intertextual intensity or, more specifically, the high degree of polyvocal intertextuality that permeates all of Dickinson's letters and letter-poems ultimately challenges, in very general terms, traditional notions of (male) literary authority, authorized discourses, and processes of authorization.

You will pardon the freedom
I use with your remarks.
—EMILY DICKINSON

Except for usurping your Copyright
—I should regive the Message,
but each Voice is it's own—
—EMILY DICKINSON

The frame is always in the
power of the framer, and . . .
there is an outrageous privilege
in the power to cite others.
—MIKHAIL BAKHTIN

Dialogue can be monological, and
what is called monologue can be
dialogical.
—JULIA KRISTEVA

5

Manipulating Multiple Voices

BOTH BAKHTIN AND KRISTEVA have argued that any text is, by definition, "a permutation of texts, an intertextuality: in the space of a given text, several utterances, taken from other texts, intersect and neutralize one another" (Kristeva, "Bounded" 37).[1] Consequently, any text can be described as "a mosaic of quotations" (Kristeva, *Desire* 66), which, in turn, leads Kristeva to conclude that all texts are ultimately "dialogic."[2] Bakhtin, on the other hand, further differentiates between dialogic prose and monologic poetry. Regarding all *language* as permeated with "a chorus of languages" (*Problems* xx) and therefore dialogic, Bakhtin nevertheless argues that lyric poetry strives to reduce this dialogicity: "Lyric poems, . . . marvellous as they can be, tend toward becoming monologues—the poet inventing a single voice, one that belies the actual polyphony of his own inner chorus" (xxii).[3] It is only the writer of prose novels, Bakhtin continues, who "allows voices into the work that are not fundamentally under the monological control of the novelist's own ideology" (xx). Therefore, according to Bakhtin, "the possibility of employing various types of discourse within a single work is typical of prose" (200).

In the past, many critics have regarded Dickinson's oeuvre—and in particular her poetry—as conforming to this dichotomy, even without explicitly invoking Bakhtin.[4] In fact, as Erika Scheurer reminds us,

> two of Bakhtin's primary interpreters, Gary Saul Morson and Caryl Emerson, allude to Dickinson as representative of the monologic lyric poet: "The poet can speak alone, and does not require interaction with other consciousnesses and with other languages in order to say what he wants to say. He selects his own society—he *is* his own society—and then he 'shuts the door,' except, perhaps to other poets and other poems. Whereas the novelist tries to represent, even exaggerate, heteroglossia, the poet escapes it in order to write in a language that is timeless" (Morson and Emerson, *Creation* 320). (Scheurer 88)[5]

Scheurer points out that Morson and Emerson's "curiously masculinized" version "not only explains Bakhtin's view of lyric poetry as single-voiced and monologic but also the popular impression of Emily Dickinson as a 'private poet' who necessarily speaks in a singular, private voice" (88).

Yet recent critical interest in Dickinson's stylistic indeterminacies has increasingly highlighted the dialogic aspects of this writer's prose *and* poetry.[6] Focusing on the element of "orality" in Dickinson's letters, Scheurer, for example, analyzes "how the oral and the textual traits of her letters combine to create a dialogic voice" (87). And Crumbley argues that it is Dickinson's highly disruptive style (in particular her use of the dash) that renders her texts dialogic: "Her punctuation, line breaks, capitalization, and chirography appear designed to isolate words and release voice possibilities that challenge the view of self as unified and single-voiced" ("Dialogic" 2–3).[7] Earlier discussions of stylistic indeterminacies in Dickinson's texts, as well as Crumbley's and Scheurer's more recent Bakhtinian analyses of the writer's style, have thus led Scheurer to conclude that "Dickinson scholarship has arrived . . . at a point where we recognize the dialogic quality of

Dickinson's textual voices in their flux and play" (90).[8] Although I agree with Scheurer and Crumbley that, from a strictly linguistic perspective, Dickinson's texts display a high degree of indeterminacy and thus dialogicity, I argue that from an intertextual or interdiscursive perspective—that is, one that focuses on the specific (literary, biblical, etc.) epistolary voices in and through which Dickinson speaks—these claims need to be further differentiated.

My analysis of Dickinson's intertextual engagement with other voices and discourses concentrates primarily on the most frequently occurring form of intertextuality in her letters: direct quotations.[9] In her correspondences, Dickinson displays a marked preference for direct quotations over indirect allusions and other forms of visually unmarked transtextuality, thus privileging heterogeneity and dialogicity. There are some exceptions to this general tendency. In her earliest letters, Dickinson still prefers indirect allusions, borrowings, and paraphrases to direct quotations. Yet even those are, for the most part, highlighted through being self-consciously introduced and apologized for. In L8, for example (dated 1845 by Johnson and Ward), an unmarked reference to "faith without works, which you know we are told is dead," is followed by the explanation: "Excuse my quoting from the Scripture, dear Abiah, for it was so handy in this case I couldn't get along very well without it." This apologetic reluctance to "quote," however, changes radically in her later letters. With respect to her poems, on the other hand, Pollak has observed that Dickinson's use of direct quotations *decreases* with time:

> Of the approximately 1775 poems by Dickinson, some fifty-one contain one or more literary allusions emphasized by quotation marks. Of these fifty-one poems, twenty-five belong to the period 1858–1861, ten to the period 1862–1865, fourteen to the period 1871–1885, and two are undated. That is, Dickinson's literary allusiveness [in her poetry] relies most on quotations during the early years 1858–1861, depends much less on these direct quotations during what is commonly taken to be her best and most productive period, 1862–1865, does without them entirely from 1866–1870, and then uses them again as a relatively insignificant feature of the poetry written from 1871–1886, the year of her death. ("Literary Allusions" 60)

In her *Valves of Attention: Quotation and Context in the Age of Emerson*, Debra Fried has noted the strikingly high density of direct quotations in Dickinson's epistolary exchanges: "The letters are often themselves a pastiche or mosaic of quotations rather than a context into which a quotation fits or from which it seems to obtrude" (150). The quotations incorporated into Dickinson's correspondences are taken from a wide range of texts, with the majority of quotations coming from the King James Bible, Higginson's writings, and Shakespeare's plays. In addition, Dickinson also quotes from a vast number of earlier and contemporary British and American, male and female authors; refers to articles in local newspapers and magazines; cites passages from her Mt. Holyoke textbooks; and recalls remarks by friends, family members, and local Amherst residents. Jack Capps has outlined the extent of Dickinson's reading in detail, emphasizing that "nineteenth-century British authors affected her poetry neither so often nor so deeply as did the Bible and the verse of the Metaphysicals and the hymn writers" (77). "On the whole," Capps continues, "Emily Dickinson found the poetry and prose of American authors less attractive than that of the British writers of the Romantic and Victorian periods. Aside from her interest in Emerson and Higginson, she showed none of the sustained enthusiasm for American prose writers that she showed for the Brontës, Dickens, and Eliot" (121). He also points out that the Dickinson family subscribed to most of the leading local and national magazines, such as *The Springfield Republican, The Hampshire and Franklin Express, The Amherst Record, Harper's New Monthly Magazine, Scribner's Monthly*, and *The Atlantic Monthly* (128), many of which have been identified by Frank Luther Mott as highly influential in the area of literary criticism. Capps also notes that *Harper's*, in particular, was filled with reprints from British publications such as the *London Times, Chamber's Edinburgh Journal*, and *Punch*, thus offering Dickinson access to the British literary scene too (129). With reference to Dickinson's own contemporaries, Capps has observed that "most of the American works that she read were written during her lifetime, and she read them soon after they appeared" (111). He expresses surprise, however, at the fact "that the religious writings of colonial America formed such a small part of Emily Dickinson's reading" (102). Multiple quoted voices from many of these sources enter Dickinson's texts throughout her entire epistolary career.

Yet both Bakhtin and Manfred Pfister have argued that it is the degree to which a direct quotation has been modified in the quoting process (including spelling, capitalization, punctuation, syntax) which ultimately determines the quoting text's intertextual and dialogic intensity. Generally speaking, the lower the degree of modification, the higher the degree of heterogeneity, and the higher, consequently, the degree of heteroglossia and dialogicity. Bakhtin distinguishes between three kinds of modification: a quotation can merge with, submit itself to, or dominate its new context. "Our practical everyday speech," he observes, "is full of other people's words: with some of them we completely merge our own voice, forgetting whose they are; others, which we take as authoritative, we use to reinforce our own words; still others, finally we populate with our own aspirations, alien or hostile to them" (*Problems* 195). More specifically, Manfred Pfister identifies six criteria that affect an intertextual reference's degree of assimilation to its new context: *referentiality* (the degree to which the quoting text explicitly marks the quotation as such [quotation marks] or directly refers to the prior context(s) of the quoted passage [title, author]); *communicativity* (the degree to which both writer and reader are able or textually enabled to recognize intertextual references); *autoreflexivity* (the degree to which the writer of the quoting text explicitly comments on her/his integration of other texts); *structure* (the formal and functional integration of quoted text into quoting text [syntax, verb form, meter, imagery]);[10] *selectivity* (the degree to which the quoted text can function as a synecdoche for—and thus metonymically refer back to and evoke—its former context); *dialogicity* (the degree to which there exist both semantic and ideological tensions between quoted text and host structure [subversion, irony].[11] In his *Poetics of Quotation in the European Novel,* Herman Meyer concludes that, generally speaking, each individual quotation displays "a unique tension between assimilation and dissimilation," since it "links itself closely with its new environment, but at the same time detaches itself from it, thus permitting another world to radiate into the self-contained world of the novel [or letter, by extension]" (6).[12]

In her correspondence, Dickinson's quoting strategies regularly combine different degrees of "assimilation and dissimilation," ranging from exact quotations (to which her own letter contexts are formally subordinated) to complete rewritings of her "quoted" voices. On the one hand, Dickinson's insistence on maintaining the formal and structural accuracy of some of her quotations occasionally even causes what Laurent Jenny has called "combinatorial incompatibilities" (52). On the other, however, many "direct quotations" are, in fact, modified to facilitate their functional integration into and their formal assimilation to their new context. It is in the specific combination of these two seemingly antithetical strategies that Dickinson's discursive critique manifests itself most distinctly.

The accuracy that Dickinson exhibits in *some* kinds of quotations suggests that inaccuracies in other cases may indeed be more than mere "slips of the pen."[13] On several occasions, for example, Dickinson insists on quoting as exactly as possible, rather than producing mere paraphrases or summaries of content. In L908, she complains to Gilbert: "I wish I could find the Warrington Words, but during my weeks of faintness, my Treasures were misplaced, and I cannot find them."[14] And the following request is directed at Forrest F. Emerson: "In a note which you sent my brother soon after the dying of our child, was a passage, our only spar at the time, and solemnly remembered. We would gladly possess it more accurately, if convenient to you" (L1018). These words are then followed by Dickinson's *recollected* version of the passage, "And I can but believe that in such a mysterious providence as the dying of Little Gilbert, there is a purpose of benevolence which does not include our present happiness," submitted to Emerson for correction. By thus insisting on utmost *textual* accuracy in this quotation (in addition to accuracy of *content*), Dickinson highlights the importance of the quoted material's texture. As Leonard Diepeveen has observed: "The less allusion and the more quotation readers encounter, the more the quoting poem [or, by extension, the quoting letter] appropriates and works with what some would call the *writing* of another text. The quotation goes beyond recording the purely intellectual content of a work . . . and calls attention to the quoted material's texture" (16).[15]

Several of Dickinson's quoting strategies illustrate this high degree of respect for the texture of others' voices. She frequently privileges short quotations over long ones, for example, including only individual words—rather than whole phrases, sentences, or stanzas—within quotation marks. This ensures a higher degree of structural accuracy, in Pfister's sense of the term, as it allows Dickinson to adapt her own text (syntax, tense, etc.) to the quoted voice, rather than requiring a modification of the quotation to suit the context of the letter. If Dickinson does include modifications of her quoted materials within quotation marks, she frequently italicizes (underlines) or otherwise foregrounds them as deviations from her respective referents, thus establishing what Pfister has termed explicit "referentiality." Very often, these modifications constitute an attempt to adapt a specific line or phrase to her addressee. In a letter to Root, for example, Dickinson quotes the opening line of *Macbeth* ("When shall we three meet again?") as, "I put my treasures away till 'we *two* meet again' " (L31). The modification, although included in quotation marks, is thus acknowledged by special emphasis. Similarly, L98 quotes a passage from Longfellow's poem "The Rainy Day." In Longfellow's version, the final two lines of the poem read: "Into each life some rain must fall, / Some days must be dark and dreary." In Dickinson's letter, however, these lines have been changed to: "Dear Emily, do not sorrow, upon this stormy day—'into each life some '*flakes*' must fall, some days must be dark and dreary' " (L98). Dickinson's substitution of "flakes" for "rain" is doubly foregrounded: by additional quotation marks as well as by italicization.[16] In addition, the very shape of Dickinson's quotation marks reinforces the visual disruption effected by their insertion: the vast majority of her quotation marks slant from top left to bottom right (\\), whereas all other characters and punctuation marks (including question marks and exclamation points) display a strong slant from bottom left to top right (/ /).[17]

All of these strategies—visible quotation marks in direct quotations, italicization, combinatorial incompatibilities, occasional references to the provenance of a quotation, or apologetic comments on the quoting process itself—heighten, as Pfister has argued, the "otherness" of the incorporated material and therefore the degree of visual dislocation and disjunction encountered by the reader. Similarly, Diepeveen has also observed that quoting "intensifies the disjunction partially introduced by allusions and accentuates a very difficult reading process that emphasizes doubleness over a univocal structure" (17).[18] Rather than striving for a complete visual assimilation or a seamless semantic and functional integration of all quotations into her own letters (and thus a domination of quoting text over quoted text), the above strategies thus seem to accentuate Dickinson's emphasis on disjunction and heterogeneity, and hence her privileging of dialogicity.

At the same time, however, Dickinson's quoting strategies also exhibit the antithetical emphasis on manipulation and hence monologization. Diepeveen has outlined this tension inherent in direct quotations: due to the visual dislocation created by quotation marks, direct quotations "work through the illusion of a lack of control" (9). On the other hand, however, "quotation marks are a sign of controlling ownership" (Diepeveen 114). This idea of quotation as control has also been advanced by Bakhtin, who points out that "the frame is always in the power of the framer, and . . . there is an outrageous privilege in the power to cite others" (*Problems* xxxvii). And indeed, Dickinson's strong preference for direct quotations, her visual indication that "each voice is it's own," stands side by side with subtle strategies of manipulation and control. These strategies manifest themselves most frequently on a microtextual level: certain quotations are formally assimilated and functionally integrated into (and thus subjected to the textual control of) Dickinson's own epistolary context through changes in spelling, capitalization, punctuation, and lineation; through the silent omission of words; through translation and recontextualization; or through metrical assimilation.[19] Such modifications, according to Diepeveen, lead to a text's monologization: "The more the quotation has been visually changed from its appearance in its original context, the more the poet adopts a lyric strategy" (113).

In some cases, Dickinson resists any modification of the quoted material, thus subjecting her own letter context to the quoted material's texture, but in others, she formally or stylistically subordinates "direct" quotations to the demands of their new context by means of "minor" morphological and syntactical changes. Replacing individual words, or adapting the quoted text's syntax, tense, verb form, verb aspect, tone, or meter to the letter context, reduces the number of combinatorial incompatibilities and therefore facilitates a less disruptive, more linear, and thus more monologic reading process. In L29, for example, Dickinson adjusts both verb aspect and tone in a passage from Bryant's "Thanatopsis." Bryant's lines "approach thy grave, / Like one who wraps the drapery of his couch / About him, and lies down to pleasant dreams" are quoted as "five minutes in all—the 'wrapping the drapery of his couch about him—and lying down to pleasant dreams' included" (L29). Dickinson's modifications and recontextualizations of this "quotation" all contribute to turning Bryant's somber meditation on death into a lighthearted remark, in keeping with the humorous tone of the entire passage in this letter to her uncle Joel Warren Norcross: "Would you like to try a duel—or is that too quiet to suit you—at any rate I shall kill you—and you may dispose of your affairs with that end in view. You can take Chloroform if you like—and I will put you beyond the reach of pain in a twinkling. The last duel I fought did'nt take but five minutes in all—the 'wrapping the drapery of his couch about him—and lying down to pleasant dreams' included" (L29).

An even more pervasive area in which Dickinson's textual striving toward monologization and control manifests itself is that of capitalization and punctuation. In many of her direct (and otherwise exact) quotations, Dickinson substitutes her own idiosyncratic use of capitals and dashes for the more conventional patterns found in her printed editions. An example is the following passage from Emily Brontë's "Last Lines": "Though earth and man were gone, / And suns and universes ceased to be, / And Thou were left alone, / Every existence would exist in Thee."[20] Dickinson quotes these lines in three letters (L940, L948, and L873). L948 introduces five changes in capitalization in addition to a semantic modification: "Did you read | Emily Bronte's | marvellous Verse? | 'Though Earth | and Man | were gone, | And suns | and Universes | ceased to be, | And Thou | wert left alone, | Every Existence | would Exist in Thee'" (Houghton MS Am 1118.10 [12]).[21] L940, however (according to Johnson and Ward, written at the same time), differs in three instances from the previous transcription: "Said that marvellous Emily Bronte | [']Though Earth and Man were gone | And Suns and Universes ceased to be | And thou wert left alone, | Every Existence would Exist in thee—.[']"[22] L873, which only quotes the final line of the Brontë passage, constitutes a third variant, its capitals differing from both L940 and Brontë's version, but being identical with those in L948: "As Emily | Bronte to her | Maker, I write | to my Lost 'Every | Existence would | Exist in Thee'" (Houghton MS Am 1118.3 [H83]). Each of these variants reflects Dickinson's habit of capitalizing key words in her texts—specifically nouns, verbs, and adjectives—irrespective of their position within a line of verse. Since each letter provides a different context for

Brontë's lines, each "quotation" thus displays a slightly different combination of capitals.

Such strategies of textual manipulation indicate the emergence of a "lyric" voice of focalization and control. Laurent Jenny has coined the term "focal text" to refer to a similar phenomenon: "the work of transformation and assimilation of various texts . . . is accomplished by a focal text which keeps control over the meaning" (39–40). Analogous to Jenny's "focal text," Dickinson's controlling "lyric" voices (a plurality of voices that can assume various manifestations and exhibit different stylistic properties in different letters) may thus be termed "focal voices." Yet in Dickinson's correspondence, this assimilative, controlling function performed by focal voices is regularly combined with and complemented by the above-described strategies of dissimilation. In many respects, Dickinson's letters thus display the simultaneous presence of, or rather an inherent tension between, dialogic and monologic impulses; they oscillate between a dialogic proliferation of voices and their monologic control. On the one hand, the proliferation of direct quotations, the presence of quotation marks (which explicitly highlight the "otherness" of the incorporated material), and the use of nonverbal discursive elements suggest an insistence on dialogization and polyvocality and thus on a plurality of speaking postures. Yet, on the other hand, Dickinson's epistolary voices also frame and manipulate these quoted voices by transforming, assimilating, and functionally integrating them into the letter context. In this way, Dickinson's letters simultaneously display a high degree of lyric or monologic control. In other words, rather than turning her letters into poetic discourse that, according to Bakhtin, "artificially extinguish[es]" the dialogicity of language, Dickinson maintains a high degree of dialogicity[23] while *simultaneously* introducing controlling or focal voices that orchestrate, frame, curtail, and thus critique some of the other "participants" in the dialogue. Hence, the result is not so much a complete monologization but rather what I would call a "monologized dialogue" or a "dialogized monologue." Similar to individual "letters" that often assume "poetic" qualities, and individual "poems" that frequently function as "letters," as I discussed in chapter 1, Dickinson's correspondence as a whole mirrors this blurring of boundaries between the lyric/monologic and the prosaic/dialogic. In this way, Dickinson's letters become lyricized letters and epistolary lyrics in a Bakhtinian as well as a generic sense.

In her correspondence, Dickinson's unique interplay between strategies of dialogization and strategies of monologization assumes a very specific function. Focal voices of control manifest themselves most pronouncedly in specific textual modifications performed on quotations from traditionally male-dominated and gender-inscribed discourses. An analysis of Higginson's works, the Bible, and Shakespeare as the three most frequently quoted groups of texts reveals that the "freedom" the writer takes with their "remarks" is grounded in her rejection of some of their historical, sociocultural, and, specifically, their gendered resonances. The relationship between Dickinson's texts and the Bible, Shakespeare, and Higginson have variously been analyzed before. Yet the vast majority of critics have all performed so-called influence studies, with a special emphasis on the effect of either the content or the style of Dickinson's "sources" on her own writings.[24] While Jay Leyda is concerned with Dickinson's use of other writers' "ideas" (1:xxii), for example, Jack L. Capps outlines the purpose of his study thus: "By fixing as accurately as possible the limits and content of her reading, her relationship to literary movements and figures can be more clearly established" (vii). Yet for Capps, this relationship consists in a one-directional effect of earlier writers *on* Dickinson: "The correlation of her reading with her letters and poems affords another significant means of focusing the understanding of intellectual and literary influences *affecting both the poetry and the poet*" (145; my emphasis).

My own focus on Dickinson's active textual engagement with and modification of her quoted materials, however, uses an intertextual approach that clearly differentiates itself from these more traditional forms of "influence studies" and "source criticism." As Frow has summarized: "Intertextual analysis is distinguished from source criticism . . . by its rejection of a unilinear causality (the concept of 'influence') in favor of an account of the work performed upon intertextual material and its functional integration in the later text" (46). To highlight this distinction even further, Kristeva explains that she has specifically introduced the term *transposition* in order to avoid a confusion between "intertextuality"[25] and "source criticism" (*Revolu-*

tion 39): "The term *inter-textuality* denotes this transposition of one (or several) sign system(s) into another; but since the term has often been understood in the banal sense of 'study of sources,' we prefer the term *transposition* because it specifies that the passage from one signifying system to another demands a new articulation of the thetic—of enunciative and denotative positionality" (*Revolution* 59–60). The following analyses of Dickinson's "work performed upon" her quotations from Higginson, the Bible, and Shakespeare will lead to a revised understanding of her response to these specific groups of texts.[26] In particular, the simultaneous presence of both dialogic and monologic strategies in the quoting process will reveal Dickinson's high degree of double-voicedness and ambivalence toward these discourses, a fact that traditional "influence studies" have tended to obscure. Capps, for example, has claimed that "although she could be impudent with the deity, she displayed remarkable reverence for mortal Shakespeare" (65). Yet Dickinson's textual treatment of quotations from the Bible and Shakespeare suggests that, although critiquing certain aspects of biblical discourse, she nonetheless regards its words as much more "sacred" (by insisting on utmost accuracy in the quoting process) than those of any other text; at the same time, she subjects Shakespeare's lines to profound textual manipulations while "revering" his thoughts. Similarly, the opinion, first advanced by Anna Mary Wells, that Dickinson's habit of quoting Higginson's images back to him constitutes a form of flattery has to be further differentiated in light of the textual critique Dickinson performs upon her preceptor's poems and prose.

THOMAS WENTWORTH HIGGINSON

Dickinson's references to her "preceptor" Higginson's essays, poems, novels, and literary criticism offer an intriguing combination of the two seemingly antithetical citation practices discussed above. Rather than directly quoting from his texts (either accurately or with modifications), Dickinson for the most part either merely refers to his titles or completely reorganizes and rewrites some of his prose and poetry passages. Whereas the latter strategy displays an extremely high degree of assimilation and thus monologic control, the former method of title citation highlights the dialogic aspect of

Dickinson's treatment of her preceptor's texts. I maintain that these two distinct forms of intertextual engagement with Higginson's writings mirror Dickinson's "double-voiced" response to Higginson in general: an oscillation between her role as "pupil" (who attempts to please her preceptor and displays her familiarity with and respect for his works by regularly quoting his titles) and that of "poet" (who competes creatively with him as "fellow author" by rewriting some of his texts).

The many references to Higginson's works occurring in Dickinson's correspondence attest to the fact that she had read most—or even all—of his published writings. Most important, however, Dickinson repeatedly quotes or refers to specific titles to let Higginson know of this fact. Already in her second letter, she informs her preceptor: "I read your Chapters in the Atlantic—and experienced honor for you" (L261). Similar references to his numerous publications in the prestigious *Atlantic Monthly* follow in subsequent epistolary exchanges: "Thank you for having written the 'Atlantic Essays.' They are a fine Joy—though to possess the ingredient for Congratulation renders congratulation superfluous" (L368). L280 concludes with a reference to an essay published in the December 1862 issue: "I trust the 'Procession of Flowers' was not a premonition" (L280).[27]

But Dickinson had also scanned other current literary magazines for Higginson's essays. L449 cites "Childhood Fancies," published in the January 1876 issue of *Scribner's Monthly:* "I had read 'Childhood,' with compunction that thought so fair—fall on foreign eyes" (L449). In addition, Dickinson does not fail to mention Higginson's fiction and literary criticism. In L405, she refers to a collection of sketches entitled *Oldport Days*: "I was re-reading 'Oldport.' Largest last, like Nature" (L405). L622 thanks Higginson for a copy of his *Short Studies of American Authors* with the words: "Brabantio's Gift was not more fair than your's, though I trust without his pathetic inscription—'Which but thou hast already, with all my Heart I would keep from thee'" (L622). At one point, Dickinson becomes even more explicit, asking for bibliographic clarification: "An article of your's, too, perhaps the only one you wrote that I never knew. It was about a 'Latch'" (L352).[28] Unsatisfied with Higginson's reply,[29] Dickinson picks up the same question again in her subsequent letter: "I saw it's notice in the Papers just before you came—Is there a magazine called the 'Woman's Journal'? I think it was said to be in that—a Gate, or Door, or Latch—" (L353). The same letter also contains a reference to another one of Higginson's essays, "A Shadow" (published in the *Atlantic Monthly*, July 1870): "I thought I spoke to you of the shadow—" (L353). And L641 even contains a reference to Higginson's wife Mary Thatcher's *Room for One More* (1879): " 'Room for one more' was a plea for Heaven" (L641). In L457, finally, Dickinson proudly informs Higginson that she can even identify his anonymous publications: "I inferred your touch in the Papers on Lowell and Emerson—It is delicate that each Mind is itself, like a distinct Bird" (L457).[30] These numerous references to Higginson's works indicate—in particular to Higginson himself—Dickinson's thorough familiarity with his writings. I suggest that here we can observe the writer speaking in her "pupil" voice, trying to please her preceptor as well as to establish her credentials as a worthy correspondent.

Direct quotations from Higginson's essays and poems, on the other hand, are surprisingly rare. Moreover, when Dickinson does quote him directly, she regularly modifies his words, introducing minor morphological changes or omissions and thus imposing monologizing and controlling gestures on her dialogic exchange with his texts. Only once does she quote a longer fragment—slightly shortened—from his essay "Letter to a Young Contributor": "Often, when troubled by entreaty, that paragraph of your's has saved me—'Such being the Majesty of the Art you presume to practice, you can at least take time before dishonoring it' " (L488).[31] Yet since this essay was specifically addressed to beginning writers, its citation suggests, again, a pupil's admiring tribute to her preceptor.[32]

All other quotations from Higginson's texts are much shorter, rarely exact, and used in a primarily allusive way. Twice Dickinson quotes from his historical novel *Army Life in a Black Regiment*. In L487, she cites a modified version of the title of chapter 8 ("The Baby of the Regiment"): "He [Austin] seems the 'Child of the Regiment' since he was so sick" (L487). L653 alludes to a longer passage of the same novel: "It [an unidentified child] reminded me too of 'Little Annie,' of whom you feared to make the mistake in saying 'Shoulder Arms' to the 'Colored Regiment' " (L653). The passage in Higginson reads: "I looked with so much interest for her small person that, instead of saying at the proper time, 'Attention, Battalion! Shoulder arms!'—it is a wonder that I did not say, 'Shoulder babies!' " (141). Another direct quotation is taken from his essay "The Life of Birds" (published in the September

1862 edition of the *Atlantic Monthly*). Higginson's passage ("And penetrating to some yet lonelier place, we find it consecrated to that life-long sorrow, whatever it may be, which is made immortal in the plaintive cadence of the Pewee-Flycatcher" [152]) is condensed to and allusively quoted as "Which is what the Essayist calls 'the Immortal Pewee' " (L692). Similarly, in L1042 (" 'Mars the sacred Loneliness'!") Dickinson modifies a line from Higginson's poem "Decoration" ("Mocks the sacred loneliness").

That the significance of these direct yet modified quotations lies in their function as the diligent and studious pupil's allusions to her mentor's writings, rather than in the quoted words themselves, is further illustrated by the fact that, twice, Dickinson's quotations from Higginson's essays are actually Higginson's quotations from a third author. Dickinson incorporates (but modifies) Keats's words, quoted in Higginson's "The Life of Birds," in L1034, as well as Higginson's quotation from Carlyle in L728.[33] By thus reflecting back to Higginson a third voice instead of his own, Dickinson emphasizes the referential function of these quotations, rather than her respect and reverence for his own "original" expressions. Whereas Dickinson's pupil voice is thus eager to quote back to her preceptor some of the more easily recognizable words, expressions, or images from his own essays in order to indicate (deferentially) her thorough familiarity with his writings, she is at the same time less willing to valorize Higginson's voice in a fully dialogic way as that of an original or originating author. This manifests itself even more strongly in Dickinson's attempts to creatively rewrite some of Higginson's prose and poetry. I suggest that these creative rewritings and, in particular, the writer's systematic efforts at condensing Higginson's verbal affluence constitute, in fact, subtle forms of competition with and criticism of Higginson's own writings. In this way, Dickinson becomes Higginson's stylistic critic almost as much as he had become hers.

Anna Mary Wells was the first to point out that Dickinson frequently plays with Higginson's own images, reflecting the results back to him: "The trick of picking up his metaphors, condensing them, and tossing the result back at him was one she perfected over the years. Of course she always said it much better than he had, but the original metaphor was his, and her use of it a subtle flattery" ("Soul's Society" 224). Several critics, including Capps, Lease, Ruth Miller, Sherwood, and St. Armand, have specifically been interested in tracing and identifying such "tossed-back" metaphors. Sherwood has noted that in his "Letter to a Young Contributor," Higginson refers to literature as "attar of roses, one distilled drop from a million blossoms," which forms the basis for J675/Fr772: "Essential Oils—are wrung— | The Attar from the Rose | Be not expressed by Suns—alone— | It is the gift of Screws—" (Sherwood 204). In addition to this poem, Miller considers two other ones ("I'll tell you how the sun rose," and "We play at paste") to be inspired by the same essay. "We play at paste," in particular, she regards as "almost like an ironic commentary on his exhortation [for patience]" (44). Miller argues that "the fact that this poem was not found in any fascicle suggests that it was composed in response to the article, for it was often the case that Emily Dickinson did not transcribe poems written for a specific occasion or to enhance or clarify a particular and private communication" (45). In addition, she cites parallels between J216/Fr124 ("Safe in their Alabaster Chambers") and some of Higginson's *Atlantic Monthly* essays (46). Both Capps and St. Armand have suggested that J1084/Fr1099 ("At Half past Three, a single Bird") responds to a passage in Higginson's essay "Water Lilies." Claiming that "it was in fact his [Higginson's] early nature essays to which she reacted most intensely" (187), St. Armand adds one more example: " 'A Route of Evanescence' (J1463/Fr1489) derives from [Higginson's] description of a hummingbird in the second paragraph of 'The Life of Birds' " (201). St. Armand continues to emphasize that "so intimate was her knowledge of Higginson's prose that in their correspondence she often had to remind him that she was merely paraphrasing his own thoughts" (202). He quotes two further examples: Dickinson's "I find ecstasy in living—the mere sense of living is joy enough" (L342a), which he traces back to Higginson's essay "Gymnastics": "health finds joy in mere existence" (qtd. in St. Armand 202); and "When she said that poetry was her only playmate and lamented after her father's death that he 'never played,' Higginson was supposed to remember his observation in 'Saints and Their Bodies' that 'We must not ignore the *play-impulse* in human nature' " (qtd. in St. Armand 202). What St. Armand and others who have engaged in tracing such parallels are primarily interested in, however, is the identification of echoes as such. Yet it is the forms and functions of Dickinson's *transformations* of Higginson's texts that are particularly intriguing.

Wells had regarded this vast array of condensed and "tossed-back" metaphors as an unambiguously deferential gesture. However, I interpret it as a more double-voiced and double-edged strategy. The fact that Dickinson does not merely quote but rather rewrites Higginson's own metaphors, "writing" them "back" to him, suggests that an underlying tone of critique emerges from this intertextual dialogue. It is in these instances of condensing and rewriting Higginson's texts that Dickinson's poet voice manifests itself most distinctly.

The most striking example of Dickinson's contestatory engagement with Higginson's texts is her rewriting of his poem "Decoration." The latter appeared in the June 1874 issue of *Scribner's Monthly*, and is reproduced in full by Johnson:

Decoration.

"Manibus date lilia plenis."
Mid the flower-wreath'd tombs I stand
Bearing lilies in my hand.
Comrades! in what soldier-grave
Sleeps the bravest of the brave?

Is it he who sank to rest
With his colors round his breast?
Friendship makes his tomb a shrine;
Garlands veil it; ask not mine.

One low grave, yon tree beneath,
Bears no roses, wears no wreath;
Yet no heart more high and warm
Ever dared the battle-storm,

Never gleamed a prouder eye
In the front of victory,
Never foot had firmer tread
On the field where hope lay dead,

Than are hid within this tomb,
Where the untended grasses bloom;
And no stone, with feign'd distress,
Mocks the sacred loneliness.

Youth and beauty, dauntless will,
Dreams that life could ne'er fulfill,
Here lie buried; here in peace
Wrongs and woes have found release.

Turning from my comrades' eyes,
Kneeling where a woman lies,
I strew lilies on the grave
Of the bravest of the brave. (qtd. in *Poems* 961)

Dickinson refers to this poem several times. In L413, she compliments Higginson: "I thought that being a Poem one's self precluded the writing Poems, but perceive the Mistake. It seemed like going Home, to see your beautiful thought once more, now so long forbade it." In a subsequent letter, she mentions "Decoration" again, this time recalling that it appeared in the same month (June 1874) during which her father died: "Your beautiful Hymn, was it not prophetic? It has assisted that Pause of Space which I call 'Father'—" (L418). Approximately three years later, Dickinson once more returns to Higginson's "hymn." This time, however, the "pupil's" compliments are replaced by the "poet's" active engagement with this text; "rereading" becomes "rewriting": "I was rereading your 'Decoration.' You may have forgotten it. | Lay this Laurel on the One | Too intrinsic for Renown— | Laurel—vail your deathless tree— | Him you chasten, that is He!" (L503; J1393/Fr1428C).[34] That these lines can be interpreted as Dickinson's "revisionist" rewriting of Higginson's poem is suggested by Higginson's own response. Millicent Todd Bingham quotes a May 1891 letter from Higginson to Todd: "One verse I copy for the pleasure of copying it, though you may have it. . . . She wrote it after re-reading my 'Decoration.' It is the condensed essence of that & so far finer" (qtd. in *Ancestors' Brocades* 129–130). In his response, Higginson gracefully admires the superiority of Dickinson's "condensed essence."

Such revisionist condensations occur in several other instances. Johnson has pointed out that "the expression 'Candor is the only wile' [L450] is ED's succinct rephrasing of the following thought in Higginson's 'Prelude' to his novel *Malbone: An Oldport Romance* (1869): 'One learns, in growing older, that no fiction can be so strange nor appear so improbable as would the simple truth'" (*Poems* 548). In J1463/Fr1489, Dickinson engages with Higginson's literary protégée Harriet Prescott Spofford's description of a hummingbird, quoted in his essay "The Life of Birds": "Or when a Humming-Bird, a winged drop of gorgeous sheen and gloss, a living gem, poising on his wings, thrust his dark, slender, honey-seeking bill into the white blossoms of a little bush beside my window, I should have thought it no such bad thing to be a bird" (131).[35] Dickinson's "condensed essence" of this passage, however, reads: "A Route of Evanescence | With a revolving Wheel— | A Resonance of Emerald— | A Rush of Cochineal— | And every Blossom on the Bush | Adjusts it's tumbled Head— | The mail from Tunis, probably, | An easy Morning's Ride—" (J1463/Fr1489E). St. Armand comments on this poem: "He [Higginson] never seems to have realized that it was his own word-painting that prompted this cameo performance, supplemented by the typically extravagant prose fragment he had quoted from a letter by Harriet Prescott Spofford, thinly disguised as 'Harriet Rohan'" (201). I argue, instead, that it is this "typically extravagant" prose and poetry style, both practiced *and* advocated ("quoted") by Higginson, to which Dickinson responds critically. St. Armand has emphasized the close affinity between Higginson's style and that of contemporary women writers such as Spofford: "[Higginson's] prose is in fact a masculine version of Spofford's mellifluous word-painting, which Henry James had rather condescendingly characterized as an exclusively feminine mode. In his *North American Review* blast, James wrote that Spofford 'uses far too many words, synonymous and meaningless words. Like the majority of female writers,—Mrs Browning, George Sand, Gail Hamilton, Mrs Stowe,—she possesses in excess the fatal gift of fluency (275)'" (197). Several of Dickinson's rewritings, on the other hand, can be characterized as exercises in conciseness, attempts to crystallize the "condensed essence" of a "mellifluous" prose passage or poem. By cutting down Higginson's thirty-line poem to a four-line stanza and by condensing his prose, Dickinson's poet voice thus openly competes with her preceptor as "fellow author."[36]

In this way Dickinson's references to, quotations from, and rewritings of Higginson's texts illustrate a strongly manipulative textual control. Her most enthusiastic praise is reserved for his essays, but it is his literary criticism and his poetry that she approaches more critically. Although eager to emphasize her familiarity with his works, Dickinson at the same time rarely valorizes Higginson's voice as such; rather, she performs numerous textual revisions and modifications, all indicative of her challenge to his tastes as literary mentor and critic, and his style as a poet. Therefore, Dickinson's "freedom" with Higginson's remarks has to be interpreted as *both* a "subtle flattery" (as Wells has suggested), and a subtle stylistic critique of her preceptor's (as well as his protégée's) verbal effusions. It is in this respect that Dickinson's engagement with Higginson's texts assumes a strongly monologic tendency and approximates Bakhtin's description of the monologic novel: "Every struggle between two voices within a single discourse for possession or dominance in that discourse is decided in advance, it only appears to be a struggle; all fully signifying authorial interpretations are sooner or later gathered together in a single speech center and a single consciousness; all accents are gathered together in a single voice" (*Problems* 204). Although Dickinson's voice never quite reaches this high degree of monologic dominance, it nonetheless frequently tends to control the intertextual dialogue with her preceptor. Quoting thus becomes Dickinson's subtle strategy of engaging with Higginson in a "stylistic struggle" and allows her to exercise discursive power without having to voice a more open or explicit form of criticism. It enables her to praise certain aspects of Higginson's writings while critiquing others; to speak in her pupil's as well as her poet's voice simultaneously, in this way enacting a truly double-voiced discourse.

In marked contrast to her quotations from Higginson, Dickinson's quotations from the Bible display a much higher degree of textual respect for the voice of God. Her scriptural quotations thus exemplify a different kind of double-voicedness, at once more subtle and more specific.

THE BIBLE

Already in 1894, Mabel Loomis Todd had commented on the pervasiveness of Dickinson's scriptural references: "Fearless and daring, she had biblical quotation at her finger-tips; . . . even if she sometimes used it in a way which might shock a conventionalist" ("Introductory" x). Subsequently, Capps's statistics have confirmed that "biblical quotations in Dickinson's letters and poems far exceed references to any other source or author" (30).[37] More specifically, "the Gospels, Revelation, and Genesis are most often cited" (Capps 30). "Verses from the Old Testament," Capps continues, "appear less than half as often . . . as do verses from the New Testament" (40).

For the most part, Dickinson's quotations from the Bible are remarkable for their high degree of textual accuracy and formal integrity, with many of the monologizing strategies of assimilation used on a much smaller scale, more subtly and more specifically. Frequently, the writer even adapts and thus subordinates her own letter context syntactically or morphologically to accommodate the quoted text or phrase. In L948, for example, Dickinson recalls that, "The 'golden bowl' breaks soundlessly," an echo of Ecclesiastes 12:6: "Or ever the silver cord be loosed, or the golden bowl be broken." In this quotation, Dickinson retains only two words of the biblical text—enough to evoke the scriptural referent and thus establish what Pfister has called "selectivity." Yet since her own syntax requires a different verb form ("breaks" instead of "be broken"), the modification is acknowledged as a deviation from the biblical phrase by being excluded from the quoted environment. A similar example is Dickinson's quotation from Psalms 147:9 ("He giveth to the beast his food, *and* to the young ravens which cry"). Her letter only marks two words of the scriptural referent as direct quotation: "The 'Ravens' must 'cry,' to be ministered to—she—need only sigh" (L668). In this way, Dickinson scrupulously distinguishes between those parts of her sentence that "belong" to the biblical context, and those contributed by herself.[38]

Occasionally, Dickinson's insistence on maintaining the formal and structural accuracy of her quotations even causes significant combinatorial incompatibilities. L708, quoting Proverbs 27:1 ("Boast not thyself of to morrow; for thou knowest not what a day may bring forth") constitutes an interesting example. In her letter, Dickinson changes the biblical pronouns from second- to first-person singular, a modification that is carefully positioned outside quotation marks; yet at the same time, she does not adapt the verb form *within* her quotation, in this way failing to establish a subject-verb agreement ("I 'knowest' "): " 'Boast not' myself 'of Tomorrow' for I 'knowest not what a' Noon 'may bring forth' " (L708). Similar combinatorial incompatibilities occur several times. An entire sentence from 1 Corinthians 15:51 ("We shall not all sleep, but we shall all be changed") is quoted verbatim in two different letters. In one instance, the capitalization of the first word of the biblical quote is maintained even in mid sentence: "Were the statement 'We shall not all sleep, but we shall all be changed,' made in earthly Manuscript, were his Residence in the Universe, we should pursue the Writer till he explained it to us" (L568).[39] Yet, generally speaking, "with the original capitalization [of any quotation] intact," as Diepeveen has suggested, "there is more disruption and less of the poet's voice [or, by extension, the letter-writer's voice] within the quotation" (114), which ultimately results in a higher degree of dialogicity.

On the other hand, however, there also emerge recurrent patterns of modification and revision. At times, these changes constitute Dickinson's playfully creative engagement with the Bible, displaying her insistence that, ultimately, no text is "sacred," that all texts are open to revision and rewriting. Dickinson's "rewritings" or creative emendations of scriptural passages often render them more dramatic or humorous. In L185, for example, she prefers a more concretely illustrative word: "carried up into heaven" (Luke 24:51) is quoted as " 'snatched up to Heaven.' " L712, while imitating biblical archaism, becomes more immediate and dramatic. The reported speech in John 7:37 ("Jesus stood and cried, saying, If any man thirst, let him come unto me, and drink") is turned into direct speech, complete with the speaker's signature: " 'And let him that is athirst come'—Jesus" (L712). Lamentations 3:22–23 ("*They are* new every morning") is augmented to " 'New every morning and fresh every evening' " (L889). As a tribute to the scriptural voice, however, Dickinson's addition carefully maintains the syntactical structure of its model. Similarly, in her quotation from Matthew 13:15 ("and *their* ears are dull of hearing, and their eyes they have closed"), Dickinson produces a stylistically more effective parallelism: " 'When our eyes are dull of seeing & our ears of hearing' " (L11). In L690, Dickinson suggests a humorous addendum to her biblical precedent. Matthew 5:3–4 ("Blessed *are* the poor in spirit: for their's is the kingdom of heaven. Blessed *are* they that mourn: for they shall be comforted") is imitated in: "Blessed are they that play, for theirs is the kingdom of heaven" (L690).[40] These examples show that Dickinson—despite her respect for the Bible's style and texture—nonetheless insists on treating it as a flexible textual construct whose authority can be challenged by rephrasing and reshaping it.

In several instances, however, Dickinson's textual modifications display an even more critical attitude. At times, these changes challenge the Bible's exclusionist language and attempt to reverse the silencing of women's voices. Specifically, Dickinson highlights the masculinist implications of the generic use of "man." Her "quotation" of Isaiah 35:8 ("the wayfaring men, though fools, shall not err *therein*") is reproduced as: "the Bible says very roguishly, the 'wayfaring Man, though a Fool—need not err therein'; need the 'wayfaring' Woman? Ask your throbbing Scripture" (L562). The fact that Dickinson, rather than answering her own (rhetorical) question, refers her reader (Judge Otis Lord) back to the Bible itself suggests that a definitive answer might be impossible to find, since, strictly speaking, the biblical phrase does not include women. A similar example can be found in the final line of J1247/Fr1353B, sent to Sue Gilbert. Here Dickinson replaces the gendered "no man" of Exodus 33:20 ("And he said, Thou canst not see my face: for there shall no man see me, and live") by the gender-neutral "none": "For None see God and live—" (J1247/Fr1353B). The silencing of women's voices in the Bible is also made explicit in L946. In this letter, Dickinson attributes the words "and I was afraid, because I *was* naked; and I hid myself" (Genesis 3:10), traditionally spoken by Adam only, to both Adam *and* Eve: "In all the circumference of Expression, those guileless words of Adam and Eve never were surpassed, 'I was afraid and hid Myself'" (L946). In this way, Dickinson grants a voice to Eve—and thus "authorizes" her to speak—since she shares Adam's experience, yet has traditionally been denied the opportunity to give expression to it.[41]

In addition to highlighting the biblical silencing of women's voices, Dickinson's textual modifications also draw attention to general discrepancies in power relations between humans and the Christian deity. Directly engaging in a highly critical dialogue with the scriptural voice of dominance and hence challenging the dominant status of God, Dickinson occasionally performs a redistribution of power through her "emendated" quotations. A recurring example is the writer's revision of Jacob's wrestling with the Angel (Genesis 32:26). The biblical precedent reads: "And [the Angel] said, Let me go, for the day breaketh. And [Jacob] said, I will not let thee go, except thou bless me." J59/Fr145A, probably mailed to Sue Gilbert, closely follows its scriptural precedent: "A little East of Jordan, | Evangelists record, | A Gymnast and an Angel | Did wrestle long and hard— || Till morning touching mountain— | And Jacob, waxing strong, | The Angel begged permission | To Breakfast—to return— || Not so, said cunning Jacob! | 'I will not let thee go | Except thou bless me'—Stranger! | The which acceded to— || Light swung the silver fleeces | 'Peniel' Hills beyond, | And the bewildered Gymnast | Found he had worsted God!" In several other contexts, however, Dickinson replays this scene in slightly different ways. A letter to Sarah Tuckerman, for example, concludes with the Angel's *voluntary* offering of blessings: "Says the blissful voice, not yet a voice, but a vision, 'I will not let thee go, except I bless thee' " (L1035). And the conclusion of L1042 enacts a complete role reversal between Jacob and the Angel, with Jacob bestowing blessings upon the Angel: "Audacity of Bliss, said Jacob to the Angel 'I will not let thee go except I bless thee'—Pugilist and Poet, Jacob was correct" (L1042). Thus Jacob has not only managed to obtain God's blessing by force—as in the scriptural precedent—but ultimately usurps the (divine) authority and power to bestow blessings himself. In this way, Dickinson directly challenges the manifest power imbalance between Jacob and the deity's representative.

Dickinson also performs such redistributions of power by playing with the strictly intratextual referentiality of pronouns. Frequently, she ascribes human (instead of divine) referents to them, in this way appropriating (for herself and others) the voice of divine authority. An example is Psalms 91:11: "For [the Lord] shall give his angels charge over thee."[42] Dickinson quotes this passage in four different letters (L820, L975, L991, and L1012), yet each time it is she herself who takes charge of "God's" angels. In L975 to Mary Warner Crowell, she asks: "Is it too late to touch you, Dear? . . . I give his Angels charge." Similarly, L1012 to Samuel Bowles Jr. declares: "I give 'his Angels Charge—.' "[43] Another variant occurs in L820, in which Dickinson not only commands the angels but usurps God's very place. To her friend Holland she writes: "Am glad Annie is well, and that Kate is sacred—Tell her with my love, 'I give my Angels charge' " (L820). Gradually, the biblical "he shall give his angels charge" has thus been transformed into "I give my Angels charge." Dickinson has erased God from and inscribed herself into the position of power: having appropriated God's "authorizing" voice, the angels become hers to command.

Similar redistributions of power occur in other letters. In L189, 1 Corinthians 3:21–22 ("For all things are your's") is translated into: "[Austin] showed me mountains that touched the sky, and brooks that sang like Bobolinks. . . . I will give them to you, for they are mine, and 'all things are mine'" (L189). In a letter to Holland, Dickinson occupies Christ's place: "But you must go to Sleep. I, who sleep always, need no Bed. Foxes have Tenements, and remember, the Speaker was a Carpenter" (L979). Even though Dickinson does not mark this passage as a direct quotation from Matthew 8:20 ("The foxes have holes, . . . but the Son of man hath not where to lay *his* head"), the biblical referent is made explicit ("the Speaker was a Carpenter"), and thus the role reversal becomes clear. In other instances, Dickinson reascribes the voice of biblical or divine authority to one of her friends. L820 quotes from Psalms 23:4: "though I walk through the valley of the shadow of death, I will fear no evil: for thou *art* with me." In her letter to Holland, however, Dickinson attributes these words to her friend: "It was sweet to touch the familiar Hand that so long had led us—'Though thou walk through the Valley of the Shadow of Death, I will be with thee,' you have taught us was no Exaggeration" (L820). In L1024, a similar appropriation of God's role occurs in Sue Gilbert's name. Jesus's speech to his father ("O righteous Father, the world hath not known thee: but I have known thee" [John 17:25]), is rewritten as: "The world hath not known her, but *I* have known her, was the sweet boast of Jesus—" (L1024). Syntactically speaking, Sue Gilbert ("her") thus occupies God's ("thee") position.

In addition to performing such morphological and syntactical changes on a microtextual level, Dickinson also frequently engages in a direct monologized dialogue with the biblical voice, disagreeing with, challenging, or simply doubting its "authoritative" message. Even though, for the most part, she maintains quotation marks, her letters nonetheless challenge the scriptural voice's "sacred" authority by subjecting it to the textual control of her own epistolary voices. The persuasiveness of the biblical claim, "For whom the Lord loveth he chasteneth" (Hebrews 12:6), for example, is twice called into question in Dickinson's letters. To Holland she declares: "'Whom he loveth, he punisheth,' is a doubtful solace finding tart response in the lower

Mind" (L369). And in a letter to Helen Hunt Jackson, she admiringly confesses: "Finding myself, no solace in 'whom he loveth he chasteneth' your Valor astounds me" (L976). Matthew's promise, "Ask, and it shall be given you; seek, and ye shall find; knock, and it shall be opened unto you: For every one that asketh receiveth; and he that seeketh findeth; and to him that knocketh it shall be opened" (7:7–8), is doubted in a letter to Holland: "If prayers had any answers to them, you were all here to-night, but I seek and I don't find, and knock and it is not opened. Wonder if God is just—presume he is, however, and t'was only a blunder of Matthew's" (L133). In L899, finally, Dickinson's choice of an interpretive adjective ("encroaching") reflects her critical attitude toward John 16:15 ("All things that the Father hath are mine: therefore said I, that he shall take of mine, and shall shew *it* unto you"). This passage is quoted as: "who reminds a perhaps encroaching Father, 'All these are mine' " (L899).

Such a direct, monologized dialogue is Dickinson's preferred way of engaging with the biblical voice of authority. In this way, her letters seek to initiate an active intertextual exchange, proposing an often critical response to the Bible. As Yaeger has put it: "As women play with old texts, the burden of the tradition is lighted and shifted; it has the potential of being remade" (18). Yet in order to "remake," to rewrite tradition, this dialogue has to be carefully orchestrated, a strategy effected by Dickinson's lyric voice of the framer. Another highly connoted traditional discursive formation whose "burden" Dickinson's texts attempt to shift and revise is iambic pentameter.

SHAKESPEARE AND IAMBIC PENTAMETER

In contrast to the Bible, whose "message" Dickinson frequently disagrees with and whose (authoritative) voice she actively challenges in direct dialogic exchanges, Shakespeare's plays occupy a much more "sacred" place in her writings. Throughout her correspondence, Dickinson repeatedly expresses her admiration for his works and thoughts: "While Shakespeare remains Literature is firm," she comments to Higginson (L368); "With the exception of Shakespeare, you have told me of more knowledge than any one living," she confesses to Sue Gilbert (L757); a letter to Todd concludes with the words, "Touch Shakespeare for me" (L1004); and to F. B. Sanborn she declares, "he has had his Future who has found Shakespeare" (L402). Sewall has summarized the extent of Dickinson's admiration for Shakespeare: "She began referring to Shakespeare in her letters, or quoting him, when she was fourteen, and never stopped. Although all but a very few quotations come after the trouble with her eyes, she may have been quoting the plays steadily in letters that are lost" (*Life* 701). At the same time, however, most of Dickinson's quotations from Shakespeare display a much higher degree of textual modification and assimilation than many of her careful attempts at formal and stylistic accuracy with biblical references. In contrast to the "word of God," the textual integrity of which Dickinson for the most part respected, yet whose message she disagreed with, it is Shakespeare's *message*, his thoughts, that Dickinson admires and quotes reverently, simultaneously challenging the sociocultural implications of the *form* in which these thoughts are presented.[44] Dickinson's strategies of incorporating Shakespearean quotations into her correspondence illustrate that she appropriates his voice(s) for her own purposes by systematically destroying their iambic pentameter structure.

In *Poetry as Discourse*, Antony Easthope defines meter as one crucial element of poetic discourse. More specifically, he describes iambic pentameter as a sociocultural code with historical and political resonances: "Promoted into dominance by the new courtly culture [in the sixteenth century], pentameter is an historically constituted institution. It is not natural to English poetry but is a specific cultural phenomenon, a discursive form" (55). Therefore, he emphasizes, it should be regarded "not as a neutral form of poetic necessity but a specific historical form producing certain meanings and acting to exclude others. These meanings are ideological" (Easthope 64–65). Similarly, Annie Finch also emphasizes the cultural inflection of meter: "Meter gains its initial significance through cultural connotations"; it has "accumulated meanings that poets can exploit as a semiological code" ("Patriarchal Meter" 167). Referring to Barthes, Finch describes meter as one of the signifying codes or "voices" that Barthes has identified for every text. As the latter suggests: "Each code is one of the forces that can take over the text (of which the text is the network), one of the voices out of which the text is woven. Alongside each utterance, one might say that off-stage voices can be heard: they are the codes: in their interweaving, these voices (whose origin is 'lost' in the vast perspective of the *already-written*) de-originate the utterance" (*S/Z* 21).

Yet in contrast to Easthope, Finch also emphasizes that meter is a highly gender-inflected discursive formulation: poetic lines, "insofar as they are metrical . . . serve[ ] . . . as signifier of a signified concept like 'epic sensibility,' 'traditional poetry,' or 'patriarchal poetry'" ("Patriarchal Meter" 167). Focusing on iambic pentameter in particular, Finch identifies the tradition of this meter as an exclusively masculine one: "By Emily Dickinson's time iambic pentameter had been in uninterrupted and nearly uncontested standard use for five hundred years. Milton's blank verse in *Paradise Lost* had given iambic pentameter an even heavier weight of authority than it had carried after Chaucer, Spenser, and Shakespeare" (168).[45] This authority, however, rests in iambic pentameter's "patriarchal" patrilineage: "Iambic pentameter codifies the force exerted on Dickinson's poetry by patriarchal poetic tradition (she associates the meter with the power of religion and public opinion, with formality, and with stasis) and demonstrates her attitudes toward that tradition (she resists the meter, approaches it with tentative ambivalence, and sometimes gains power in it)" (166).[46] Finch further illustrates how Dickinson's poetry displays an acute awareness of this gendered connotation of iambic pentameter. Rather than avoiding it altogether, Finch argues, Dickinson uses this meter to a very specific purpose. In all instances, Dickinson employs iambic pentameter to critique the very patriarchal institutions and traditions it has come to be associated with: "In fact she appears to have scrupulously avoided five-stress lines except . . . where iambic pentameter evokes patriarchal concepts, particularly Christianity and traditional patriarchal poetic and other 'authority'" (170).[47]

Yet it is not only in *writing* poetry, as Finch has demonstrated, but also in *quoting* from other poets—specifically, from Shakespeare's plays—that Dickinson scrupulously avoids five-stress lines. Instead, she frequently either breaks up pentameter units by quoting only shorter fragments or, alternately, she adds material to turn them into longer lines (hexameters, etc.). Occasionally, she also changes five-stress lines into her own preferred hymn measure (alternating iambic tetrameters and trimeters) or variations thereof. Such metrical assimilations occur in L478 and L937, for example. Both letters "quote" the pentameter line: "The robb'd that smiles steals something from the thief" (*Othello* 1.3. 208) as hexameter or two trimeters. In L478, the hexameter is preceded by an additional trimeter consisting of Dickinson's own words: "Beloved Shakespeare says, 'He that is robbed and smiles, steals something from the thief.' "[48] In L937, the quotation has undergone more significant modifications; in this letter, Shakespeare's line has been truncated to a catalectic pentameter, while Dickinson's additions turn the entire sentence into a hexameter: "He who is 'slain and smiles, steals something from the' Sword." Similarly, in L551, Dickinson fuses two quotations from *Macbeth* in order to create an iambic hexameter: " 'I thought that Birnam Wood' had 'come to Dunsinane.' " The phrase "Therein the patient / Must minister to himself" (*Macbeth* 5.3.45–46), quoted in three different letters (L332, L669, L986), becomes—with the exception of minor differences in capitalization—in all three versions: " 'That sort must heal itself' " (L332). In L1012, the line "O, speak of that; that I do long to hear" (*Hamlet* 2.2.50) is quoted as " 'Speak that I live to hear.' "[49] Desdemona's words "Nobody; I myself; farewell: / Commend me to my kind lord" (*Othello* 5.2.127–128) are shortened to "Should she ask who sent it [the flower], tell her as Desdemona did when they asked who slew her, 'Nobody—I myself' " (L1010). In this way, Dickinson regularly superimposes her own metrical units (predominantly three-foot lines) onto the Shakespearean pentameter.[50]

All of these examples illustrate Dickinson's avoidance of not only writing in but also quoting in iambic pentameter units. An even more interesting variant of this strategy can be observed in cases where Dickinson seems to quote a complete five-foot line. Easthope has argued that iambic pentameter, more than any other meter, "enforces coherence and unity" (70): "While the four-stress line tends to break down into two-beat units as well as building cohesively into two- and four-line units, the pentameter line resists both dismantling into smaller units (since if it does divide, the units are unequal, one of two and one of three stresses) and cohesive assemblage into larger units. Each pentameter line tends to retain its separate identity" (71). Yet it is exactly this "separate identity" of the pentameter line which Dickinson destroys or obscures in her manuscript lineations. Rather than respecting the five-foot unit(y), she regularly imposes her own line breaks on the quoted material. This strategy results in a "dismantling" of the pentameter line into smaller units of primarily two and three syllables. The line "For

Brutus, as you know, was Caesar's Angel" (*Julius Caesar*), for example, is lineated as "For Brutus, | as you know, | was Caesar's | Angel" (Houghton MS Am 1118.5 [B34]; L448). In addition, several of Dickinson's quotations combine elements taken from two or more *different* Shakespearean lines, thus heightening Shakespeare's own counterpoint between the flow of longer textual passages on the one hand and the pentameter line as a self-contained unit on the other. The exclamation "And, for his ordinary, pays his heart, / For what his eyes eat only" (*Antony and Cleopatra*), for example, is quoted as "Susan's Calls are | like Antony's | Supper— | 'And pays his | Heart for what | his Eyes eat, | only'" (Houghton MS Am 1118.5 [B24]; L854).[51] In this quotation, the first Shakespearean line (a regular pentameter) is shortened to a dimeter ("'And pays his | Heart'"); this dimeter is then supplemented by a catalectic tetrameter ("'for what | his Eyes eat, | only'"). Although the result thus resembles a hypercatalectic iambic pentameter line, it consists of elements taken from two *different* Shakespearean lines and is rearranged as four different lines in Dickinson's letter, in this way completely challenging the "unity" that, according to Easthope, is generally associated with iambic pentameter.[52]

These attempts at breaking up the iambic pentameter unit, however, are not restricted to Dickinson's quotations from Shakespeare. Most of her epistolary quotations from other poems illustrate the same preference for either selecting non-pentameter lines or modifying the lineation and metrical structure of the five-foot unit. Given the predominance, as Finch has shown, of iambic pentameter as the most widely used meter during the nineteenth century, Dickinson's large number of non-pentameter quotations is striking. These quotations include iambic tetrameters ("'so I shall see it in just three days,'" L547; "and one Day more I am deified," L1015; "'his part in all the pomp that fills / The circuit of the Southern Hills, / Is that his Grave is green,'" L967; "John—Lad—and 'here's a health to *you*,'" L184), trimeters ("'But the last Leaf fear to touch,' says the consummate Browning," L966), and catalectic iambic hexameters ("'My Days that are at best but dim and hoary,'" L653). William Cowper's poem "Light Shining out of Darkness" (a poem set to hymn tunes) already provides Dickinson's preferred hymn measure for her quotation in L97, one of her most extensive epistolary quotations of verse passages: "Yet we should not repine—'God moves in a mysterious way, his wonders to perform, he plants his foot upon the sea, and rides upon the storm.' "

In addition to this explicit preference for quoting non-pentameter lines, Dickinson also performs frequent metrical assimilations. In L315, for example, she splits apart Wordsworth's iambic pentameter line "The light that never was, on sea or land" (from *Elegiac Stanzas*) to produce two dimeters and a trimeter (consisting of both Wordsworth's and her own words), which eventually scan like Dickinson's hymn measure: "Here is the 'light' the Stranger said 'was not on land or sea.' " In L801, the writer fuses two quotes from Tennyson: "Can trouble live with April days" (*In Memoriam* 81), and "Of love that never found his earthly close, / What sequel?" ("Love and Duty"). Any trace of a five-foot unity is submerged in the fusion of the two quotes (underlined by the omission of the capital in "what") and the rearranged line breaks: " '*Can* Trouble dwell | with April Days?' | 'Of Love that never | found it's earthly | close, what sequel?' " (Houghton bMS Am 1118.99c; L801).[53]

By thus truncating, expanding, or re-lineating and reorganizing five-foot units in the quoting process, Dickinson carefully obscures, and at times eliminates, their pentameter-ness and therefore also the patriarchal resonances traditionally associated with this meter. In this way, to use Jenny's expression, Dickinson "speaks in order to cancel": "Since it is impossible to forget or neutralize the discourse, one might as well subvert its ideological poles, . . . intertextuality thus forces [other discourses] to finance their own subversion" (59). Through specific modifications in her quotations of pentameter lines, Dickinson thus manages to "subvert" its gender-inscribed ideology.

This subversion of the connotations of iambic pentameter as a discursive formation also has implications for Dickinson's own texts. Easthope has argued that "since coherence in the subject is an effect of meaning intended along the syntagmatic chain, iambic pentameter in verse will support and promote coherence in the subject" (71). Dickinson's challenge to the unity and coherence of the five-foot line is thus an additional strategy to undermine the coherence of her epistolary subject positions. According to Easthope, it is the pentameter line that encourages the identification of the subject of enunciation with the subject of the enounced, an identification that—as I have demonstrated in chapters 3 and 4—Dickinson's "supposed persons" tend to avoid at all costs: "the pentameter would render poetic discourse transparent, aiming to identify the speaking of a poem with the speaking of a represented speaker or a narrator" (75). In this way, "pentameter promotes the 'realist' effect of an individual voice 'actually' speaking" (76). Yet Dickinson's choice of different (non-pentameter) types of meter in her quotations—ranging from rhythmical prose to iambic passages to hymn measure—"forces attention to the words as words and so shatters any effect of transparency" (74). It therefore also shatters any coherence of the subject, thus enabling a proliferation of multiple subject positions and multiple epistolary voices to prevail.

DICKINSON'S treatment of quotations from texts by Higginson, Shakespeare, and the Bible illustrates her double-voiced interrogation of these specific discursive formations and their sociocultural connotations. In each case, Dickinson displays extreme accuracy with some of their features while engaging in a careful manipulation of others. Claiming to admire Higginson's work, Dickinson nonetheless also engages competitively with her mentor's texts and subtly critiques the contemporary "popular" literary style exemplified and advocated in his writings; she disagrees with the Bible's exclusionist language and authoritative status while treating the word of God with the utmost textual respect and accuracy; and she rejects (i.e., manipulates) the patriarchal resonances of (Shakespearean) iambic pentameter while revering the thoughts expressed in these lines. In all of these intertextual negotiations, Dickinson, to modify Bakhtin, does allow oppositional voices into her texts; yet at the same time, she consistently brings them under a quasi-monological control, thus producing framed or monologized dialogues.

This exertion of the power of the framer, however, is not restricted to quotations from Higginson, Shakespeare, and the Bible. In fact, Dickinson's dialogic juxtaposition and monologic control of a wide variety of intertextual gestures affects all of the voices entering her correspondences. And it is her framing of these voices that ultimately interrogates the status of (male) authority, authoritative voices, and authorized (canonical) discursive formations on a very general level. Barthes has argued that any text—by definition—challenges conventional notions of authority and originality, since it "is not a line of words releasing a single 'theological' meaning (the 'message' of the Author-God) but a multi-dimensional space in which a variety of writings, none of them original, blend and clash" ("Death of the Author" 146). Kristeva highlights the extent to which this blending of writings may have a "neutralizing" effect: "in the space of a given text, several utterances, taken from other texts, intersect and neutralize one another" ("Bounded" 37). This "neutralization," however, is a result of the texts' dialogic juxtaposition. As Anne Herrmann has argued:

> The dialogic represents the struggle between opposing discourses arising out of different contexts, either semantic or sociohistorical. Unlike the dialectic, which seeks to transcend oppositions by means of a synthetic third term, the dialogic resists the reconciliation of opposites by insisting on the reciprocity of two or more antagonistic voices. Both the dialectic and the dialogic are based in theories of conflict, but the former attempts to resolve antitheses in a utopian synthesis while the latter seeks to disrupt the assimilation of differences sought by a monologic discourse. (15)[54]

Valorizing (an albeit monologized) dialogicity instead of "assimilating differences" completely, Dickinson thus insists on maintaining and foregrounding discursive oppositions by respecting each quoted voice within her letter as a discrete entity, irrespective of its provenance. As she explains in a letter to her friend Sue Gilbert: "Except for usurping your Copyright—I should regive the Message, but each Voice is it's own" (L909). Dickinson is unwilling to "usurp" Sue's words, since, in her opinion, "regiving" her friend's message would amount to seizing it forcefully and without legal rights, and would therefore constitute an infringement of "Copyright." The writer's use of legal discourse in this context suggests her treatment of Sue's words—and, by extension, of discourse in general—as legal property in a Foucauldian sense.[55] Yet in contrast to Foucault, who restricts the "system of ownership for texts," including "strict rules concerning author's rights . . . [and] rights of reproduction" (148) to specific discourses, Dickinson extends this notion of text as legally protected property to *all* texts and voices. In this way, the unpublished words of Sue, for example, are as much "copyrighted" material as the words of the Bible or Shakespeare cited above. For Dickinson, quoting thus ultimately becomes a gesture of democratization.

By granting each voice equal textual treatment, and by refusing to reconcile opposing discourses, Dickinson intends her letters ultimately to function as sites for multilayered dialogues between widely divergent discursive voices. Two central dialogues foregrounded in Dickinson's letters are the hierarchically inflected ones between "high" canonical male literature and contemporary "popular" women's writing, and those between published and unpublished texts.[56] That Dickinson is indeed aware of "elitist" connotations inscribed in specific canonical texts is indicated by her way of utilizing the "authority" traditionally associated with the Bible and Shakespeare. Dickinson's "pupil" voice, for example, frequently signals her respect for Higginson's writings by placing his words (directly or indirectly) in the company of these two groups of texts. In L593, she declares: "I have known little of Literature since my Father died—that and the passing of Mr Bowles, and Mother's hopeless illness, overwhelmed my Moments, though your Pages and Shakespeare's, like Ophir—remain—." L457 compares Higginson's words to Revelations: "But two had mentioned the 'Spring' to me—yourself and the Revelations." In L488, Dickinson again links quotations from Higginson and Shakespeare: "Often, when troubled by entreaty, that paragraph of your's has saved me—'Such being the Majesty of the Art you presume to practice, you can at least take time before dishonoring it,' and Enobarbus said 'Leave that which leaves itself.' "

Dickinson's juxtaposition of quotations from two contemporary popular American women writers and two highly respected British authors in a letter to her friend Holland can be interpreted as such a challenge to the traditional elitist status of canonized texts:

> "Douglass, Douglass, tender and true" who never swindled me! I am ashamed and sorry. I meant hypothetic tomorrows—though are there any other? I deserve to be punished. I am—in regret. . . . Austin was pleased and surprised, that you wished for him, and still hopes he may go, but not now—but "Beyond," as the Vane says—You remember Little Nell's Grandfather leaned on his Cane on the Knoll that contained her, with "She will come tomorrow." That was the kind of Tomorrow I meant—I hope I have not

tired "Sweetest Eyes were ever seen," for whose beloved Acts, both revealed and covert, I am each Day more fondly, their Possessor's Own. (L491)

The quotation from Dinah Maria Craik's popular poem "Douglas" is followed by a reference to Florence Vane's poem "Are we almost there?," before the letter turns to Dickens's *The Old Curiosity Shop*. In addition to explaining her mistake in her own words, Dickinson appropriates both Vane's notion of "Beyond" and Dickens's idea of "tomorrow," expressed through the voice of Nell's Grandfather, to apologize to her friend. Her own explanation, "I meant hypothetic tomorrows," is thus reinforced, its importance doubly underlined by two additional voices. Both "external" voices thus contribute equally to a clarification of Dickinson's own point and are thus functionally "equated." Finally, the concluding reference to Elizabeth Barrett Browning's poem "Catarina to Camoens" offers a second British voice to counterbalance the two earlier American ones. In a democratizing gesture, this letter thus brings together both male and female, British and American, "serious" and popular contemporary writers, all "speaking to" the same issue.

Throughout Dickinson's correspondence, biblical messages are in this way combined with snatches of conversations from family members; Shakespeare's lines are placed next to quotations from contemporary, popular women's literature; Dickinson's own poems are cited in the context of George Eliot's and Elizabeth Barrett Browning's verses. It is by juxtaposing these voices that Dickinson's correspondence initiates a dialogue comparable to the ones described by Yaeger: "Women writers have incorporated men's texts in their own and entered into dialogues with these texts that these male writers have refused to initiate" (30). Dickinson's intertextually dialogized correspondences thus illustrate on yet another level that, as Showalter (quoting Bakhtin) has argued, "women's writing is a 'double-voiced discourse' that always embodies the social, literary, and cultural heritages of both the muted and the dominant" (263). By embodying such a wide variety of external (muted *and* dominant) voices within her own texts and by valorizing all of them equally, Dickinson's letters therefore call into question the hierarchy and authority traditionally inscribed in and ascribed to dominant voices.

Yet in addition to traditional notions of literary, social, or cultural "authority," Dickinson also destabilizes the very concept of authorization associated with conventionally authored (published) texts. Occasionally, for example, she inserts her own poem as a deliberately unidentified voice (albeit without quotation marks) into a letter:

> I infer from your Note you have "taken Captivity Captive," and rejoice that that martial Verse has been verified. He who is "slain and smiles, steals something from the" Sword, but you have stolen the Sword itself, which is far better. . . . I shall watch your passage from Crutch to Cane with jealous affection. From there to your Wings is but a stride—as was said of the convalescing Bird, And then he lifted up his Throat And squandered such a Note—A Universe that overheard Is stricken by it yet—I, too, took my summer in a Chair, though from "Nervous prostration." (L937)

Embedded within a reference to Ephesians 4:8, a line from *Othello*, and a quotation from her physician, there emerges a variant of four lines of Dickinson's J1600/Fr1663B: "And then he lifted up his Throat | And squandered such a Note | A Universe that overheard | Is stricken by it yet—."[57] The expression "as was said," however, while obscuring Dickinson's authorship, at the same time implies a more widely "known" or even "public" provenance of her unpublished lines. Dickinson's own words are thus both "de-authored" (the author remains unidentified), as well as "authorized" (they are granted "authority" by being placed on a par with Shakespeare's and the Bible's lines). In her analysis of this letter, Fried has commented that "to the friend [Helen Hunt Jackson] who most urged her to share her work with the public, Dickinson coyly quotes herself as if she were already as eminent as Shakespeare" (159). In addition, she also highlights the process through which such "eminence" can traditionally be achieved: publication.

An even more daringly ambivalent attribution of her own words to another "author(ity)" occurs in a letter to her friend Samuel Bowles, the editor of the *Springfield Republican*. In this letter, Dickinson introduces J1398/Fr1432B ("I have no Life but this—") with the following words: "I went to the Room as soon as you left, . . . recalling the Psalmist's sonnet to God, beginning I have no Life but this—To lead it here—Nor any Death—but lest Dispelled from there—Nor tie to Earths to come—Nor Action new Except through this extent The love of you" (L515).[58] The expression "recalling the Psalmist's sonnet to God" both de-authors and reauthor(ize)s Dickinson's unpublished poem. By attributing it to the "Psalmist," whose voice carries scriptural authority, Dickinson refers to her "own" work as a well-known, "quotable" text in the public domain.

This strategy of reattributing her own words to another "author(ity)," however, ultimately results in an ambiguation of author attributions in general, and thus, in a challenge to the status that is generally granted (published) texts on the basis of their author. The very concept of a single, identifiable, potentially "canonized" author is being interrogated. Foucault has pointed out that "there was a time when the texts that we today call 'literary' . . . were accepted, put into circulation, and valorized without any question about the identity of their author"; by the seventeenth century, however, "literary discourses came to be accepted only when endowed with the author-function. We now ask of each poetic or fictional text: from where does it come, who wrote it, when, under what circumstances, or beginning with what design? The meaning ascribed to it and the status or value accorded it depend upon the manner in which we answer these questions. And if a text should be discovered in a state of anonymity . . . the game becomes one of rediscovering the author" (149–150). Yet it is precisely this "status or value accorded" to a text on the sole basis of its author attribution that Dickinson's quoting practices call into question.

Dickinson's challenge to the concept of a single, identifiable "author" manifests itself most explicitly in her decontextualized "quoting" of other voices within her letters in the form of enclosing dried flowers from her garden and conservatory; newspaper clippings; and cutouts from her Bible, her *New England Primer*, and her father's edition of Dickens. Examples include a cutout of a robin from the *New England Primer* attached to Sue Gilbert's copy of the poem "Whose cheek is this?" (J82/Fr48A); an illustration taken from the same book and pasted at the beginning of L214 to Sue;[59] and two pictures from *The Old Curiosity Shop* appended to Sue's copy of "A poor—torn Heart—a tattered heart" (J78/Fr125A).[60] Martha Nell Smith has discussed these cutouts as Dickinson's strategy of undermining the inviolability granted these texts by virtue of their (author's) status: "These manipulations of texts are transformations, opportunities for Emily Dickinson and her readers to exert control over expression by remaking supposedly fixed utterances and thereby challenge conventional authorities in a constructive way" (*Comic Power* 71–72). Yet in addition to profaning the "authoritative" words of God (or Dickens) by cutting them to pieces, Dickinson's strategy of attaching these textual fragments as unattributed clippings to her letters also effectively obscures their "author" and "origin." This intertextual gesture thus shifts the emphasis away from the author(ity) of these texts and accentuates their texture instead. The status and value of authority is thus superseded by the status and value of textuality.

Dickinson's strategy of de-author(iz)ing discourse becomes most explicit in the context of newspaper clippings, which, in their decontextualized form, completely obscure their former "author." The first page of the manuscript of J1167/Fr1174A, for example, displays a postage stamp and two cutouts from *Harper's Magazine*;[61] L751 shows a clipping from the *Springfield Republican* pasted onto the top of its first page; enclosed with L719 is an unidentified (newspaper) clipping; L1007 is accompanied by an excerpt from the *Springfield Republican;* and L33, according to Johnson and Ward, contains "small cuts clipped from old books and papers, one cutting taken from the *New England Primer*" (*Letters* 91). Moreover, the wording of the following letter to Higginson also suggests a newspaper enclosure, which is now lost, however: "The Hope of seeing you was so sweet and serious—that seeing this—by the Papers, I fear it has failed" (L546).[62] In each of these instances, the cutout becomes an integral part of Dickinson's own text: the demonstrative pronoun in L546, for example ("seeing this—by the Papers") depends on the enclosure as its referent; and J1167/Fr1174A plays with the texture of its clippings, as their careful arrangement on the page suggests: the stamp is pasted sideways onto the sheet of paper, with the strips attached to its top and bottom left-hand corners. Johnson and Holland have both emphasized that "the poem was written after the stamp and strips were pasted onto the sheet, for the lines accommodate themselves to the occupied space" (Johnson, *Poems* 816).[63] Though texture is thus foregrounded in the visual arrangement of these cutouts on the page, the former "author" of these excerpts has completely lost her/his significance.

Yet this loss of significance, this de-authorization of the respective originating author, is ultimately accompanied by a concomitant "authorization" of the compiler of this intertextual or interdiscursive environment. Jenny has argued that "the most common variety of intertextual construction is that in which the multiplicity of discourses is accommodated in a narrative framework, which is coherent, if not traditional, and this keeps the work from following the borrowed forms in an aimless proliferation and reassures the reader" (46–47). Such a "narrative framework," however, is established by the "power of the framer" who orchestrates, coordinates, and ultimately controls this multiplicity of discourses. Hence, beneath the dialogic polyvocality, the seemingly endless proliferation of (de-author(iz)ed) voices in Dickinson's letters, there always emerges the focal voice of the framer, which—even though it cannot be equated with the voice of a single, unified author or, in Bakhtin's words, with "the monological control of the" letter-writer's "own ideology" (*Problems* xx)—nonetheless exerts a high degree of textual control.

The ways in which Dickinson appropriates (literary) authority as such an orchestrator of voices can be observed in her transcription of two stanzas of George Herbert's poem "Matin Hymn," published in the October 28, 1876, *Springfield Republican* under the title "Mattens." Dickinson's transcription systematically changes Herbert's punctuation, capitalization, and spelling. Herbert's version reads: "My God, what is a heart? / Silver, or gold, or precious stone, / Or starre, or rainbow, or a part / Of all these things, or all of them in one? / / My God, what is a heart, / That thou shouldst it so eye, and wooe, / Powring upon it all thy art, / As if that thou hadst nothing els to do?" Dickinson transcribes these stanzas as: "My God—what is a Heart, | Silver—or Gold—or precious Stone— | Or Star—or Rainbow—or a part | Of all these things—or all of them in one? || My God—what is a Heart— | That thou should'st it so eye and woo | Pouring upon it all thy art | As if that thou had'st nothing else to do—" (qtd. in Bingham, *A Revelation* 108). Dickinson's insertion of ten dashes (her habitual punctuation mark), as well as her use of capitals in six additional instances created such an effect of "stylistic unity" that, as Lease has noted, "Millicent Todd Bingham . . . —on discovering these stanzas among Dickinson's poems—publish[ed] them, in the first edition of *Bolts of Melody*, as Dickinson's own poem" (63).

What Dickinson's "quotation" of "Mattens" has thus effected is a challenge to Herbert's author identity (and attendant status). In her transcription, the poem differs substantially from Herbert's version; at the same time, it cannot be described as having been "authored" by Dickinson alone either. Dickinson's method of assimilative quoting thus accomplishes a partial subversion of Herbert's authorship and a concomitant partial appropriation of authority. Without invoking a Foucauldian approach, Werner has come to a similar conclusion: "Dickinson's translations of printed passages from Swinburne, Emerson, and Herbert into her own 'peculiar handwriting' attest both to her desire to stay inside the original source and her desire to sign the work as her own" (*Open Folios* 50). Yet, although Dickinson has *stylistically* "signed" Herbert's poem "as her own"—it has at least once been attributed to the author "Dickinson"—she has nonetheless simultaneously abolished the possibility of ascribing it to a specific, individual author. This indeterminacy of attribution ultimately results in a depersonalization and a de-authoring of "Herbert's" poem.

An additional strategy that emphasizes this indeterminacy of author attribution is Dickinson's practice of quoting other quotations. An example of a "quoted quotation" can be found in L1034, in which Dickinson cites a passage from Higginson's essay "The Life of Birds" (published in the September 1862 issue of *Atlantic Monthly*), which, in turn, constitutes a quotation from Keats's *Endymion.* Higginson's passage reads: "There is one favourite bird,—the Chewink, or Ground-Robin,—which, I always fancied, must have been known to Keats when he wrote those few words of perfect descriptiveness,—'If an innocent bird / Before my heedless footsteps *stirred and stirred / In little journeys*'" (152). Dickinson's (modified) version becomes: "perhaps like Keats's bird, 'and hops and hops in little journeys'?" (L1034). Similarly, in L728, Dickinson quotes Higginson citing Carlyle. Her question, "Does she coo with 'discraytion'?," refers to Higginson's essay "Carlyle's Laugh" (*Atlantic Monthly,* October 1881), in which he had quoted Carlyle sporting a Scottish accent: " 'yes, my little fellow, r-r-roll at discraytion!' " (9). And in L564 to Jonathan L. Jenkins, Dickinson observes: "as Lowell quotes from the Stranger 'Live—live even to be unkind'—" (L564).[64] In addition to modifying and thus lyricizing these quotations, Dickinson also obscures their provenance. With the exception of the first example, in which she identifies Keats as the first "author" of the quoted quotation, Dickinson regularly omits this information (L728) or explicitly ambiguates any attribution ("as Lowell quotes from the Stranger," L564).[65] Moreover, this method of quoting the quotation of a quotation also leads to an infinite regression of "origins." If, as Worton and Still have pointed out, a single quotation "distorts and redefines the 'primary' utterance by relocating it within another linguistic and cultural context" (11), a double quotation thus multiplies this effect, resulting in an even more "infinite deferral . . . of meaning" (11). Ultimately, as Culler has argued, "there are no moments of authority and points of origin except those which are retrospectively designated as origins and which, therefore, can be shown to derive from the series for which they are constituted as origin" (117).

A similar challenge to the concepts of "origin" and "original" can also be observed in Dickinson's production of multiple variants of individual passages by quoting the "same" phrase on several occasions, yet each time in a slightly "different" version. Matthew 6:28 ("Consider the lilies of the field"), for example, is quoted in six different letters, all of which show varying degrees of morphological and syntactical changes. L213 ("Even the 'Lilies of the field' have their dignities") and L904 (" 'Consider the Lilies' ") alter capitalization; L119 (Houghton MS Am 1118 [1]: "please accept the 'Lily of the field' for the blossoms of Paradise") and L824 (" 'The lily of the field!' I never pass one without being chagrined for Solomon, and so in love with 'the lily' anew") revert from plural to singular; and L897 ("Thank you for 'considering the Lilies' ") syntactically assimilates the quoted text to its new context. By thus producing multiple variants of the "same" passage, Dickinson's letters challenge what Worton and Still have called a "belief both in original and originating integrity" (11). Although the referent (Matthew 6:28) is still identifiable in each instance, Dickinson's proliferation of variants obscures the notion of one single "original" version.

A similar effect is created by Dickinson's fusion of two or more "sources" for one quote. L732 ("Death has mislaid his sting—the grave forgot his victory") and L967 ("Oh, Death, where is thy Chancellor?") are modifications of both 1 Corinthians 15:55 ("O death, where *is* thy sting? O grave, where *is* thy victory?") and Pope's version of this passage in "The Dying Christian to His Soul." Moreover, Dickinson's phrase, " 'taken Captivity Captive' " (L937), recalls, according to Capps, Ephesians 4:8 ("led captivity captive"). In addition, it also echoes the subtitle of Xavier Boniface Saintine's

Picciola: The Prisoner of Fenestrella or, Captivity Captive (a novel Dickinson had mentioned in L27). All of these quotations thus ambiguate their "origins" and "authors," calling into question the very concept of a single, determinable "origin" guaranteed by a definitive attribution to a specific, identifiable "author."

In Dickinson's correspondence, the objective of de-authoring discourse and thus privileging the textuality and textual agency of the framer—the orchestrator of voices—over conventional notions of a unified, single author is ultimately achieved through the complementary strategies of dialogization and monologization. In other words, Dickinson's letters enact an oscillation between a dialogic proliferation of textual voices and the controlling agency of monologic "frames." On the one hand, Dickinson accents the "otherness" and heterogeneity of her quoted materials. Her insistence on the premise that "each voice is it's own" (L909) allows for what Genette has called the "coprésence" (8) and thus the equal valorization of a wide variety of historically and socioculturally divergent texts. In this way, Dickinson is able to initiate an intertextual dialogue between authoritative and nonauthoritative voices; between canonized and popular authors; between published and unpublished texts; between, in Elaine Showalter's terms, "dominant" male and "muted" female discourses (11). On the other hand, Dickinson's letters contain strategies of assimilation and monologization, which underscore the emergence of focal voices of control (a plurality of voices that can assume various manifestations and exhibit different stylistic properties in different letters and cannot be reduced to a single monologic consciousness). Yet these focal voices not only critique the gendered inscriptions inherent in canonical texts and discourses but also orchestrate Dickinson's intertextual epistolary dialogues by undermining the concepts of "originality" and "originating author" in a more general sense. In this way, Dickinson challenges the "authoritative" (canonical) status traditionally accorded published (literary) texts due to their author's status by reascribing literary "authority" to "textuality" itself. Rather than favoring conventional modes of literary production and authorization in her "letters to the world," Dickinson thus prefers to exercise the (more subtly subversive) power and authority of the framer, a preference that may indeed explain her insistence that "I have a vice for voices" (PF19).

This is my letter to the World

—EMILY DICKINSON

CONCLUSION

Dickinson's Letters to the World

THIS BOOK has been prompted by two impulses: to outline the generic transgressions—in both form and function—at work in Dickinson's manuscript correspondence, and to explore the proliferation, the dialogic interaction, and the critical potential inherent in Dickinson's epistolary voices in individual letters as well as throughout entire correspondences. Both aspects have formed the basis for my claim to reconsider the status and function of Dickinson's "letters" within her canon: I have attempted to demonstrate throughout that these texts constitute literary writings in their own right and are most productively read in an intergeneric dialogic exchange with Dickinson's "poems," rather than as mere vehicles or explanatory companions to her poetic writings or as supplementary sources of predominantly auto- or psychobiographical value. Ultimately, this revisionist reading thus argues for regarding correspondence as Dickinson's central (because "authorized" and "published") form of literary expression, while challenging the superior status that her fascicle poems (unpublished during her lifetime) have enjoyed in the past in both print and manuscript format. Domhnall Mitchell has only recently reiterated the difficulties in "working with documents that derive from the author but were never authorized by her for publication" ("Diplomacy" 51). Yet the overly strong critical focus on Dickinson's "unauthorized" fascicles all too easily tends to obscure the fact that her *correspondence* was indeed "authorized" by the poet herself, if only for an alternative ("private") form of publication, that is, for circulation among friends and family.

The fact that Dickinson constantly blurs generic boundaries between poetic and epistolary discourses suggests that her correspondence resists any facile alignment with traditional nineteenth-century "personal" and "private" women's letters as described in contemporary letter-writing manuals. By subverting—in both form and function—nineteenth-century epistolary conventions, her letters ultimately appropriate elements of "literary" and "fictionalized" discourses. This becomes especially clear in the context of Dickinson's "supposed" epistolary persons, which are based on and negotiate the narrowly circumscribed subject positions available to women in nineteenth-century sociocultural discourses. A particularly striking feature of these negotiations is Dickinson's initiation of an intergeneric dialogic exchange between authoritative and nonauthoritative voices in which her poems mailed to a specific correspondent either complement (Holland, Sue Gilbert) or subtly subvert (Austin, Higginson) her letter messages. Yet these "double-voiced" discourses are only part of Dickinson's more comprehensive critique of specific gender-inscribed and power-differentiated discursive formations, accompanied by her challenge to the hierarchical distinction between conventionally author(iz)ed (published, canonical) and nonauthoritative voices. Dickinson's "vice for voices," the high intertextual intensity of her correspondence, her oscillation between dialogic forms of juxtaposition and monologic strategies of control, as well as her repeated subversion of traditional processes of authorizing discourse ultimately all contribute to an interrogation of established forms of literary production and publication in general.

Dickinson's adamant resistance to the publication process has most forcefully been expressed in her poem J709/Fr788A:

Publication—is the Auction
Of the Mind of Man—
Poverty—be justifying
For so foul a thing

Possibly—but We—would rather
From Our Garret go
White—unto the White Creator—
Than invest—Our Snow—

Thought belong to Him who gave it—
Then—to Him Who bear
It's Corporeal illustration—sell
The Royal Air—

In the Parcel—Be the Merchant
Of the Heavenly Grace—
But reduce no Human Spirit
To Disgrace of Price—

Although this poem can be read as Dickinson's rejection of (literary) publication in general, the pervasive use of economic metaphors ("poverty," "invest," "belong," "sell," "Merchant," "Price") also suggests that it may be the crudely economic, commercial aspect of the publishing industry that Dickinson primarily objects to: in her opinion, "Thought," an insubstantial ("Royal Air"), sacred gift bestowed by God, cannot be measured in dollars and cents; to "reduce . . . Human Spirit / To Disgrace of Price" thus constitutes almost a sacrilege.

This pronounced resistance to conventional (i.e., commercial) forms of publishing, however, cannot be interpreted as Dickinson's general unwillingness to share her own work with an audience. As we all know, she prolifically circulated both letters and letter-poems among her own "private" readers. Yet in addition to the often-advanced argument that Dickinson resisted print culture because of a highly experimental manuscript calligraphy, I suggest that what she may also have objected to is the irreverent treatment that the most precious fruits of the mind incur as a result of their public exposure to the marketplace. Rather than a public, anonymous mass consumption of texts, Dickinson's ideal form of reception is a much more reverential, private act, best epitomized in the perusal of a personal letter: "The Way I read a Letter's—this— | 'Tis first—I lock the Door— | And push it with my fingers—next— | For transport it be sure— || And then I go the furthest off | To counteract a knock— | Then draw my little Letter forth | And slowly pick the lock—" (J636/Fr700A). The private "publication" of poems as integral parts of such letters might thus also guarantee a similarly reverential treatment for them by their recipients.

Dickinson's insistence on utmost privacy in the reading process is explained by her conviction that words, especially her own words, are sacred, quasi-immortal beings: "A word that breathes distinctly | Has not the power to die (J1651/Fr1715A). Similarly, to Louise and Frances Norcross she writes: "We must be careful what we say. . . . A word left careless on a page | May consecrate an eye" (J1261/Fr1268B; L379); and again to her Norcross cousins: "A word is dead when it is said, | some say. | I say it just begins to live | that day" (J1212/Fr278A.1; L374). Yet this "aliveness" of words depends to a not insignificant degree on the existence of someone to receive them. The day a word "begins to live," Dickinson seems to imply, is the day it has been spoken or addressed *to* someone, in particular to someone known and dear to her. This interpretation is suggested by the context of the above lines. According to Franklin, they had accompanied the poem "Going to them, happy letter!" (*Poems* 1:297):

> Going—to—Her! | Happy—Letter! Tell Her— | Tell Her—the page I never wrote! | Tell Her, I only said—the Syntax— | And left the Verb and the Pronoun—out! | Tell Her just how the fingers—hurried— | Then—how they—stammered—slow—slow— | And then—you wished you had eyes—in your pages— | So you could see—what moved— them—so— || Tell Her—it was'nt a practised Writer— | You guessed— | From the way the sentence—toiled— | You could hear the Boddice—tug—behind you— |

> As if it held but the might of a Child! | You almost pitied—it—you—it worked so— | Tell Her—No—you may quibble—there— | For it would split Her Heart—to know it— | And then—you and I—were silenter! || Tell Her—Day—finished—before we—finished— | And the old Clock kept neighing—"Day"! | And you—got sleepy— | And begged to be ended— | What could—it hinder so—to say? | Tell Her—just how she sealed—you—Cautious! | But—if she ask "where you are hid"—until the evening— | Ah! Be bashful! | Gesture Coquette— | And shake your Head! (J494/Fr277B)[1]

In many ways, this letter-poem—a generic hybrid in itself—constitutes a celebration of the epistolary act.[2] The word that "begins to live" after having been said is the word contained in the "happy letter," sent on its way to its recipient. And indeed, the letter-poem itself is fully alive, endowed with emotions, with various perceptory senses, and with the capacity for speech. Yet this power to speak refers not only to the letter-poem's actual (i.e., written) part, but also to the unwritten words emerging from "the page I never wrote." Strictly speaking, this unwritten page (containing the thoughts of the letter writer) is hidden from the recipient's view. At the same time, however, due to the letter's directedness at a specific addressee who is most likely on familiar terms with the writer, the "Syntax" may be enough for the reader to recover "the Verb and the Pronoun" that were left out. In other words, a written exchange between friends can communicate on a written as well as an unwritten level. For an anonymous (public) reader, on the other hand, the "unwritten" part of the communication would be nonrecoverable. Ultimately, this letter-poem thus epitomizes Dickinson's preference for a specific, familiar audience rather than the anonymous marketplace. It highlights her privileging of a "private" form of publication.

Accepting such texts as an argument for the centrality of epistolary writing within Dickinson's canon might finally also enable us to revisit two frequently recurring and hitherto unresolved questions that have long occupied a central place in the textual and feminist branches of Dickinson criticism: first, is it possible to identify a purpose or an underlying organizational principle for Dickinson's hand-sewn manuscript collections of poems, the so-called fascicles;[3] and second, how can we interpret the writer's decision to "withdraw from the world" and turn her letters into the primary mode of social interaction? A reevaluation and reconfiguration of "correspondence" as Dickinson's central form of artistic expression and a concomitant challenge to the conventional privileging of literary poems over quasi-autobiographical letters may offer a fresh perspective on these issues.

Current scholarly interest in the materiality of Dickinson's texts has drawn much critical attention to her fascicles, first published in a two-volume facsimile edition by Ralph W. Franklin in 1981. Franklin summarizes the central questions raised by these manuscript booklets thus: "interest has developed in the fascicles as artistic gatherings—as gatherings intra-related by theme, imagery, emotional movement. In general, we need to understand why she assembled the fascicles—by what principles and for what purposes" (*Manuscript Books* 1:ix).[4] The most frequently advanced explanation for their purpose was initially suggested by Franklin himself: "to reduce disorder in her manuscripts" (1:ix).[5] Additionally, Franklin was also the first to propose that the fascicles might have constituted Dickinson's form of "private publication": "In her isolation and poetic silence, these manuscript books, known as fascicles, may have served privately as publication, a personal enactment of the public act that, for reasons unexplained, she denied herself" (1:ix).[6] Based on this and similar views of the fascicles as Dickinson's collection of the most "important" part of her creative output (her poems), and possibly as her form of manuscript "publication," a number of critics have concentrated on identifying organizational and structuring principles either within a given fascicle or across fascicle boundaries, and have insisted on emphasizing the centrality of an audience for the poetic processes at work in these gatherings.[7]

Yet most of these hypotheses about purpose, structure, and audience involvement raise several fundamental questions. If the fascicles were indeed intended as Dickinson's "private form of publication," why, then, do the majority of fascicle poems appear as unfinished drafts, with words crossed out and variant readings unresolved?[8] Why, in contrast to her letter-poems, did Dickinson never circulate these manuscript booklets among her friends? And why has it been impossible so far—despite numerous and scrupulous attempts—to identify and agree upon a convincing underlying organizational principle (or the absence thereof)?

One reason for this critical impasse, I believe, is the fact that Dickinson's fascicles have almost always been treated as self-contained units, independent of and unrelated to the writer's other creative work, specifically her letters. Yet if we are willing to suspend an exclusionist privileging of "poems" and instead entertain the possibility of "correspondence" as Dickinson's major form of composition, some tentative answers might emerge. This approach might explain, for example, the unfinished status of many fascicle poems. Martha Nell Smith is representative of a number of textual critics who interpret the multiplicity of unresolved variants as an indication of audience addressivity and audience involvement in the production of meaning: "By leaving variants among which readers may pick and choose, Dickinson may have been extending her work toward her audience, demanding a kind of performance" ("Manuscripts" 123).[9] Yet the crucial question is: how can we know that Dickinson actually *wanted* her audience to read her fascicle collections? Isn't it also possible that these fascicles were not intended for "publication" or for an "audience" at all, but were conceived of as "private" gatherings, as a "scrapbook"[10] for Dickinson's own perusal? After all, as far as we know, Dickinson never actually shared either her fascicles or any draft versions of her poems with her "audience." Smith herself has emphasized elsewhere that Susan Gilbert (who, according to Smith, may have collaborated with Dickinson in the composition process) was the only correspondent to ever receive a poem in the semifinal state that is characteristic of so many of the fascicle poems.[11] In the process of incorporating her poems into or enclosing them with letters to any other recipient, however, Dickinson always resolved variant readings to produce a "final," "fair-copy" version of a poem. Moreover, although she freely distributed (and thus "published") her letters and letter-poems to correspondents, Dickinson consistently rejected entreaties from both Helen Hunt Jackson (L937a and L976a) and Thomas Niles (L813b) to share parts of her fascicle collection with them, sending them finalized "letter-poems" instead.[12] Hence it seems plausible that, due to their very "draft"-like quality, Dickinson was unwilling to allow anyone (with the possible exception of Sue) access to these unfinished versions and preferred to "publish" (circulate) her texts in an "authorized," finalized version instead. This view is confirmed by Bruce Clary's most recent study of the fascicles as "poetic scrapbooks," in which he emphasizes "Dickinson's failure to mention or otherwise regard her fascicles as works of art" (145).

Ultimately, Clary—echoing Franklin—views Dickinson's fascicles "as a pragmatic afterthought" (153), a device "to discipline the product of her spontaneous, creative process—to manage the chaos, the wildness, of manuscript scraps" (5). Of particular interest is his observation that, for Dickinson, the significance of fascicle making *decreases* with time: "The fascicles are, in fact, anomalies, the experiment of a youthful poet still insecure with her natural abilities and innate creative processes" (153). The more Dickinson matures as a writer, the more these fascicles seem to have lost their importance for her.

Yet if we accept this view of Dickinson's fascicles as "scrapbooks" containing semifinal drafts (rather than "intentionally" unresolved variants to involve her readers in the meaning-making process) and agree further that sharing her work with her audience was nonetheless important for Dickinson, a potential organizational principle may suggest itself, not dependent on *intra*textual (structural, thematic), but on *inter*textual—or rather inter*generic*—criteria: Dickinson might initially have started to group her fascicle poems according to the people she intended to share them with; that is, within any one fascicle she might have included poems she had mailed to or considered suitable for a specific correspondent.[13]

To determine the probability of this hypothesis, it is useful to compare both fascicle and correspondence versions of poems. As far as the relative time between the production of the fascicle version and the epistolary version of a poem is concerned, Johnson and Franklin are partly in disagreement. In 1955, Johnson had come to the conclusion that the fascicle copy in most cases precedes the respective copies sent to addressees. In 1981, Franklin had agreed, surmising that the fascicles might therefore have served "as a record from which Dickinson made copies to send to friends" (*Manuscript Books* 1:x). In 1998, however, Franklin restricts this hypothesis to Dickinson's earlier poems, pointing out that her first poems to Higginson, for example, were indeed "gleaned from fascicles" (*Poems* 1:24). It might thus be possible that during this early time of collecting poems in fascicles, and then drawing upon fascicles to find poems suitable for inclusion with/in letters, Dickinson may have adopted a correspondence-specific principle of organization, grouping poems according to specific recipients' interests.

From the time of increased poetic production during the 1860s onward, however, Franklin maintains that, generally, "copies for friends do precede the fascicle" (*Poems* 1:14–17): "Further into her poetic career, when the fascicle copies no longer had to be finished versions, the fair copies sent to others may be succeeded by a fascicle copy with alternative readings" (1:18). At the same time, however, Franklin also points out that Dickinson's fascicles were still "the source for further copies" (1:27), in other words, that some poems were "finalized" *after* the fascicle copy had been produced: "Confident that she could produce fair copies as needed, she did not care that poems were unfinished in the fascicles, where they were sometimes simply the working draft transcribed" (1:18). All of this leads Franklin to argue that the "first" (i.e., epistolary) version of a Dickinson poem was often produced in response to specific occasions: "Common sense suggests that fair copies would have been sent near composition, when the poem was fresh and a particular occasion at hand" (1:17). Although Franklin thus emphasizes the event-specific (and hence potentially addressee-specific) form of poetic production, his observation might also make an event-specific or addressee-specific form of organization or "storage" not seem entirely unlikely.

For all we know, however, this hypothesis will probably always have to remain conjectural. The fact that only sixty-seven poems survive in both a fascicle version and a "finished" version incorporated into or mailed as a letter may indeed be an indication of addressee specificity. In other words, it may suggest that the majority of those poems that had already been sent to someone were so addressee- or event-specific that she did not consider transcribing them into her fascicles, as she was not planning on mailing them to someone else later on. At the same time, though, this small number, of course, also leaves us with material insufficient either to prove or disprove such speculations. It is interesting to note, however, that of these sixty-seven poems surviving in both a fascicle and a "letter" version, those grouped within any given fascicle were never sent to more than two different correspondents, and in twenty-three out of thirty-three fascicles,[14] poems contained therein were only mailed to one correspondent.

A second, and perhaps even more controversial, issue in Dickinson studies is the speculation about the writer's "withdrawal from the world." Initially, psychobiographical and psychoanalytical critics such as Theodora Ward, Clarke Griffith, and John Cody turned to Dickinson's letters, specifically to the famous "I had a terror—since September" letter (L261, addressed to Higginson), to identify a psychological crisis (Ward), metaphysical causes (Griffith), or a personal neurotic disposition (Cody) at the root of her "seclusion." Sandra Gilbert, Susan Gubar, and Maryanne Garbowsky even suggest an agoraphobic syndrome as the cause for Dickinson's way of acting out the cultural myth of the "madwoman." Biographical critics such as Cynthia Griffin Wolff, Richard Sewall, Barbara Antonina Clarke Mossberg, and Vivian Pollak, among others, have located the reasons for Dickinson's reclusiveness and subsequent commitment to poetry in her mother's shortcomings and/or a thwarted love affair.

Several feminist scholars, however, have taken issue with this view of Dickinson as being "victimized" by psychological or psychosocial factors. Adrienne Rich and Suzanne Juhasz, in particular, have challenged "the traditional view of Dickinson as a victim forced into seclusion and renunciation by a failed love affair" (Erkkila, "Dickinson and Rich" 553), and have argued instead that Dickinson's "withdrawal" constituted a deliberate choice, based on her commitment to writing.[15] As Juhasz summarizes, Dickinson "devises a life that will enable her to be a woman poet on her own terms: rejecting the life for which society had prepared her, choosing the life of the mind" (*Naked and Fiery Forms* 14).[16]

Although these refutations of the "frustrated spinster" approach constitute crucial correctives in their emphasis on Dickinson's lifestyle as a deliberate choice rather than a psychological necessity, I nonetheless maintain that many of them still reflect two problematic assumptions. First, some critics tend to imply that Dickinson's only form of engagement with and resistance to the strictures of her society consisted in passive capitulation and withdrawal into, as Bennett formulates it, a poet's "life of self-indulgence and self-gratification" (*My Life* 17). Second, all of these theories, though highlighting Dickinson's commitment to writing, still, to modify Juhasz's words, lodge *poetry* at the center of Dickinson's creativity, suggesting that for Dickinson, creative writing was located in a space completely removed from social activities (Juhasz's "life of the mind").

Based on my discussion of the function and status of Dickinson's correspondence within her canon, I challenge such an exclusively "poetocentric" view. The fact that Dickinson was actively engaged in epistolary exchanges with more than ninety-nine correspondents throughout her life suggests that, rather than "cut[ting] herself off from the social interactions of life in this world" (Budick n.p.), Dickinson actively and extensively participated in a highly popular nineteenth-century form of social exchange: letter writing. The objects of Dickinson's social outreach included, among many others, prominent contemporary writers (Helen Hunt Jackson), editors (Thomas Wentworth Higginson, Thomas Niles), clergymen, and members of Amherst College. As Wolosky has emphasized: "The letters vividly face Dickinson's work outward toward people and events. They strengthen the sense of Dickinsonian poetics as profoundly enmeshed in her daily life, her social norms, her interests and relationships with the people around her and the world in which she, and they, lived. The letters, then, are an essential theatre for seeing Dickinson's work not as reified artifacts, but as acts of address, rhetorical fields, historical engagements, and cultural events" ("Manuscript Body" 90). Moreover, by regarding these letter-poems and poem-letters distributed ("published") widely to specific addressees, rather than her unpublished "poems," as Dickinson's major form of composition, and by acknowledging the writer's constant blurring of the formal and functional boundaries between poetic and epistolary discourses, I challenge the mutual exclusivity between a "socially active life" and Dickinson's "literary productivity" implicit in both Bennett's and Juhasz's statements. On the contrary, Dickinson's letter-poems and poem-letters illustrate that she effectively fused a more strictly "literary" with a predominantly socially sanctioned form of writing. Her "letters" thus become "literary writings" as much as her "poems" partake of the realm of social activities. Rather than reflecting a view of Dickinson as "writing poetry" in the seclusion of her room, her texts thus highlight the public aspect of Dickinson's creative activities.

In this way, I also take issue with critics who regard Dickinson's commitment to writing as a form of "self-indulgence and self-gratification" (Bennett, *My Life* 17),[17] disengaged from and unrelated to social issues. As I have attempted to demonstrate, it is in her letters that Dickinson actively and critically engages with some of the prevailing male-dominated and gender-inscribed nineteenth-century discourses. Her strategies of discursive self-fashioning constitute a powerful gesture toward redefining and rewriting the possibilities of being female in nineteenth-century New England society.

Therefore, rather than viewing Dickinson as someone who passively withdraws from a society according to whose scripts she refuses to perform, I contend that she actively uses her correspondences to rewrite these scripts. In this way, Dickinson's epistolary engagement with questions of gender and gendered power relations becomes a performative act, in Butler's sense. In and through her letters, Dickinson exerts textual control over her correspondents and actively shapes and rewrites her friendships according to her own terms. In this way, Dickinson the letter writer, far from conforming to the critical construction of the "shy reclusive poet," emerges as a

> woman, masculine
> in single-mindedness,
> for whom the word was more
> than a symptom—
> . . .
> [you] chose to have it out at last
> on your own premises.
>
> ADRIENNE RICH, "I Am in Danger—Sir—"

Notes

INTRODUCTION: TWO CENTURIES OF CRITICAL RESPONSES TO DICKINSON'S LETTERS

1. According to Ellen Louise Hart and Martha Nell Smith, there is only one notable exception: Dickinson's epistolary exchange with Sue Gilbert. Part of this correspondence, the editors maintain, consists of draft poems, submitted to Sue for critical commentary and professional feedback (see *Open Me Carefully*). Yet even the draft quality of these materials has recently been contested by Franklin (*Poems* 1:31–32).

2. See Cameron (*Choosing* 13–14) and McGann ("Visible" 43, 45), who writes about Dickinson's "scriptural and epistolary" medium for dissemination.

3. According to Richard Sewall, these extant materials constitute "only a fraction, and probably a small one" of Dickinson's total epistolary output (*Life* 2:750).

4. Several textual Dickinson critics, including Martha Nell Smith, Marta Werner, Ellen Louise Hart, Susan Howe, Paul Crumbley, Paula Bennett, and McGann himself, have empha-

sized the importance of this observation for Dickinson studies. However, most of them primarily concentrate on manuscript features such as dashes, capitalization, line breaks, or variants that are lost in print translations.

5. By March 1891, six issues of *Poems* had been published in less than four months. Three months from the publication of the first issue, *Poems* had elicited more than one hundred reviews and notices across the United States and Great Britain (Buckingham, "Readers" 164).

6. These two volumes contained only a small selection of Dickinson's correspondence. The most comprehensive compilation to date, Thomas H. Johnson and Theodora van Wagenen Ward's three-volume variorum edition *The Letters of Emily Dickinson*, was not published until 1958. Its 1,049 letters and 124 prose fragments, addressed to then-known 93 correspondents, constitute all the material extant to its publication date.

7. See also Mark Antony de Wolfe Howe Jr.'s review in *The Book Buyer*: "Ethereal in life, just as her poems are, these *Letters* must, in a certain way, be a disappointment to those who were expecting to find in them the tangible solution of her many mysteries" (Buckingham, *Reception* 335, item 398). The *Boston Herald* regrets "there is very little biography in these letters" (Buckingham, *Reception* 362, item 429).

8. A more detailed analysis of this aspect, based on nineteenth-century letter-writing manuals, follows in chapter 1.

9. For Tuckerman, the ideal writer of personal correspondence was the seventeenth-century author Madame de Sévigné, since her letters "constantly exhibit the woman" (105). In this context, it is interesting to note that Janet Gurkin Altman has identified Madame de Sévigné (together with Mother Chantal) as instrumental in initiating a crucial shift "toward biography" ("Letter Book" 52) in the history of the French familiar letter: "For each of them [Sévigné and Chantal] the letter was an essentially intimate communication, opening up on an interior space where a highly personal self evolves over time in interaction with close relations" ("Letter Book" 48). Cf. also Klaus Lubbers, who has suggested that "the arrangement [of Dickinson's letters] according to correspondents found more criticism than praise. It reduced the autobiographical value of the letters, since the history of Emily Dickinson's life receded behind that of her friendships" (64).

10. This notion of the (Western) private letter as an unmediated revelation of the speaker's soul can be traced back to the personalized style and contents of Cicero's correspondence; according to Rosenthal ("Courtesan's Voice" 4), it continues to dominate the cultural function of correspondence until the twelfth century. During the thirteenth century, however, as Karen Cherewatuk and Ulrike Wiethaus have argued, the proliferation of so-called formularies or *dictamina* (model letter books) and the rise of professional letter writers indicate a shift in the social role of correspondence: the letter now becomes a rhetorical construct with a predominantly public or political function. It is during the fourteenth century that a two-tiered system of correspondence emerges. Although the humanist tradition of epistolary writing continues to privilege refinement of style over revelation of self (Anderson and Ehrenpreis 274–276; Henderson 339; Constable 40), the rise of the vernacular as a written means of communication

simultaneously initiates the reemergence of the confessional/private letter (Cherewatuk and Wiethaus 4), which then flourishes during the sixteenth century (Altman, "Letter Book" 28). Yet the Renaissance's privileging of individual self-consciousness and, consequently, of the intimate, self-revelatory letter, is temporarily reversed during the following century ("Letter Book" 32–47), until the renewed public interest in the personal and the familiar during the eighteenth century induces a concomitant shift in epistolary writing toward privileging the "biographical" again (Altman, "Letter Book" 52; cf. Saintsbury, *Letter Book* 85–86). Ruth Perry and Robert Adams Day both point out that booksellers, using the device of "intercepted correspondence" as a marketing strategy even for fictional letters, "traded on the implication that letters could give a more unguarded, natural picture of a life than memoirs which were written with a public audience in mind" (Perry, *Women* 70).

Although the above remarks sketch the European tradition of the personal letter until the end of the eighteenth century, Tuckerman's delineation of the "ideal correspondent" as well as then-contemporary critical responses to Dickinson's letters suggest that many of these conceptions about the private letter as "confessional" discourse were still shared by mid nineteenth-century New England readers.

11. As Altman commented: "By the nineteenth century . . . the letter of the living writer has effectively become private property, with the advent of copyright laws and other measures to protect writers: the interval between posting of the missive letter and publication of an author's collected letters during the nineteenth century is typically extended by a long posthumous protection period" ("Letter Book" 60).

12. No doubt it is partly the personal letter's amorphous discursive status that has contributed to a perpetuation of this critical impasse well into the twentieth century. As Altman summarizes: " 'Real' letters have an ambiguous status among literary critics" ("Letter Book" 17). Early twentieth-century studies of nonfictional correspondence frequently tend to assume uncritically that private letters function as confessional discourse. George Saintsbury, for example, suggests in his "Introduction on the History and Art of Letter Writing" in *A Letter Book* that in the correspondence of any writer "you get . . . your character at first hand; . . . you get, except in cases of willful deception or great carelessness, the most trustworthy accounts of fact; and you can, or ought to be able to, hear the man talking" (86–87). And Herbert Davis prefaces his analysis of *The Familiar Letter in the Eighteenth Century* with these remarks: "For a biographer there can hardly be any documents more reliable, more valuable, and more essential than the whole corpus of a writer's correspondence" (2). More recent critical discussions either provide only selective interpretive readings of individual (predominantly pre-nineteenth-century) correspondences or do not differentiate generically between (unpublished) personal letters and (published) fictive ones. Each of the three major studies centrally concerned with theorizing the epistolary genre, Janet Gurkin Altman's *Epistolarity*, Linda S. Kauffman's *Discourses of Desire*, and Peggy Kamuf's *Fictions of Feminine Desire*, focuses primarily on fictional letters, which somewhat reduces their applicability to private correspondence. Altman's description of the ambivalent nature of the epistolary genre,

however, provides a good introduction to and rationale for the diversity, vacillation, and ambivalence exhibited by critical approaches to Dickinson's correspondence during the twentieth century: "the letter can be either portrait or mask . . . [it] is a totally amorphous instrument in the hands of its creator" (*Epistolarity* 185).

13. To refer to this edition of Dickinson's *Letters* in a way that adequately represents the contributions of both Thomas H. Johnson, editor, and Theodora Ward, associate editor, proves somewhat difficult. My arguable decision to treat Johnson and Ward as coeditors for reference purposes throughout the text—which somewhat tends to overemphasize Ward's role—thus requires some qualifications. Most readers who are accustomed to refer to the 1958 edition of *Letters* as the "Johnson edition" do so because it was Johnson who brought to this project his substantial editorial expertise acquired through preparing Dickinson's three-volume edition of *Poems* three years earlier. In *Poems*, he acknowledges that Ward had already assisted him in this task, pointing out that she "acted as counselor in all matters of plan and execution, while devoting her time chiefly to the letters" (*Poems* 1:xv). At the same time, however, the fact that Ward was instrumental in identifying and describing the changes in Dickinson's handwriting, which formed the basis for an accurate dating of the poet's manuscripts in both *Poems* and *Letters* (see the section on "Characteristics of the Handwriting" in *Poems* 1:xlix–lix, written by her), deserves to be emphasized. Even more important, however, it was Ward's 1951 edition of *Emily Dickinson's Letters to Dr. and Mrs. Josiah Gilbert Holland* (published four years prior to Johnson's edition of *Poems* and seven years prior to their joint edition of *Letters*) that set many of the editorial parameters that were subsequently adopted in the 1958 edition of *Letters* (into which Ward's edition of the Holland correspondence was integrated, albeit with an occasionally shortened critical apparatus). I thus believe—without intending to obscure Johnson's unarguably more substantial contributions to the 1958 edition of *Letters*—that a case can be made for giving Ward's editorial role more credit than she has commonly received in the past.

14. The only exceptions to date are Marta Werner's *Emily Dickinson's Open Folios* and her *Radical Scatters*; Ellen Louise Hart and Martha Nell Smith's *Open Me Carefully*; and the continually expanding *Dickinson Electronic Archives*, edited by Smith, Hart, and Werner, at: http://jefferson.village.virginia.edu/dickinson. Since most of these projects are very recent, however, their revisionist influence on Dickinson's critical reception is only beginning to manifest itself at this time.

15. The critical reception of Dickinson's so-called Master letters, three unfinished and most likely unmailed drafts written between 1858 and 1861, is a case in point. For a more detailed discussion of these letters, see chapter 4.

16. McKinstry's reason for classifying Dickinson's letters as biography rather than autobiography is the writer's heightened self-awareness and self-interpretation in her correspondence (195).

17. This argument is echoed by Paul Ferlazzo: "Another aspect of her art reveals how conscious she always was of her audience, trying to send to her correspondents what best

fitted their minds and needs . . . she also 'posed' herself for various members of her audience" (127).

18. Juhasz's concept of language is based on the notion that "any telling must always constitute some form of disguise. Because words cannot help but rearrange things, they can be used accordingly" ("Reading" 170).

With some exceptions (detailed below), all quotations from Dickinson's letters follow the text of Thomas H. Johnson and Theodora van Wagenen Ward's three-volume edition of *Letters* and are identified by their Johnson number, with "L" indicating "letter," and "PF," "prose fragment." All quotations from Dickinson's poems follow the text of Ralph W. Franklin's revised three-volume edition of *Poems* (1998), yet for easier reference are identified by both Johnson number ("J" plus poem number) as well as Franklin number ("Fr" plus poem number). Ten letters to Abiah Root (L5, L6, L8, L9, L12, L14, L23, L39, L69, L91) have recently been revised by Franklin, who had access to Mabel Loomis Todd's first (more accurate) transcriptions that were unavailable to Johnson in 1958. Quotations from these letters thus follow Franklin's reconstructed versions in *The Emily Dickinson Journal* 4, no. 1 (1995):1–43.

19. Echoing Miller's argument about the "constructedness" of the roles of both speaker and addressee in Dickinson's letters, William Merrill Decker also highlights the perfectionability of epistolary relationships enabled by this strategy: "it is not the friend's unconstructed presence for which Dickinson longs. The scenes of immediate contact that she projects are remarkable in that, beyond the vision of friends reunited, they commonly depict a perfection of relations . . . such an understanding as may never in this life take place" (87).

20. See also Ferlazzo, who points out that "Emily Dickinson's methods of writing were perhaps even more consciously artistic than those belonging to many of her correspondents. Her letters were creations, some of which might begin to take shape years before they were mailed" (126).

21. Also see her remarks in "Emily Dickinson's Letters: The Making of a Poetics": "Intimate and literary experience came together in instances of Victorian correspondence with spectacular dramatic and romantic force" (8).

22. See also Renza, who argues that "autobiography, in short, transforms empirical facts into *art*ifacts; it is definable as a form of 'prose fiction' " (269).

23. Some feminist critics object to the implications inherent in a poststructuralist concept of the subject "as a fictive entity constituted in images or words that cannot refer back to the 'real' world because of the inherently nonreferential nature of all signs" (Benstock, *Self* 37). Its major problem, they claim, is its tendency to sabotage feminist attempts to reconstruct a female speaking self based on individual experience. Nancy K. Miller, in particular, reads women's autobiographies as a genre that can offer privileged access to an individualized experience and is concerned with constituting a female subject: "The postmodernist decision that the Author is dead, and subjective agency along with him, does not necessarily work for women and prematurely forecloses the question of identity for them. Because women have not

had the same historical relation of identity to origin, institution, production, that men have had, women have not, I think (collectively) felt burdened by too much Self, Ego, Cogito, etc. Because the female subject has juridically been excluded from the polis, and hence decentered, 'disoriginated,' deinstitutionalized, etc., her relation to integrity and textuality, desire and authority, is structurally different" (106). Yet, rather than circumscribing the female speaking self, I would argue that Dickinson's construction of multiple epistolary subject positions allows her to express herself in powerful voices other than her own. As Benstock has suggested, "such writings serve as a means by which to create images of 'self' through the writing act, a way by which to find a 'voice'—whether private or public—through which to express that which cannot be expressed in other forms" (*Self* 5–6). In this way, a multiplication of subject positions, a "fracturing of the narrated 'I' into multiple speaking postures" (S. Smith 47), serves as an empowering strategy for the speaker to expand the number of roles available to her.

24. Consider also this comment from Bakhtin: "Every struggle between two voices within a single discourse for possession or dominance in that discourse is decided in advance, it only appears to be a struggle; all fully signifying authorial interpretations are sooner or later gathered together in a single speech center and a single consciousness; all accents are gathered together in a single voice" (*Problems* 204).

25. Based on my analysis of the blurring of genre boundaries within Dickinson's oeuvre in chapter 1, I treat as "correspondence" all texts defined by Johnson and Ward as "letters" and included in their edition of *The Letters of Emily Dickinson* (1958) as well as all "poems" from *The Poems of Emily Dickinson* (1998) that Franklin has identified as having been mailed to a specific recipient.

CHAPTER 1. THE CONTEXT OF NINETEENTH-CENTURY EPISTOLARY CONVENTIONS

1. Newman's was one of the textbooks that Dickinson had used during her stay at Mt. Holyoke Female Seminary.

2. Sometimes this gender link is merely indirect, as in *Aids to Epistolary Correspondence*, which uses female pronouns as the generic referent for the two parties engaged in an epistolary exchange: "A correspondence between two persons, is simply a conversation reduced to writing; in which one party says all that *she* has to communicate, replies to preceding inquiries, and, in *her* turn, proposes questions, without interruption by the other; who takes precisely the same course in *her* answer" (4; emphases added). Karen Cherewatuk explains that these gendered connotations can be linked to the rise of the vernacular in fourteenth-century Europe, which initiated a two-tiered system of letters: public letters written in Latin, predominantly by men, and visionary or personal vernacular letters, written by women (8). This distinction was reinforced, according to Josephine Donovan, by the fact that a classical education was mainly reserved for men, while women's education focused primarily on the vernacu-

lar (42). During the Renaissance, as Altman observes, no distinctions were drawn between men's and women's letters, but "in the seventeenth century . . . women's letters begin to be published and marketed as such, as emanating from a space that is separate from that of men and even more narrowly confined" ("Letter Book" 42). See also Goldsmith, who argues that "by the end of the seventeenth century France, this notion of a feminine affinity for a certain kind of epistolary writing was becoming a critical stereotype. Compilers of model letters were including an increasing number of letters by women in their collection" (*Writing* 46).

3. A copy of John Bennett's 1824 *Letters to a Young Lady*, inscribed to Dickinson's mother, Emily Norcross, can be found among Dickinson's books at the Houghton Library, Harvard.

4. See also Lovelace's false "etymological" explanation of the word *correspondence* as derived from Latin *cor* (heart) in Richardson's *Clarissa:* "I loved familiar letter-writing, as I had more than once told her, above all the species of writing: it was writing from the heart (without the fetters prescribed by method or study), as the very word correspondence implied" (2:431).

5. In this context it is interesting to note that, though Dickinson's poetry was frequently faulted for grammatical errors by nineteenth-century reviewers, the same critics unanimously praised her prose style.

6. In another letter to her brother, she exhorts him: "Dont tell them, *will* you Austin; they are all asleep soundly and I snatch the silent night to speak a word to you" (L66).

7. Also see the guidelines in *Aids to Epistolary Correspondence:* "Ease and simplicity, an even flow of unlaboured diction and an artless arrangement of obvious sentiments, have been pronounced to be the qualities most frequently required" (1). And the *Young Lady's Own Book* recommends: "Ease is the grace of letter-writing: far-fetched words, and studied phrases, are by no means to be accepted as legitimate ornaments in the epistolary style. A passage which is at once brilliant and brief, enriches a letter; but it must be artless, and appear to flow without effort from the writer's pen" (109).

8. See also Bilworth (13), *The Young Lady's Book of Classical Letters* (14), and *Aids to Epistolary Correspondence* (7). Newman is somewhat more specific, but comes to the same conclusion: "[Letters] hold a middle rank between the unrestrained flow and carelessness of conversation, and the preciseness and formality of dignified composition, approaching however nearer to the former, than to the latter" (198).

9. Refer also to the *Young Lady's Book of Classical Letters:* "Many persons make a rough draft of the letter they design to write; which, when they have corrected and improved it as much as they can, they transcribe. On occasions of particular difficulty or importance, this practice is not to be condemned. It is frequently recommended, or allowed, to children and young persons, in their first epistolary essays, though on the most trivial subjects: but if it should be long continued, or become habitual, it will prove a great hinderance to facility and dispatch in writing; which are always useful, and often absolutely necessary, in the commerce of the world" (15).

10. See also L179: "I fear I grow incongruous."

11. Additional examples include: "How are your Hearts today" (L189); "The Hearts in

Amherst—ache—tonight—You could not know how hard" (L259); "How hard to thank you—but the large Heart requites itself" (L300); "The Heart wants what it wants—or else it does not care—" (L262).

12. See also L532 to Samuel Bowles, which contains half rhymes ("own," "done," "long"), assonance ("own," "Bowles"), and a full rhyme ("do," "new"): "To remember | our own | Mr Bowles | is all we | can do— | with grief | it is done | so warmly | and long, | it can | never be | new" (Dickinson ms. 712 and ms. 713c-18, Amherst). L184 to John Graves: "Glad I was, to get it—and gladder had I got them *both,* and glad indeed to see—if in your heart, *another* lies, bound one day to me." And L977: "So Madonna | and Daughter | were incomplete, | and Madonna | and Son, must | supersede!" (Houghton MS Am 1118.3 [H93]). L149 contains an example of isocolon: "Then New Year the sweetest, and long life the merriest, and the Heaven highest." Additional instances of internal rhymes include L951, L175, L58, L117, L155, L432, L767, L329.

13. Dickinson's use of rhythmical prose had been noted earlier by David Porter, Lewis Turco, and Robert Graham Lambert. Porter comments in *The Art of Dickinson's Early Poetry:* "The rhythms of poetry, she seems to be demonstrating, so pervade her consciousness that she cannot make the distinction between them and unmetered prose" (8). And Turco's creative response to Dickinson's correspondence (he selects passages from Dickinson's letters and arranges them as "verse") similarly demonstrates the close metrical affinity between Dickinson's "prose" and her "poetry." The most extensive compilation of Dickinson's rhythmical prose can be found in chapter 5 of Lambert's *Critical Study of Emily Dickinson's Letters.* Lambert distinguishes between two different forms of rhythmical prose: "gatherings" (or "pre-stanzas") and "semi-stanzas": "Gatherings occur in the sentences just preceding a poem included in the body of a letter. Essentially, these gatherings are iambic lines that prepare the reader for the leap into poetry" (175–176). Lambert identifies the following letters as containing gatherings: L173, L219, L251, L266, L338, L339, L354, L364, L374, L379, L630, L695, L890, L967 (177). "Semi-stanzas," according to Lambert, occur primarily in letters to Sue Gilbert, Samuel Bowles, and Thomas Wentworth Higginson, and consist of passages or entire paragraphs that scan in hymn meter (176). Lambert identifies semi-stanzas in L238, L247, L261, L265, L266, L268, L275, L276, L288, L292, L333, L750 (187). Although Lambert's compilation of examples of iambic prose in Dickinson's letters proves a useful resource, he nonetheless omits non-iambic metrical patterns and fails to explain the function of these "gatherings" and "semi-stanzas" in the context of Dickinson's correspondence. In addition, I also disagree with some of his metrical analyses (he regularly neglects to distinguish between full and half stresses, for example, and accepts both lexical and promoted stress as "regular" patterns without explaining instances of and reasons for the promotion of an otherwise unstressed syllable).

The reasons Dickinson's iambs rarely develop into iambic *pentameter* have been analyzed by Annie Finch. In "Dickinson and Patriarchal Meter," later expanded in *The Ghost of Meter,* Finch regards the iambic pentameter as a "signifying code" ("Patriarchal Meter" 173), sparingly yet effectively employed by Dickinson in poems that both metrically as well as semantically constitute an explicit critique of patriarchal metrical conventions. This issue is explored more fully in chapter 5.

14. The following examples of iambic prose may be added to Lambert's relatively short list: L33, L146, L183, L203, L229, L247, L249, L259, L262, L266, L276, L277, L323, L324, L333, L339, L351, L359, L364, L371, L397, L399, L450, L513, L516, L532, L542, L591, L609, L621, L643, L671, L706, L715, L730, L732, L735, L745, L750, L794, L802, L806, L820, L832, L868, L890, L891, L951, L955, L977, L978, L1014, L1020, L1045. In addition, an intricate combination of iambs and anapests can be found in L532 to Mary Bowles on Samuel Bowles's death: "With grief it is done, so warmly and long, it can never be new."

Cristanne Miller has pointed out that "Dickinson is most apt to write in meter when she is responding to a crisis or is particularly upset" (*Grammar* 11).

15. Interestingly enough, Dickinson's own manuscript line breaks here approximate lines of verse. Neither Johnson nor Franklin have included this as a poem. For additional iambic notes, see also L397: "Without the | annual parting | I thought to | shun the | Loneliness that | parting ratifies. | How artfully | in vain! | Your Coffee | cooled un | touched except | by random | Fly. A one armed | Man conveyed | the flowers. | Not all my | modest schemes | have so perverse | a close" (Houghton MS Am 1118.5 [B123]); L247: "I am so | far from Land— | To offer *you* the | cup—it might some | Sabbath come *my* | turn—Of wine how | solemn—full!" (Dickinson ms. 675, Amherst); L262 (to Mary Bowles during her husband's absence): "When the Best is gone—I know that other things are not of consequence—The Heart wants what it wants—or else it does not care—You wonder why I write—so—Because I cannot help—I like to have you know some care—so when your life gets faint."

16. Hymn measure (and its variants) can also be found in L259, L277, L516 (on the death of Mary Channing Higginson), L643, L750, and L794; L266: "You go away—and where you go, we cannot come—but then the Months have names—and each one comes but once a year—and though it seems they never could, they sometimes do—go by"; L399: "The Giant in | the Human | Heart was | never met | outside. | The Sun came | out when you | were gone. | I chid him for | delay— | He said we had | not needed him" (Houghton MS Am 1118.2 [32]); L609: "Labors as endeared may engross our lost. Buds of other days quivered in remembrance. Hearts of other days lent their solemn charm. Life of flowers lain in flowers—what a home of dew! And the bough of ivy; was it as you said? Shall I plant it softly? There were little feet, white as alabaster"; L802: "I hope the mis | sing Health is | rapidly returning— | and grieve that | any faintness should | waste your second | Home— | It acclimates | our thought of | you to see your | Noble Sons—" (Houghton MS Am 1118.2 [75]); L276: "That you return to us alive, is better than a Summer. And more to hear your voice below, than News of any Bird"; L333: "To take away our Sue leaves but a lower World, her firmamental quality our more familiar Sky. . . . The Bird would be a soundless thing without Expositor. Come Home and see your Weather. The Hills are full of Shawls, and I am going every Day to buy myself a Sash"; L820: "but we must bring no Twilight to one who lost her Dawn—"; L955: "The Thank you in

my heart obstructs the Thank you on my Lips. How little of our depth we tell, though we confide our shallowness to 'every passing Breeze—.'"

17. I contend that Dickinson's letters-as-poems show a tendency toward the monologic and that her poems-as-letters (see below) approximate the dialogic end of the spectrum. At the same time, however, neither one becomes fully "monologic" or "dialogic" in a Bakhtinian sense. This proposition to regard Dickinson's letters as "monologized dialogues" and "dialogized monologues" is explored more fully in chapter 5.

18. See also G. P. Quackenbos: "The date of a letter, which should always be distinctly stated, must stand at the right of the first line" (359); the *Young Lady's Own Book* warns: "It is very improper to omit dating a letter" (132).

19. See also H. O. Ward: "Upon friendly notes nothing more than the day of the week, with the street and the number, is absolutely necessary" (14).

20. See also Linda S. Kauffman, who points out that "the particularity of material existence in a specific historical moment . . . is one of the hallmarks of epistolary writing-to-the-moment" ("Special Delivery" 226).

21. Mark Jeffreys associates such an atemporal existence of a text with the lyric genre that has frequently been regarded as unrelated to its (cultural or political) time and place of writing (199–202).

22. For a list of all the poems mailed to more than forty correspondents (organized by recipients), see Franklin's Appendix 7 in *Poems*, vol. 3; for a more detailed survey of critical discussions of this issue, see chapter 2 of this book.

23. I am here primarily concerned with an accurate editorial representation of poems mailed as or in letters. I am not, however, arguing against separate "poetry" editions of, for example, those poems that Dickinson had collected in her fascicles and sets. Whenever a poem occurs within a letter as well as a fascicle context (there are about sixty such poems), this poem would have to be included in both a letter and a fascicle edition, since, in my opinion, it constitutes two different or differently contextualized texts.

24. The nonreferential quality of Dickinson's poetry has frequently been pointed out. Roland Hagenbüchle, in particular, discusses Dickinson's "metonymically constructed metaphors" ("Precision and Indeterminacy" 40), which he defines as metaphors that have no discernible referent in the external world and thus cannot produce a "stable" meaning but rather lead to ambiguity and multiplicity of meaning. Among such instances of "pure *deixis*," Hagenbüchle analyzes Dickinson's "'absolute' use of the pronoun" (43). Sarah Wider has specifically commented on poems enclosed in letters: "by themselves, these poems are markedly without personal reference. Any connection with the correspondent's situation belongs to the prose alone" (28).

25. See also L444 to Helen Hunt Jackson (the relative pronoun in the first line of the poem "Who fleeing from the Spring" is preceded by the lines "Have I a word but Joy? | E. Dickinson," thus suggesting as its referent Dickinson herself); L449 to Higginson (the sentence "Mr Bowles lent me flowers twice, for my Father's Grave" introduces the poem "To his simplicity |

To die—was little Fate—"); L776 to James D. Clark (the poem "Obtaining but his own extent" is quoted in the context of discussing their mutual friend Wadsworth); L893 to Higginson (the line "In memory of your Little Sister" introduces "Who 'meddled' with the costly Hearts"); L1042 to Higginson in discussing Helen Hunt Jackson ("Not knowing when Herself may come"); L1043 to Higginson in the same context ("The immortality she gave").

26. In its manuscript lineation, the combination of the salutation and the first line of the poem looks exactly like the beginning of a letter, with the first line after the salutation indented. Further addressee-specific examples include L229 to Bowles ("Would you like Summer? Taste of our's—"); L249 to Bowles ("[Sh]ould you but fail [at]—Sea—"); L155 to Henry V. Emmons ("Please, Sir, to let me"); L515 to Bowles ("I have no Life but this—"); L868 to Susan Gilbert ("Pass to thy Rendezvous of Light,"); L937 to Helen Hunt Jackson during her time of recovery ("Pursuing you in your transitions"); L946 to Mr. and Mrs. E. J. Loomis at the time of their departure ("Parting with Thee reluctantly"); L975 to Mary Warner Crowell ("Is it too late to touch you, Dear?").

27. Martha Nell Smith has drawn attention to the fact that a large number of poems were indirectly addressed to Sue Gilbert, with "Sue" written on the verso (*Rowing* 183). For a compilation of these materials, see Hart and Smith's *Open Me Carefully*. In these instances it is impossible to determine whether the poems were sent to Sue for critique and feedback or whether they contained "messages" specifically addressed to her.

28. Since these two notes constitute the only reference to a possible estrangement between the two women, some critics have challenged this interpretation (Martha Nell Smith and Ellen Louise Hart, among others). Additional examples of "occasional" letter-poems include: L246 to Edward S. Dwight on the memory of his late wife ("Sufficient troth—that she will rise—"); L305 to Sue Gilbert upon the death of her sister ("Unable are the Loved—to die—"); L371 to Higginson upon the death of his brother ("Of Heaven above the firmest proof"); L630 to Higginson on the death of his daughter Louisa ("The Face in evanescence lain"); L517 to Higginson on the death of his wife ("Perhaps she does not go so far | As you who stay—suppose—").

29. Additional examples have been noted by Wider, who quotes L967 and L970 as well as L585 and L677. L967 is a tribute to the late Judge Otis Lord, addressed to their mutual friend Benjamin Kimball: "On my way to my sleep, last night, I paused at the [Lord's] Portrait. Had I not loved it, I had feared it, the Face had such ascension." This line is followed by the poem "Go thy great way! | The Stars thou meetst | Are even as Thyself— | For what are Stars but Asterisks | To point a human Life?" (J1638; Fr1673). While commemorating the post-mortem passage of Lord in L967, the "same" poem celebrates the life of another friend in L970. The letter addressed to Mrs. James S. Cooper closes with "To thank you would profane you—There are moments when even Gratitude is a desecration," before continuing with "Go thy great way!" (without any changes to the earlier version).

30. The strikingly different context for this poem has also been noted by Cristanne Miller ("A Letter" 33).

31. Brita Lindberg-Seyersted is one exception. She insists on regarding these poems as "occasional" in each case: "One [poem] which can be described as occasional in the full sense of the word, is directly addressed and sent to an actual person" (27). Later, however, she seems to contradict her earlier statement by suggesting that "a perusal of Emily Dickinson's later poems and letters would indicate that the *occasion* itself seldom or never prompted the initial composition of the poems; the first drafts of poems, unfinished or fragmentary, probably already existed in the poet's scrap basket; a special event, or the need to reply to a friend's note, then afforded the necessary impetus for a decision on the final form of the often fragmentary lines" (29).

32. See also Bingham, *Ancestors' Brocades* 45; Franklin, *Editing* 132; T.H. Johnson, *Poems* 1:xxxiv.

33. Related to this aspect is Elizabeth C. Goldsmith's emphasis on "the feminine cultivation of letter writing as a vehicle for both practical and artistic expression" ("Authority" 54).

34. Smith emphasizes the importance of this point: "Reconceptualizing notions of 'publication' to include Dickinson's circulation of her poems to her correspondents places her in an active, cultured network, and calls into serious question the prevailing image of the isolated, withdrawn poet" (*Rowing* 92). Lazer suggests a similar idea in his discussion of the letter-poem as "a gesture and an attempt to defeat the poet's isolation" (240).

35. McGann, for example, explains that "in the late nineteenth century 'publication' only came when a poet followed certain textual conventions. These conventions—they are strictly bibliographical rather than more broadly formal—were so dominant that most poets and readers could not imagine poetry without them. (Tennyson and Dante Gabriel Rossetti, for example, both said that they could not really begin to see their own poetry until it was put into print.)" ("Composition" 123).

36. Generally speaking, though, Dickinson's "prose" more often approaches the realm of poetry than vice versa, a fact that had already been pointed out by one nineteenth-century reviewer who suggested that "it is much truer that her prose ran into verse than that her verse ran into prose" (Buckingham, *Reception* 427, item 490). The fact that she once defined her age in terms of the number of poems she had written—to Higginson she writes, "You asked how old I was? I made no verse—but one or two—until this winter—Sir—" (L261)—suggests that Dickinson prefers to move epistolary discourse toward the "poetic" end of the spectrum. And while her early letters frequently attempt to render her "prose" more "poetical" by *adding* specific rhetorical elements, her later letters, on the other hand, more often concentrate on *omitting* epistolary features.

37. In this context it is interesting to note that most if not all of Dickinson's letter recipients were most likely unaware of her double mailing practice. Thus Dickinson's addressees inevitably perceived each letter-poem they received as a private, personalized "message" (in its "epistolary function"), while only Dickinson was aware of its predominantly nonreferential or polyreferential ("literary") aspects.

CHAPTER 2. EDITING DICKINSON'S CORRESPONDENCE, 1894–1999

1. The first, in fact, to comment on the poetic quality of Dickinson's letters was Thomas Wentworth Higginson. In an 1890 letter to Mabel Loomis Todd he exclaims: "I am distressed exceedingly to find that among E.D.'s countless letters there are poems as good as any we printed. . . . This shows we *must* have another volume by and by & this must include prose from her letters, often quite as marvellous as her poetry" (qtd. in Bingham, *Ancestors' Brocades* 72).

2. Dickinson's earliest editors, Thomas Wentworth Higginson and Mabel Loomis Todd, divided her writings into three editions of *Poems* (1890, 1891, 1896, edited by Todd and Higginson) and two editions of *Letters* (1894 and 1931, edited by Todd). From a generic perspective, the problematic fact that Dickinson frequently mailed poems as letters, or incorporated poems or lines of poetry into her letters, was resolved typographically. In both editions of *Letters*, Todd prints poems incorporated into letters in a smaller font size to distinguish them visually from their letter context. If the poem, however, constitutes the entire missive, it is printed in letter-font size, but indented in order to distinguish it from "prose" letters. This typographical convention was, with minor variations, adopted by all subsequent editors. Martha Dickinson Bianchi's *The Life and Letters of Emily Dickinson* (1924) and her 1932 sequel, *Emily Dickinson Face to Face*, are largely based on Todd's editions. Bianchi's only typographical change consists in using the same font size for both poems and their letter context, yet all poems are again visually marked by indentation. Millicent Todd Bingham's *Ancestors' Brocades* as well as her later *Emily Dickinson: A Revelation* and *Emily Dickinson's Home: Letters of Edward Dickinson and His Family* share the same typographical conventions of visually separating "poems" and "letters." Theodora Ward's *Emily Dickinson's Letters to Dr. and Mrs. Josiah Gilbert Holland* and Thomas H. Johnson and Ward's three-volume variorum edition maintain a strict generic distinction between poems and letters. "Letters" are printed margin to margin, while "poems" and poems incorporated within letters are indented and arranged in hymn stanza form. Although Marta Werner's (1995, 1999) and Ellen Louise Hart and Martha Nell Smith's (1998) editions attempt to challenge this distinction, Franklin (1998) continues to maintain it by editing three volumes of Dickinson's "poems," at times featuring an even more "conservative" notion than Johnson of what does or does not constitute a Dickinson poem.

3. Most of Bianchi's work had been based on Todd's editions, as her letter to Houghton Mifflin's editor Ferris Greenslet demonstrates: "What fun I've had doing Emily by proxy" (qtd. in Horan 96). Horan explains further: "When in 1922 the copyright on the Todd-edited *Letters of Emily Dickinson* expired, putting the text in public domain, Madame Bianchi used the occasion to draw freely and without acknowledgment from Todd's work. . . . Madame Bianchi did not actually possess the originals of many of the letters" (95–96). Franklin further comments on Bianchi's editions: "Neither she nor Hampson was notably competent in dealing with Emily Dickinson's handwriting. Her editions are marked by maladroit misreadings or

errors . . . and numerous alterations in the interests of sense and sensibility, but she refrained from extensively rewriting the poems as she published them, in particular leaving words to rhyme in the way Dickinson had. Her texts were regularized as to spelling, capitalization, and punctuation, if sometimes idiosyncratic in lineation. . . . Bianchi made only desultory attempts to compare texts with the manuscripts in her possession" (*Poems* 1:5).

4. *Ancestors' Brocades, Emily Dickinson: A Revelation,* and *Emily Dickinson's Home: Letters of Edward Dickinson and His Family.*

5. Bingham explains: "One packet brought by Mr. [Austin] Dickinson was different from all the others. In a used brown envelope, addressed in an unknown hand . . . the canceled stamps an issue of the early 1880's, it is labeled in my mother's [Todd's] writing, 'Rough drafts of Emily's letters.' She told me that when Mr. Dickinson gave her this envelope he indicated that it was something very special and personal. . . . Obviously love letters, my mother did not ask Mr. Dickinson how they came to be in his possession" (*A Revelation* 1). Cf. Anna Mary Wells, however, who argues that the letters in *A Revelation* are forgeries; and William H. Shurr's critique of Bingham in *The Marriage of Emily Dickinson.* The latest response to Bingham's edition of the Lord correspondence is Marta L. Werner's 1995 edition, *Emily Dickinson's Open Folios* (discussed below).

6. One of the impulses behind these narratives was no doubt the infamous family feud—between Susan Gilbert Dickinson (Austin Dickinson's wife) and Mabel Loomis Todd (Austin Dickinson's mistress) that began over a strip of land—which resulted in a division of the manuscripts between the two families and an attempt by each of their daughters (Bianchi and Bingham) to vindicate their respective mothers.

7. The 1,049 letters and 124 prose fragments constituted all the material extant to its publication date, 1958.

8. As Bornstein has pointed out, "We cannot hope through textual scholarship to recover an ideal text like a well-wrought urn, but only to increase the self-awareness and internal consistency of the choices that we make in constituting the monument for our own time" (2).

9. As McGann emphasizes: "When we come to edit [Dickinson's] work for bookish presentation, . . . we must accommodate our typographical conventions to her work, not the other way round" ("Composition" 135). Hart and Smith further justify this position by highlighting the fact that "Dickinson used the page itself, and the placement of words in relation to embossments, attachments, and margins to convey meaning, and in ways that typography cannot sufficiently transmit" (*Open Me* xxiii). Curiously, several earlier editors had already identified such a change in medium as a potential source of misrepresentations. Todd, for example, explains in her 1894 introduction to Dickinson's *Letters:* "In more recent years, dashes instead of punctuation and capitals for all important words, together with the quaint handwriting, give to the actual manuscript an individual fascination quite irresistible. But the coldness of print destroys that elusive charm, so that dashes and capitals have been restored to their conventional use" ("Introductory" 342). Similarly, Theodora Ward remarked that "the task of rendering Emily Dickinson's manuscripts into print can be compared to trying to

represent a watercolor in an engraving. The lines, the spacing, the punctuation, as well as the highly individual forms of the script, all play a part in the effect on the reader" (*Emily Dickinson's Letters* 239). Yet each of these editors eventually endorsed print conventions over manuscript idiosyncrasy.

10. The archives are located at: ⟨http://jefferson.village.virginia.edu/dickinson⟩. Smith explains the advantages of these archives thus: "In hypermedia, texts are electronically stored and managed. . . . Texts appear on the screen, not the page, and that creates new possibilities for analysis. . . . Through various windows simultaneously displayed on the screen more than one or two pages can appear at once, and they can be from a variety of [primary and/or secondary] sources" ("Importance" 77). For a more detailed discussion of this project, see Smith, "Because the Plunge" and "Electronic Resources." To date, readers can access materials compiled under four different headings: "(1) *Writings by the Dickinson Family,* which features Emily Dickinson's writings as well as those of Susan Dickinson, Ned Dickinson, and Martha Dickinson Bianchi; (2) *Responses to Dickinson's Writings;* (3) *Teaching with the Archives;* and (4) *Citations and Research Resources*" (Smith, "Electronic Resources" 13). Smith's ultimate goal is to provide facsimile images and electronic text versions of all Dickinson's manuscripts in the groups in which they were left at her death, including all the "books" sent to various correspondents, as well as fascicles, sets, and ungathered poems (see Hart, "Elizabeth" 45; Smith, "Dickinson's Manuscripts" 133). In addition, these archives will also contain the publication history of all documents, all subsequent print editions and their critical reception, their representation in popular culture and other media (music), as well as audio streams of contemporary American women poets reading and responding to Dickinson's writings. Particular emphasis is placed on "making available and visible marks routinely erased in typography"—including Dickinson's calligraphic experiments, slanting dashes, interlinear variants, unusually formed letters, or mixed-media layouts—in order to allow readers to "decide for themselves" the significance of these features (Smith, "Electronic Resources" 26). Viewing this archive as complementary to, rather than contestatory with, Franklin's variorum edition, Smith is fully aware that "the *Dickinson Electronic Archives* is not an ultimately 'authoritative' edition but serves as a valuable resource for exploring theoretical implications of the material structures of Dickinson's texts (both individual documents and the organization of their relationships to one another)" ("Dickinson's Manuscripts" 132). Highlighting the archive's perpetual updatability, she particularly invites readers to engage in an "online critical exchange that is . . . dynamic, where critical positions can be constantly deepened and updated rather than become fixed and entrenched" (Smith, "Electronic Resources" 26).

11. Werner's edition engages, in particular, with Millicent Todd Bingham's representation of these texts in *Emily Dickinson: A Revelation.* Summarizing Bingham's and others' earlier editorial practices of incorporating these scraps and fragments into a biographical context, Werner explains the different purpose of her own edition: "My work initiates a break with this critical line by proposing that the most powerful 'revelations' of the drafts and fragments are not biographical but, rather, *textual*" (*Open Folios* 301 n. 3).

12. Werner talks about Dickinson's "word-paintings" (*Open Folios* 23), her "iconography of the page" (29), and the "shift from the lexical toward the visual" (15). This emphasis on the visual component of Dickinson's compositions is shared by Jerome McGann, who points out that Dickinson "decided to use her text page as a scene for dramatic interplays between a poetics of the eye and a poetics of the ear" ("Composition" 120).

13. An online version is also available at: ⟨http://www.hti.umich.edu/d/dickinson/⟩.

14. Combining "elements of popular storytelling, biographical analysis, textual theory, and close reading," *Open Me Carefully* makes use of advances both in feminist Dickinson criticism and in textual reproduction ("such as photographic representations of the fascicles that show Susan's marks on the poems") to present this "biography of a literary liaison" (Smith, " 'Open Me Carefully' " 22). Hart and Smith also point out that "twenty poems and one letter not previously associated with Susan are reproduced in this collection" (*Open Me* xxii).

15. See also McGann, who states that it "does no good to argue, as some might, that these odd lineations are unintentional—the result of Dickinson finding herself at the right edge of the page, and so folding her lines over" (*Black Riders* 28).

16. A related observation had already been made earlier by Franklin in his introduction to Dickinson's poems collected in fascicles. In the context of an ongoing controversy with Howe, Franklin asserts that the compositional unit of Dickinson's fascicles is the sheet (i.e., two leaves; *Manuscript Books* xii) and that line breaks of individual fascicle poems are "accidents of physical line breaks on the paper" (letter from Franklin to Howe, qtd. in Howe, "Some Notes" 12).

17. Mitchell also compares the manuscript of "Remembrance has a Rear and Front" contained in Set 10 with Susan's transcript of this poem, observing that "Susan dispensed with Dickinson's own lineation" ("Revising the Script" 727). He acknowledges, though, that "the Dickinson version I print . . . may not be the same one Susan received" (727). Mitchell also cites David Porter as another "conscientious objector" who hypothesizes that a possible explanation for Dickinson's line breaks may be medically inflected: "In the aesthetics of her scriptural forms, then, what is the function of Dickinson's disabling eye trouble and the probability that, as she wrote in pen then pencil, her impaired peripheral vision could not measure out spaces or reliably ascertain a sheet's edges where her hand-written lines began or finished or were interrupted?" (qtd. in Mitchell, "Revising the Script" 707; Porter, "Review Essay" 127).

18. This has also been noted by Franklin (*Poems* 1:32) and Mitchell ("Revising the Script" 717).

19. See also Loeffelholz's observation that "Franklin is much bolder than Johnson ever was in establishing a boundary between Dickinson's poetry and her prose" (458).

20. A wide range of critical responses to Franklin's edition of *Poems* can be found in the 1999 special issue of *The Emily Dickinson Journal* (8.2). One of the most frequently welcomed aspects is Franklin's decision to abandon Johnson's hierarchically inflected practice of determining

one copy text for each poem, and instead to print all known versions of any one poem in the same font size in chronological order, in this way "presenting those versions just about as democratically as the machinery of the book will allow" (Smith and Hart, "Gifts & Ghosts" 26; cf. also Crumbley, "*Variorum*" 12). Another highly appreciated feature is Franklin's scrupulous recording of the complex material details of Dickinson's texts (including fascicle placement, letter context, manuscript lineation, page breaks, stanza breaks, dating and transmission information, as well as publication history of each document) in the critical apparatus. At the same time, however, Smith and Hart, Crumbley, Mitchell, Wolosky, and others have also raised several points of criticism, all of which converge on the misleading impression of textual "stability" that Franklin's edition conveys. In several respects, these critics argue, Franklin's *Poems* proceeds to "fix" too quickly what in fact is and might always remain highly unstable. Examples include his at times arguable decisions on capitalization (Mitchell 42–43); his occasionally too precise dating, which occludes the fact that chronology might still be problematic (Smith and Hart 26; Wolosky 88); his decision to give titles to poems (Crumbley 16); the problem that textual details have to be reconstructed from the critical apparatus rather than having been incorporated into the copy texts (Smith and Hart 29; Wolosky 88); the ideological implications of having a separate critical apparatus for recording line breaks and word divisions (Mitchell 51); the imprecise description of paper size and embossments, paper wear, stains, pinholes, etc. (Smith and Hart 32); the reductive explanation of certain manuscript features that does not leave room for equally plausible alternative explanations (Smith and Hart 34–35); or "the new variorum's seeming resistance to the possibility of poetic innovation" (Crumbley 16).

21. Sometimes multiple variants of one poem (now only surviving in transcripts made by the respective recipients) were mailed to different addressees. See also Franklin's Appendix 7 for an exhaustive list of poems mailed to identifiable recipients.

22. Generally speaking, most prose or poetry manuscripts that were mailed to correspondents can be identified by some form of address. "When a manuscript is not addressed," Martha Nell Smith points out, "the fact that it has been folded does not necessarily mean that it was ever sent to a reader. Evidence suggests that Dickinson folded paper before writing on it to avoid writing directly over folds" (*Open Me* xxvii–xxviii).

23. Although he presents seventeen additional poems not contained in Johnson's *Poems*, including some of Johnson's prose fragments and metrical scraps from letters (such as Fr1676), Franklin also excludes five poems that had been included by Johnson (see Franklin's Appendix 9).

24. The complete context in the manuscript version reads: "She [the sky] will smile and look happy, and be full of | sunshine *then*—and even *should* she frown upon | her child returning, there is *another* sky ever | serene and fair, and there is *another* sun- | shine, tho' it be darkness there—never mind | faded forests, Austin, never mind silent fields— | *here* is a little forest whose leaf is ever green, | here is a *brighter* garden, where not a frost | has been, in its

unfading flowers I hear | the bright bee hum, prithee, my Brother, into *my* | garden come!" (Dickinson ms. 573–573a, Amherst; L58). This example has also been noted by Shurr (*New Poems* 4).

25. Johnson's *Poems* repeatedly tends to break up textual or syntactical units in order to extrapolate a "poem" from its "letter" context. Another illustrative example is his transcription of J1390 (Fr1416), variants of which were integrated in three different letters. In the manuscript version of L544, the text reads as follows: "These held their | Wick above the | West— | Till when the | Red declined— | Or how the | Amber aided it— | Defied to be | defined— || Then waned | without disparage | ment | In a disembling | Hue | That would not | let the Eye decide | Did it abide | or no—" (Houghton MS Am 1118.2 [46]; L544). In two other letters, however, Dickinson omits the first nine lines of the poem, while expanding the ending: "To wane | without | disparagement | In a dissembling | hue | That will not | let the Eye | decide | If it abide | or no | is Sunset's— | perhaps—only" (Houghton MS Am 1118.5 [B54]; L480). The variant in L486 differs slightly in lineation and capitalization but contains the same added final lines. Johnson, however, chooses L544 as the sole basis for his edition of J1390 in *Poems;* he edits the lines "is Sunset's— | perhaps—only" as "prose" in both L480 and L486, and fails to mention their existence as a variant of J1390 in his critical apparatus for this poem. Not only does such an insistence on fixed generic boundaries obscure contextual and intertextual references that play an important role in Dickinson's correspondence, it also invariably refuses to acknowledge the existence of Dickinson's generic borderblur. This problem is resolved in Franklin's edition (Fr1416), which lists all three versions copied into letters as well as a fourth version found among Dickinson's manuscripts and gives equal weight to each extant version. Furthermore, the line divisions, although relegated to the critical apparatus, nonetheless allow for an exact identification of the multiple variations of these lines by Dickinson's hand. Additional examples of Johnson's breakups of contextual units include J1265 (Fr1285) in L391; J1139 (Fr893) in L336; J1637 (Fr1674) in L975; J1584 (Fr1625) in L871; J739 (Fr737) in L294; J1222 (Fr1180) in L353; and J691 (Fr272) in L229. In the case of J691 (Fr272), Todd arranges these lines as prose paragraphs in both of her editions (1894, 214; 1931, 202), as does Bianchi in *Life and Letters* (247). McGann has commented on this passage that "in this case . . . the poem slips into the prose without any marginal signals that the textual rhythms are about to undergo a drastic shift" ("Visible Language" 258).

Sometimes Johnson's own lineation remains ambivalent as to the genre of a specific text, as for example in L912, or in L250. The latter consists of J1072/Fr194 ("Title divine—is mine!") and concludes with the lines "*Heres* —what I had | to 'tell you'— | You will tell no other? | Honor—is it's | own | pawn—" (Dickinson ms. 678a, Amherst; L250). Yet whenever Johnson is unable to make a definitive editorial decision, he adds an explanatory note indicative of his uneasiness. On J1637/Fr1674, incorporated in L975, for example, he comments: "It is impossible in such a *jeu d'esprit* to be sure where the prose leaves off and the poetry begins" (*Poems* 1122).

26. It is important to note, however, that Franklin only prints a short excerpt of the original

letter (the two sentences immediately preceding the "poem"), thus providing only part of rather than the entire context. This has also been critiqued by Martha Nell Smith and Ellen Louise Hart ("Gifts & Ghosts" 30) as well as Shira Wolosky ("Manuscript Body" 90) in relation to other examples. Smith and Hart cite Franklin's "40%" reduction of Sue's "Pony Express" letter, which deletes passages related to everyday activities and thus effectively "separates [Dickinson's] production of art from her conduct of everyday life" ("Gifts & Ghosts" 30).

27. Cf. also J1568/Fr1597, incorporated in L802: Dickinson's manuscript lineation de-emphasizes the triple anaphora and isocolon in lines 1–3 and the double anaphora in lines 5–6, whereas Johnson's lineation has the effect of specifically foregrounding those features of the poem. Additional changes in lineation that highlight rhymes in Dickinson's letter-poems can be found in J809/Fr951, incorporated into L305, and in L41. Dickinson's lineation regularly de-emphasizes rhymes by relegating them to an internal rather than an end position. J825/Fr898, for example, incorporated into L312, reads in its manuscript lineation: "An hour is a Sea | Between a few, and me— | With them would | Harbor | be—" (Houghton MS Am 1118.5 [B78]). Johnson's version of J825 in *Letters*, however, changes Dickinson's lineation to: "An Hour is a Sea | Between a few, and me— | With them would Harbor be—" (L312). The manuscript version of L356 reads like a prose note (with justified left and right margins): "Lest any doubt | that we are glad | that they were born | Today | Whose having lived | is held by us | in noble Holiday | Without the date, | like Consciousness | or Immortality— Emily—" (Houghton MS Am 1118.5 [B33]). In Johnson, however, it is lineated, arranged in heptameters, with a focus on end rhymes: "Lest any doubt that we are glad that they were born Today | Whose having lived is held by us in noble Holiday | Without the date, like Consciousness or Immortality— | Emily—" (L356).

28. For all these reasons, I have, throughout this study, provided my own transcriptions of Dickinson's manuscript letters and poems (with line breaks indicated by a vertical line [|]) whenever I specifically discuss manuscript features, and when I have been able to access the manuscript in question. If manuscript features do not bear directly on my interpretations, my quotations follow Johnson's and Franklin's respective print editions.

CHAPTER 3. THE "FEMALE" WORLD OF LOVE AND DUTY

1. See also Gilmore, who maintains that "the discourses and materials through which one may represent identity are culturally marked" (11). Altman specifically focuses on epistolary discourse when pointing out that "correspondences . . . have a great deal to tell us about the ways in which a culture's linguistic choices have promoted its social values and constructed the social identity of its citizens" ("Letter Book" 62).

2. An explanation for this definition of "woman" in exclusively relational terms is provided by Nancy F. Cott: "The identification of woman with the heart meant that she was defined *in relation to* other persons" (164–165).

3. Her letters to Jane T. Humphrey (1829–1908), who graduated from Mt. Holyoke Female Seminary in 1848, were written between 1842 and 1855. Emily Ellsworth Fowler Ford (1826–1893) and Abiah Palmer Root (1830–?) were Dickinson's schoolmates at Amherst Academy. The writer's correspondence with Fowler spans the years 1850–1854, with one extant letter written in 1874 and a final one in 1882; her epistolary exchange with Root lasts from 1845 to 1854. Dickinson's letters to other members of her Amherst circle of friends (Abby Wood, Harriet Merril, Sarah Tracy) are no longer extant.

4. Questions of religious conversion assumed particular urgency in the context of frequent revivals sweeping over Amherst during those years: "Last winter there was a revival here" (L10, 1846); "There is now a revival in College" (L11, 1846).

5. In the previous letter, Dickinson also confesses her inability to perform a frequently practiced exercise: "I cannot imagine with the farthest stretch of my imagination my own death scene" (L10). See also: "I tremble when I think how soon the weeks and days of this term will all have been spent, and my fate will be sealed, perhaps. I have neglected the *one thing needful* when all were obtaining it, and I may never, never again pass through such a season as was granted us last winter. . . . I regret that last term, when that golden opportunity was mine, that I did not give up and become a Christian" (L23); and: "I try to be right and good, and he [God] knows every one of my struggles" (L31).

6. Obligated, nonetheless, to perform *some* domestic duties, Dickinson envisions herself as martyr: "I have been at work, providing the 'food that perisheth,' scaring the timorous dust, and being obedient, and kind. . . . Father and Austin still clamor for food, and I, like a martyr am feeding them. Would'nt you love to see me in these bonds of great despair, looking around my kitchen, and praying for kind deliverance. . . . *My* kitchen I think I called it, God forbid that it was, or shall be my own—God keep me from what they call *households"* (L36).

7. See also Cott: "Religious activities can be seen as a means used by New England women to define self and find community" (138).

8. Although Dickinson regrets losing her friends, she nonetheless expresses a growing certainty about her own "deviant" path: "We are growing away from each other, and talk even now like strangers," she writes to Root. However, she self-confidently continues: "The shore is safer, Abiah, but I love to buffet the sea—I can count the bitter wrecks here in these pleasant waters, and hear the murmuring winds, but oh, I love the danger!" (L39). The "danger" Dickinson courts is indirectly associated with the writing of poetry: "Somehow or other I incline to other things—and Satan covers them up with flowers, and I reach out to pick them . . . it is so much easier to do wrong than right—so much pleasanter to be evil than good, I dont wonder that good angels weep—and bad ones sing songs" (L30). Dickinson's path is strewn with the flowers of rhetoric; she becomes the "bad" angel who sings songs. See also: "I have dared to do strange things—bold things, and have asked no advice from any—I have heeded beautiful tempters, yet do not think I am wrong" (L35).

9. Dickinson's differentiation between "woman" and "child" is an interesting one. Through its juxtaposition to womanhood, childhood becomes a state that not only precedes but pre-

vents the writer's transformation into the culturally constructed role of "woman." Yet this antithetical interpretation stands in marked contrast to the Victorian synonymity between "woman" and "child." As Grace Greenwood (Sara Jane Clarke) has pointed out: "True feminine genius is ever timid, doubtful, and clingingly dependent; a perpetual childhood" (qtd. in Welter 29). And Welter, citing *A Young Lady's Guide to the Harmonious Development of a Christian Character,* explains that "females should 'become as little children' and 'avoid a controversial spirit' " (30). Yet for Dickinson, childhood denotes a freedom from the constraints of female adulthood, a stage during which gender ascriptions are still suspended. To her brother, Austin, she writes in 1853: "I wish we were children now. I wish we were *always* children, how to grow up I dont know" (L115). Thus "childhood" constitutes Dickinson's temporary refusal to adopt the socially constructed role of woman before she eventually uses her letters to negotiate a wider range of different subject positions for herself.

10. Several letters to Abiah Root and Jane Humphrey cast the young women in the role of Dickinson's confidantes, privy to the writer's most intimate secrets. To Root Dickinson writes: "Please not let S. or any one see this letter. It is only for you" (L11). Similarly, her friend Jane Humphrey is also addressed as her "only" confidante: "Oh I have needed my trusty Jane . . . Oh Jennie, it would relieve me to tell you all, to sit down at your feet, and look in your eyes, and confess what *you only* shall know" (L35).

11. The last extant letter to Abiah Root concludes: "I thank you Abiah [for your invitation], but I dont go from home, unless emergency leads me by the hand, and then I do it obstinately, and draw back if I can. Should I ever leave home, which is improbable, I will with much delight, accept your invitation; till then, my dear Abiah, my warmest thanks are your's, but dont expect me. I'm so old fashioned, Darling, that all your friends would stare. I should have to bring my work bag, and my big spectacles, and I half forgot my grandchildren, my pincushion, and Puss—Why think of it seriously, Abiah—*do* you think it my *duty* to leave?" (L166). Johnson comments on this letter: "There is a finality to the last paragraph which suggests that this letter terminated the correspondence between them" (*Letters* 299). Farr has claimed that it is Root and Humphrey rather than Dickinson who end these friendships, yet the tone of finality in Dickinson's own letters suggests otherwise.

12. There are two additional letters addressed to Emily Fowler. Johnson notes that one letter (L421, written in 1874), "probably acknowledges a note of condolence from Emily [Fowler], written after the death of [Dickinson's father] Edward Dickinson" (*Letters* 530); the second letter (L728, 1882) was a thank-you note after Fowler had presented an inscribed copy of her book of poems, *My Recreations* (1872), to Sue and Austin Dickinson (*Letters* 748).

13. The degree of indefiniteness that Dickinson associates with the term *sometime* becomes explicit in Higginson's account of his visit to the Homestead. In a letter to his wife, he notes: "When I said I would come again *some time* she said 'Say in a long time, that will be nearer. Some time is nothing' " (L342b).

14. The following critics have identified a wide range of "masks" in Dickinson's texts. In his study *Emily Dickinson's Use of the Persona,* John Emerson Todd distinguishes between four

basic types of "supposed persons": "Little Girl," "Lover-Wife-Queen," "Personae in Death and Eternity," and "Personae Involving Psychology and the Divided Personality." These types are echoed by Robert Graham Lambert, who focuses on the little girl, the erotic child, the regal queen, and the martyr to love (xiv). Jane Eberwein, discussing Dickinson's patterns of "symbolic behavior" (17), augments this list by including, in addition to "child" and "bride," the roles of "aristocrat," "daisy," "corpse," "gothic figures," Judah, Khedive, "quester," "scholar," "sentimental figures," Socrates, and "watcher over the dying" (94–127). Paul Ferlazzo concentrates on the "tone" of Dickinson's roles: he distinguishes between playful, childish, and imperious personae, and discusses the three poses of Emilie, Scholar, and Rascal. In their analysis of Dickinson's self-mythologizing strategies, Sandra Gilbert and Susan Gubar concentrate on the tragic, and, specifically, the gothic aspects of the poet's roles. Other critics who have focused on questions of self-mythologizing are Cynthia Griffin Wolff, Judith Farr, S. Jaret McKinstry, and Elizabeth Phillips. The latter explores ways in which Dickinson employs dramatic monologues to dramatize her own life in literature through her "histrionic imagination" (4). Wolff analyzes how Dickinson's voices of child and wife "originate in a need to compensate for the indifference, inadequacies, or hostilities of an absent God" (*Emily Dickinson* 471). Most recently, Beth Maclay Doriani has suggested that, ultimately, all of Dickinson's poetic voices are based on biblical prophetic writings; she distinguishes between Dickinson as traveler to eternity, indicter, and consoler. Paul Crumbley regards "child" and "Queen" as the two poles of a continuum of personae, with "bride" at the center: "In the following chapters I divide Dickinson's speakers according to the voices of the child, the bride, and the Queen in order to represent paradigmatic relationships speakers have with conventional discourse, rather than as labels for unified identities. In general terms, the child communicates shock at the discovery that discourse limits personal power; the bride seeks to acquire personal power by conforming to discourse; the Queen proclaims personal power that exceeds containment in discourse" (*Inflections* 2–3).

15. This high degree of constructedness, performativity, and self-fashioning can often only be appreciated by reading her letters to different addressees in the context of one another (a privilege not available to most recipients of her letters). Thus, although the following examples of individual correspondences are discussed consecutively, they nonetheless have to be understood contextually.

16. The question of how to cite Susan Gilbert's name posits an interesting problem. As Martha Nell Smith explains: " 'Sister Sue' entered this life as Susan Huntington Gilbert and went through her early years as Susan Gilbert. Though she added Dickinson when she married, and of Gilbert kept only the initial G., styling herself Susan G. Dickinson, she dropped her married name for a while and was, though a wife, again Susan Gilbert; then she used Susan Gilbert Dickinson or dropped her father's name and was Susan Dickinson; finally she reassumed her middle name and died as Susan Huntington Dickinson" (*Rowing* 134–135). Given this complex history of her name, most critics, including Smith, have thus adopted the convention of referring to "Sue" by her first name only.

17. Erkkila has argued that "experiencing herself as hungry and insufficiently nurtured by either God the Father or her biological mother, in the early stages of their relationship Dickinson turned to Sue as a compensatory source of mother-religion and mother-love" (*Wicked Sisters* 33). I demonstrate, however, that it is Elizabeth Holland rather than Sue Gilbert who fulfills this role. Never delineated in "maternal" images, Sue usually tends to occupy the position of lover/beloved.

18. See also: "I tried to write to you. I had rather have *talked*" (L102); "Sometimes when I do feel so, I think it may be wrong, and that God will punish me [for asking for too much] by taking you away; for he is very kind to let me write to you, and to give me your sweet letters, but my heart wants *more*" (L85).

19. See also: "Susie, will you indeed come home next Saturday, and be my own again, and kiss me as you used to?" (L96); "Will you let me come dear Susie—looking just as I do, my dress soiled and worn, my grand old apron, and my hair—Oh Susie, time would fail me to enumerate my appearance, yet I love you just as dearly as if I was e'er so fine, so you wont care, will you?" (L73); "Oh my darling one" (L73); "I would nestle close to your warm heart" (L74); "Thank you for loving me, darling, and *will* you 'love me more if ever you come home'?—it is enough, dear Susie, I know I shall be satisfied. But what can I do towards you?—*dearer* you *cannot* be, for I love you so already, that it almost breaks my heart—perhaps I can love you *anew*, every day of my life, every morning and evening—Oh if you will let me, how happy I shall be!" (L74); "And I do love to run fast—and hide away from them all; here in dear Susie's bosom, I know is love and rest, and I never would go away, did not the big world call me, and beat me for not working" (L85); "Loved One, thou knowest" (L88); "I add a kiss, shyly, lest there is somebody there! Dont let them see, *will* you Susie?" (L94); "I love you as dearly, Susie, as when love first began, on the step at the front door, and under the Evergreens" (L177). Dickinson's love for Sue at times becomes overpowering: "Oh Susie, I often think that I will try to tell you how very dear you are, and how I'm watching for you, but the words wont come, tho' the *tears* will, and I sit down disappointed—yet darling, you know it all . . . in thinking of those I love, my reason is all gone from me, and I do fear sometimes that I must make a hospital for the hopelessly insane, and chain me up there such times, so I wont injure you" (L77).

20. A poem included in L105 is introduced with the lines: "*Write! Comrade, write!*"

21. Erkkila follows Farr and Sewall, among others, in reading L173 as an indication for a break in their relationship, arguing that "a difference of class and privilege" might have been at the root of this problem (*Wicked Sisters* 34). Paula Bennett distinguishes between Dickinson the woman and Dickinson the poet, suggesting that the woman's relationship to Sue may have become strained, whereas to the poet, Sue remained the same ("Orient" 117). Martha Nell Smith and Ellen Louise Hart, on the other hand, maintain that no breach in the Dickinson-Sue friendship occurred (Hart, "Encoding" 251; cf. Smith, *Rowing* 164–167). Dorothy Huff Oberhaus has suggested a possible explanation for the theory of an estrangement between the two women; she regards it as a malignant rumor created by Mabel Loomis Todd (Sue's husband's

lover), and later upheld by her daughter Millicent Todd Bingham, who "pictured Sue as cruel and vindictive and claimed that Sue and Emily Dickinson's relationship was distant, even hostile" ("In Defense" 5). Oberhaus points out that none of Dickinson's letters to Sue, for example, had been printed in either of Todd's editions of Dickinson's letters (6), and that Todd never responded to Higginson's suggestion to use Sue's obituary as a preface (Oberhaus, "In Defense" 6; Bingham, *Ancestors' Brocades* 61–62, 178–179). Hart and Smith's most recent edition of Dickinson's intimate letters to Sue strives to confirm their own earlier position, highlighting both the literary as well as the emotional bond and enduring intimacy between the two women by drawing attention to the significance of the high degree of informality (untypical of other epistolary exchanges) to be found in their letters (*Open Me* 148).

Most recently, however, this argument has again been challenged by Agnieszka Salska and Ralph Franklin. The latter notices a reduction in the number of poems sent to Sue over the years (*Poems* 1:29), an observation corroborated by Salska, who argues that with the beginning of Dickinson's correspondence with Higginson, "Sue's role as Emily's literary authority seems here to have come to an end" ("Dickinson's Letters" 170). Whether or not Higginson actually displaced Sue in the role of literary advisor remains arguable; yet what becomes clear from Dickinson's letters and poems to Sue is that their (love) relationship had not been without tensions—in spite of, or maybe rather because of, the fact that Dickinson's love and desire for her sister-in-law seems not to have abated over the years.

22. See also the letter-poem (addressed "Sue"), "Could *I*—then—shut the door— | Lest *my* beseeching face—at last— | Rejected—be—of *Her?*" (J220/Fr188A, 1861); and "To own a Susan of my own | Is of itself a Bliss— | Whatever Realm I forfeit, Lord, | Continue me in this!" (J1401/Fr1436A, 1877).

23. At the same time, Hart and Smith highlight the later resolution of these differences, thus striving to "discount the popular claim that the two women had nothing to do with each other in these final years" by pointing out that "it is Susan who nurses Emily through her last days" (*Open Me* 203, 204).

24. Johnson remarks that " 'Dollie' was a pet name for Sue" (*Poems* 113).

25. The term "Child" was specifically chosen for the version sent to Sue. The fascicle variant of this line reads, "The Love a Life can show Below" (Fr285B).

26. Dickinson's love for Sue is expressed in less equivocal terms in several other poems directly addressed or mailed to her (several of them were often specifically personalized for her—in contrast to extant fascicle copies). J809/Fr951A: "Unable are the Loved—to die— | For Love is immortality— | Nay—it is Deity—" (J809/Fr951A, 1865). Several times, she envisions a mystical marriage with Sue/God: "Given in Marriage unto Thee | Oh Thou Celestial Host— | Bride of the Father and the Son, | Bride of the Holy Ghost" (J817/Fr818A, 1864). A similar thought is echoed in J1072/Fr194B. Here, however, the marriage ends on the deathbed ("shrouded"); the bride becomes "Empress of Calvary": "Title divine, is mine. | The Wife without the Sign— | Acute Degree conferred on me— | Empress of Calvary— | Royal, all but the Crown— | Betrothed, without the Swoon | God gives us Women— | When You

hold Garnet to Garnet— | Gold—to Gold— | Born—Bridalled—Shrouded— | In a Day— | Tri Victory— | 'My Husband'— Women say | Stroking the Melody— | Is this the Way" (J1072/Fr194B, 1865). In addition, J446/Fr346A can be read as a failed attempt at seduction. Only at the moment of her death can Dickinson secure the addressee's attention: "I showed her Hights she never saw— | 'Would'st Climb,' I said? | She said—'Not so'— | 'With *me*—' I said—With *me*? | I showed her Secrets—Morning's Nest— | The Rope the Nights were put across— | And *now*—'Would'st have me for a Guest?' | She could not find her Yes— | And then, I brake my life—And Lo, | A Light, for her, did solemn glow, | The larger, as her face withdrew— | And *could* she, further, 'No'?" (J446/Fr346A, 1862).

27. In L88 (1852), even prior to Sue's engagement, Dickinson had already reflected upon the ways in which a textual representation could be a possible replacement for the physical person "lost" to a husband: "I have heard all about the journal. . . . I want you to get it bound—at my expense—Susie —so when he takes you from me, to live in his new home, I may have *some* of you. I am sincere."

28. Martha Nell Smith has pointed out that after Sue and Austin Dickinson had moved into the Evergreens (where they lived from 1858 until 1886, the year of Dickinson's death), Dickinson sent 405 items next door to Sue, compared with 3 to her brother (*Rowing* 247 n. 16). Many critics have commented on Dickinson's textual interaction with her sister-in-law. Juhasz emphasizes the aesthetic advantage of physical distance: "Paradoxically, literal or physical separation promotes and provokes aesthetic union, so that while Dickinson the seducer wishes Sue to love her enough to come to her, Dickinson the writer needs the very physical distance she decries" ("Reading" 179). She further argues that "Dickinson's tendency to associate her correspondence with Sue with literary figures and techniques suggests that conducting this relationship is as much an aesthetic problem as an emotional one" (179). This opinion is also shared by Sullivan, who describes L912, in particular, as "a curious example both of Dickinson's extreme attachment to her friend, and her self-acknowledgment that such an attachment can prevent, rather than foster, interviews" (48). Sullivan concludes that "Sue's name begins to stand for an abstract idea of friendship rather than a particular friend" (45). Smith, arguing that Sue became Dickinson's poetry critic, collaborator, and possibly coauthor, views their exchange of letters as an extension of their collaboration: "Dickinson makes sharing language with one another central to her intimacy with Sue. Therefore, her dreams of physical intimacy with Sue evolve into reverie imagined in a setting suggesting linguistic coition" (*Rowing* 167). Smith thus regards Dickinson and Sue as participating in a "literary dialogue" (130), taking place in an "imaginary world insulated from society" (169). She refers to the poem "Wild Nights," for example, as a place constructed by the imagination (170).

29. Sue's distance and inaccessibility are emphasized in poem after poem addressed to her: "Distance—is not the Realm of Fox | Nor by Relay of Bird | Abated—Distance is | Until thyself, Beloved" (J1155/Fr1128A, 1866); or: "I sometimes remember we are to die, and hasten toward the Heart which how could I woo in a rendezvous where there is no Face?" (L856, about 1883). In J1664/Fr1708A, Death prevents the encounter: "I did not reach Thee

| But my feet slip nearer every day | Three Rivers and a Hill to cross | One Desert and a Sea | I shall not count the journey one | When I am telling thee || Two deserts but the Year is cold | So that will help the sand | One desert crossed— | The second one | Will feel as cool as land | Sahara is too little price | To pay for thy Right hand || The Sea comes last—Step merry feet | So short we have to go | To play together we are prone | But we must labor now | The last shall be the lightest load | That we have had to draw | The Sun goes crooked— | That is Night | Before he makes the bend | We must have passed the Middle Sea | Almost we wish the End | Were further off | Too great it seems | So near the Whole to stand | We step like Plush | We stand like snow | The waters murmur new | Three rivers and the Hill are passed | Two deserts and the sea! | Now Death usurps my Premium | And gets the look at Thee" (J1664/Fr1708A, undated).

30. I thus disagree with critics such as Adalaide Morris, who defines Dickinson's relationship with Sue in terms of "equality" and "reciprocity" (102, 107).

31. Cf. also: "Savior! I've no one else to tell— | And so I trouble *thee*. | I am the one forgot thee so— | Dost thou remember me?" (J217/Fr295A, 1862); "'Remember me' implored the Thief— | Oh Magnanimity! | My Visitor in Paradise | I give thee Guaranty. || That Courtesy will fair remain | When the Delight is Dust | With which we cite this Mightiest case | of Compensated Trust. || Of All, we are allowed to hope | But Affidavit stands | That this was due, where some, we fear, | Are unexpected friends" (J1180/Fr1208C, 1873).

32. Dickinson also uses references to *Antony and Cleopatra* in her correspondence with Judge Otis Lord, which induces Farr to argue: "In this way Dickinson makes of *Antony and Cleopatra* a referential world in whose exhilarated light her own emotions might be measured and expressed. . . . [S]he . . . links personal to Shakespearean contexts" ("'Engulfing'" 235). Paula Bennett, having examined the Shakespeare edition in Dickinson's family library, comments that it "shows signs of habitual use"; in particular, Bennett continues, the two tragedy volumes "have broken spines and loose pages," and *Antony and Cleopatra* seems the most well-read of all plays ("Orient" 108). Bennett suggests that "Dickinson used the playwright's ambiguity to find mirrors for herself" (108). Farr, maintaining that Dickinson's preference for this play "sheds light on Emily Dickinson as a person and a poet" ("'Engulfing'" 231), argues that "it was typical of Dickinson to assign to *Antony and Cleopatra* a private set of meanings, which she explored in letters and poems for those she knew" (232).

33. Dickinson's strategy, as Bennett and Farr have demonstrated, is—rather than quoting entire passages—to rely on Sue's familiarity with the context of the quoted lines; it is for this reason that Dickinson's allusions to *Antony and Cleopatra* are "exceedingly cryptic, . . . designed to set off reverberations in the reader's mind" (Bennett, "Orient" 110). Farr has pointed out that this was one of two passages Dickinson had marked in Sue's copy of *Antony and Cleopatra*. The other passage was the "Age cannot wither her" speech ("'Engulfing'" 240).

34. A similar idea is expressed in L554: "Susan knows she is a Siren—and that at a word from her, Emily would forfeit Righteousness."

35. Similarly, J299/Fr418A also reverberates in the context of the above quoted passage

from *Antony and Cleopatra.* In this poem, the "Queen" is no longer metonymically referred to as just "Egypt," but becomes a conglomerate of places associated with gold and treasures. The letter-poem concludes with the remark, "Dear Sue— | You see I remember— | Emily" (qtd. in Franklin, *Poems* 1:441), and reads: "Your—Riches—taught me—poverty! | Myself, a 'Millionaire' | In little—wealths—as Girls can boast— | Till broad as 'Buenos Ayre' | You drifted your Dominions— | A Different—Peru— | And I esteemed—all—poverty— | For Life's Estate—with you! || Of 'Mines'—I little know—myself— | But just the *names*—of *Gems*— | The *Colors*—of the *Commonest*— | And scarce of Diadems— | So much—that did I meet *the Queen*— | Her glory—I should know— | But *this*—must be a *different Wealth*— | To miss it—beggars—so! || I'm sure 'tis *'India'*—all day— | To those who look on you— | Without a stint—without a blame— | Might I—but be the Jew! | I know it is 'Golconda'— | Beyond my power to dream— | To have a smile—for mine—each day— | How *better*—than a *Gem*! || At least—it solaces—to know— | That there *exists*—a *Gold* | Altho' I prove it, just in time— | It's distance—to behold! | It's far—far—Treasure—to surmise— | And estimate—the Pearl— | That slipped—my simple fingers—thro' | While yet a Girl—at School!" (J299/Fr418A, 1862). Beginning as a celebration of the wealth Sue contributed to their friendship, the poem's second half, however, focuses on the "Queen's" absence, which reduces Dickinson to a "beggar"; no longer among those who are privileged to "look" on her, the writer's only "solace" is "to know— | That there *exists*—a *Gold.*"

36. A translation of the *Vita Nuova,* introduced and discussed by Charles Eliot Norton, was serialized in the *Atlantic Monthly* between January and March 1859 under the title *The New Life of Dante.*

Mirabeau's love letters to Sophie were written while he served a sentence for their illicit love affair and elopement; Swift's *Journal* was composed at a time when the addressee, Esther Johnson, was living in Ireland with her companion Rebecca Dingley; and Dante's *Vita Nuova* talks about his youthful love for a woman who eventually gets married to someone else and later dies.

37. Mirabeau develops a secret code for their correspondence, using the pet name "Mimi" for Sophie; Beatrice is likewise acknowledged as a code name; and Swift writes under the pseudonym "Presto" (Italian for "Swift"), addressing Esther as "Stella."

38. A large number of poems thematize nature (which is frequently personified as female): J716/Fr495 ("The Day undressed—Herself"), J1075/Fr1121 ("The Sky is low—the Clouds are mean," ending with the lines, "Nature, like Us is sometimes caught | Without her Diadem"), J1265/Fr1285 ("The most triumphant Bird I ever knew or met"), J1333/Fr1356 ("A little Madness in the Spring"), J1336/Fr1371 ("Nature assigns the Sun"), J1363/Fr1411 ("Summer laid her simple Hat"), J1405/Fr1426 ("Bees are Black, with Gilt Surcingles"), J1514/Fr1544 ("An Antiquated Tree"), and J1570/Fr1600 ("Forever honored be the Tree"). In addition, domestic imagery is emphasized in J17/Fr66 ("Baffled for just a day or two"). A third cluster of poems concentrates on issues of faith, afterlife, and the Bible—issues typically gendered female within the discourse of "true womanhood": J1162/Fr1178 ("The Life we

have is very great. | The Life that we shall see | Surpasses it, we know, because | It is Infinity"), J1491/Fr1525 ("The Road to Paradise is plain"), and J1569/Fr1598 ("The Clock strikes one that just struck two— | Some schism in the Sum— | A Vagabond for Genesis | Has wrecked the Pendulum"). Moreover, J1334/Fr1352 ("How soft this Prison is"), J1396/Fr1453 ("She laid her docile Crescent down"), J1515/Fr1564 ("The Things that never can come back, are several"), J1517/Fr1567 ("How much of Source escapes with thee"), and J1606/Fr1632 ("Quite empty, quite at rest, | The Robin locks her Nest, and tries her Wings") concentrate on death, with J88/Fr78 describing the task of watching over the dying, a task primarily performed by women in nineteenth-century New England: "As by the dead we love to sit, | Become so wondrous dear— | As for the lost we grapple | Tho' all the rest are here."

39. L866 (1883) is signed "your dependent Emily."

40. Erkkila has argued that Dickinson plays the role of the *rebellious* daughter in her letters to Holland (*Wicked Sisters* 25), yet the postures assumed by Dickinson highlight much more her *dependency*. Holland is the only correspondent with whom Dickinson maintains this role of dependent "child" throughout her life—they span a much larger time period than her "child" poses in her letters to Sue.

41. Throughout Dickinson's correspondence with Holland, references to spiritual issues as well as Bible quotations abound.

42. Dickinson also, curiously enough, asks Holland for advice on matters related to *her own* area of expertise, letter writing: Having "fled" from visitors, she intends to send a note of apology, and asks Holland: "I write a little note to him, saying I am sorry, and will he forgive me, and remember it no more? Now will I ask so much of you, that you read it for me, judge if it is said as yourself would say it, were *you* rude instead of me" (L202).

43. See, among others, L133, L181, L318, L399, L487, L544, L731, L738, L792, L802; L182, L195, L207, L492, L502, L542, L619, L689, L721, L888, L901.

44. According to Jay Leyda, a copy of Coventry Patmore's *The Angel in the House* was owned by Sue Gilbert, with whom Dickinson regularly exchanged books. Leyda quotes from Sue's *Annals of the Evergreens*, in which she recalls Emerson's visit to her home in December 1857: "He seemed greatly pleased to find Coventry Patmore's "Angel in the House" . . . on the library table, which we were just reading, and praised it with great warmth" (1:351).

45. Tingley quotes from Harriette Merrick Plunkett's 1895 biography of Holland's husband, in which Holland's appearance is described at the time of their marriage: "She was of medium height, but looked fairly petite beside the tall and stalwart figure of her husband" (25–26, qtd. in "Holland Letters" 196 n. 4). See also "my tiny friend" (L269); "our little sister" (L311; L377); "I take Mrs Browning's little Basket to bring the note to you . . . Your little Note protected . . . Your little Trip still lingers, for is not all petite you do—you are such a Linnet?" (L547); "Little Mrs Holland" (L619); "my Little Sister" (L687); "You always seemed to me like David and Goliath, and if Goliath is not as strong, David is needed more, but David is competent—in his—her—small—pathetic Hands, there is strength for both" (L687); "your little hand" (L742); "I hope the large sons are docile to their little Mother" (L792); in L805,

Dickinson asks for "a little news of the ill Linnet"; "You always were a Wren, you know, the tenant of a Twig—" (L950); "Little Child Wife" (L738); "Little Sister. I miss your childlike Voice" (L399).

CHAPTER 4. THE "MALE" WORLD OF POWER AND POETRY

1. The vast majority of Dickinson's letters to Austin are written during the years 1842–1854, when he had left Amherst to attend Williston Seminary and, later, to teach at Sunderland and at the Endicott School in Boston. There are only three extant letters written after 1854: L240 (1861), L954 (1882), and L997 (1885). Though it is possible that Austin simply did not save Dickinson's later letters, it seems equally likely that Dickinson stopped writing to her brother once he had moved into the Evergreens because they saw each other frequently enough to render any large-scale epistolary role reconstructions futile. It may also be the case that Dickinson no longer felt compelled to redefine sibling relations once Austin's engagement to Sue (in November 1853) signals his intention to start his own family.

2. She also refers to her father as "my rheumatic sire" in this letter.

3. Cf. Dickinson's reference to Austin's conflicts with his father: "I do think it's so funny—you and father do nothing but 'fisticuff' all the while you're at home, and the minute you are separated, you become such devoted friends; but this is a checkered life" (L108).

4. Austin's public life as a teacher is frequently identified with power and kingdoms. Dickinson calls him "Rabbi-Master" and says: "Oh how I wish I could see your world and it's little kingdoms, and I wish I could see the King—Stranger—he was my *Brother!*" (L48). Austin had already been associated with Jove "sitting on great 'Olympus'" in an earlier letter; upon his graduation from Amherst College in 1850, Dickinson regards him as her superior and expresses envy at his elevated status: "Suppose 'Topknot' should come down, and speak to his brothers, and sisters, . . . suppose he should doff his crown, and lay down his lofty sceptre, and once more a patient child receive reproof, and correction, salute the insulted rod, and bow to the common Lord! . . . Permit me to tie your shoe, to run like a dog behind you. . . . Permit me to be a stick, to show how I will not beat you, a stone, how I will not fling, musquito, I will not sting. . . . Herein I 'deign to condescend to stoop so low,' what a high hill between me, and thee, a *hill*, upon my word, it is a *mountain*, I dare not climb. Let's call it 'Alp,' or '*Ande*,' or yet the 'Ascension Mount.' I have it!—you shall be 'Jove' a sitting on great 'Olympus,' a whittling the lightnings out, and hurling at your relations. Oh, 'Jupiter'! fie! for shame! *Kings* sometimes have fathers and mothers" (L37). Juhasz was the first to point out that Dickinson's relationship with her brother is characterized by a certain degree of competition based on gender differences: Austin "inspired her jealousy because he was male and therefore able to be and do, with ease, those things she wanted for herself" ("Reading" 173).

5. In another poem addressed to her brother, Dickinson expresses her dissatisfaction with her own role: "The Grass so little has to do— | A Sphere of simple Green— | With only Butterflies to brood | And Bees to entertain— || And stir all day to pretty Tunes | The

Breezes fetch along— | And hold the Sunshine in it's lap | And bow to everything— || And thread the Dews, all night, like Pearls— | And make itself so fine | A Duchess were too common | For such a noticing— || And even when it dies—to pass | In Odors so divine— | Like Lowly spices, lain to sleep— | Or Spikenards, perishing— || And then, in Sovreign Barns to dwell— | And dream the Days away, | The Grass so little has to do | I wish I were a Hay" (J333/Fr379).

6. Crumbley sees Dickinson's first letter to Higginson as the beginning of her employment of "distinct voices as strategic attempts to elicit certain responses or test reader acuity" (*Inflections* 79). Yet in order to orchestrate specific relationships, she had utilized voices earlier, as we have seen in particular in her correspondence with Austin.

7. As explained below, Dickinson employs the term *scholar* in the sense of "student" or "pupil" rather than that of independent, established "expert."

8. A variant of this statement was also included in a letter to James Clark (L788). Cf. also the above-quoted statement, "When I state myself, as the Representative of the Verse—it does not mean—me—but a supposed person" (L268). Marlene Kadar has pointed out the unusualness of this strategy: "autobiography, letters, diaries, and anthropological life narratives [are] genres in which the conventional expectation is that the author does not want to pretend he/she is absent from the text" ("Coming to Terms" 12).

9. See also Erika Scheurer, who describes speech as a "closed" instance of enunciation, associated with voice and presence: "At the moment of speech, then, the stratifying and unifying forces in language unite" (89).

10. "I should have liked to see you, before you became improbable. War feels to me an oblique place—Should there be other Summers, would you perhaps come?" (L280).

11. Dickinson would later use Higginson's own authority in the same way, asking him to support her refusal to contribute a poem to Roberts Brothers's *No Name Series* on Helen Hunt Jackson's request: "Are you willing to tell me what is right? . . . She [Jackson] was so sweetly noble, I would regret to estrange her, and if you would be willing to give me a note saying you disapproved it, and thought me unfit, she would believe you" (L476). And in the following letter: "But may I tell her just the same that you dont prefer it? Thank you, if I may, for it almost seems sordid to refuse from myself again" (L477).

12. After his first visit, Dickinson repeatedly expressed a desire to see Higginson again (see, for example, L546 and L553). Later, however, she returns to her former hesitancy: "I should rejoice to see you, and had earnestly asked you to my Home with your sweet friend, but for a Cowardice of Strangers I cannot resist, and my Mother's illness" (L735). Higginson's second—and last—visit took place on December 3, 1873.

13. As I demonstrate below, the tension apparent in Dickinson's ambivalent self-description as "small" (insignificant) yet "bold" (self-confident) is at the center of her discursively constructed subject positions throughout her entire correspondence with Higginson.

14. In a letter to Louise Norcross, Dickinson repeats her preference for words as being more "vivid" than actual faces: "Do you remember what you said the night you came to me? I secure

that sentence. If I should see your face no more it will be your portrait, and if I should, more vivid than your mortal face. We must be careful what we say" (L379). Referring to J170/Fr174 as "Dickinson's tribute to portrait painting," Farr emphasizes that the poet "regards a good portrait as more evocative of the inner self than the appearance of a subject in real life" (*Passion* 21). Farr ultimately relates this preference to Dickinson's regard for the artistic use of language as "a mysterious form of revelation" (23) by drawing attention to an article in the *Leipziger Anzeiger*, published around the time of Dickinson's letter to Higginson: "Wanting to hold fast to transitory mirror-pictures is . . . blasphemy. Man is created in the image of God, and God's image cannot be captured in any man-made machine" (qtd. in *Passion* 22).

15. Higginson, on the other hand, had made a point of assuring Dickinson of his stable identity: "I am always the same toward you" (L330a).

16. Whereas the form "E. Dickinson" also occurs in letters to other correspondents, Higginson is the only addressee for whom Dickinson adopts this form before her father's death.

17. Ironically, Dickinson's own father failed to perform this role: "Father, too busy with his Briefs—to notice what we do—He buys me many Books—but begs me not to read them" (L261).

18. Martha Nell Smith has kindly supplied me with the information that the card in question was one of Dickinson's calling cards, bearing her full name in the form of "Emily E. Dickinson."

19. See also R. Miller 43.

20. See also Martha Nell Smith, who has emphasized that "the women writers so popular [during the nineteenth century] were routinely characterized in periodicals and newspapers as not really producing literature" (*Rowing* 136).

21. That she did not adopt a (male) pseudonym might have been the result of Higginson's own disparaging remarks in his "Letter to a Young Contributor," the article to which Dickinson's first letter was a direct response. In this essay, Higginson mockingly refers to "My dear young Cecil Dreemes of literature who superscribe their offered manuscripts with very masculine names in very feminine handwriting" (qtd. in R. Miller 43). Advocating utmost simplicity and directness, Higginson also strongly objected to pseudonyms, poking fun at Abigail Adams, who "wrote a letter asking John Adams to buy her a supply of cheap pins, and signed it 'Portia' " ("Women's Letters" 114). Thus a viable and inoffensive strategy to defer the revelation of her (female) identity was to enclose her name in an extra envelope.

22. From the second letter onward, Dickinson invites Higginson to become her "friend." She signs L261 as "Your friend, E—Dickinson," and addresses him in the following letter as "Dear friend" (L265); the signature in this, as in L290, is again "Your friend E Dickinson."

23. Cf. also L261, L319, L457, L503.

24. See also Shira Wolosky, who reads Dickinson's decision not to publish as an indication that "she both would and would not incarnate herself in texts" (95). Ultimately, for Wolosky, "Dickinson's inhibition against inhabiting textual body is deeply inscribed within her contemporary (and in many ways, our continuing) women's culture" (95).

25. Crumbley has related Dickinson's use of dashes to "the frequency of voice shifts and the degree to which Dickinson grants or challenges Higginson's authority at any particular moment" (*Inflections* 79).

26. I thus disagree with the more one-dimensional interpretations of the Higginson-Dickinson relationship, such as Lambert's, for example: "Emily's need for masculine domination is further reflected in her choice of Higginson as her ostensible literary advisor" (xiv).

27. Cf. also: "You spoke of Pippa Passes—I never heard anybody speak of Pippa Passes—before. You see my posture is benighted" (L268); "You say I confess the little mistake, and omit the large—Because I can see Orthography—but the Ignorance out of sight—is my Preceptor's charge" (L271).

28. Dickinson also frequently refers to Higginson as "Master": "There is no one so happy her Master is happy as his grateful Pupil" (L575); "That it is true, Master, is the Power of all you write" (L449); "Twice you have gone—Master—Would you but once come" (L413).

29. Cf. also: "I will be patient—constant, never reject your knife and should my . . . slowness goad you, you knew before myself that Except the smaller size" (L316); "If you truly consent, I recite, now" (L268); "I am happy to be your scholar, and will deserve the kindness, I cannot repay" (L268).

30. "Who were 'the Father and the Son' " (J1258/Fr1280), also comments on Dickinson's lack of faith. And in L268, she encloses J324/Fr236, "Some keep the Sabbath going to Church— | I keep it, staying at Home." This pronounced disinterest in religious matters is even more striking in the context of the fact that Higginson "had graduated from Harvard's Divinity School and had been a pastor of a Unitarian Church in Newburyport from 1847 to 1849 and of a 'Free Church' in Worcester from 1852 to 1861" (Ferlazzo 135), and that Dickinson constantly emphasized her need of Elizabeth Holland's spiritual guidance. The—first and last—time Dickinson expressly refers to Higginson's former career as a pastor and asks for religious instruction is much later in their friendship: "Would you explain it [immortality] to me? I was told you were once a Clergyman. It comforts an instinct if another have felt it too" (L503).

31. In some ways, this metaphor has an even more critical implication: like the compass's needle, Higginson may only be capable of pointing in one direction (the traditional way of writing poetry); he is unable to appreciate the more experimental forms.

32. Another poem sent to Higginson also dwells on the self-destructive aspect of her poetic voice: "Dare you see a Soul *at the White Heat?* | Then crouch within the door— | Red—is the Fire's common tint— | But when the vivid Ore | Has vanquished Flame's conditions, | It quivers from the Forge | Without a color, but the light | Of unannointed Blaze. | Least Village has it's Blacksmith | Whose Anvil's even ring | Stands symbol for the finer Forge | That soundless tugs—within— | Refining these impatient Ores | With Hammer, and with Blaze | Until the Designated Light | Repudiate the Forge" (J365/Fr401).

33. Cf. also Porter: "She was encouraged in her choice by the wording in the critic's article,

encouraged even to represent her work by a greater proportion of irregularly formed verses than in fact existed in the whole of her work to that date" (*Art* 10).

34. This was pointed out to me by Martha Nell Smith.

35. See also: "I hope you will not cease to trust me and turn to me; and I will try to speak the truth to you, and with love" (L405a). That Higginson's efforts to please Dickinson are not entirely genuine, however, can be inferred from his less charitable comments to his sister. On December 28, 1876, he refers to "one imaginary letter to me from my partially cracked poetess at Amherst, who writes to me & signs 'Your scholar' " (qtd. in Johnson and Ward, *Letters* 570). And on December 9, 1873: "I saw my eccentric poetess Miss Emily Dickinson . . . I'm afraid Mary's [his wife's] other remark 'Oh why do the insane so cling to you?' still holds" (qtd. in Johnson and Ward, *Letters* 519).

36. Thus I disagree with critics such as Lambert who regard Dickinson's relationship with Higginson as growing in confidence (75).

37. That Dickinson was indeed acutely concerned with maintaining a power differentiation between herself and Higginson is illustrated by the following poem, mailed to Mary Bowles, which uses closely related patterns of metaphor and semantic fields to sketch a quite divergent self-articulation: "My River runs to thee— | Blue Sea! Wilt welcome me? | My River waits reply— | Oh Sea—look graciously— | I'll fetch thee Brooks | From spotted nooks— | *Say*—Sea— | Take *Me*!" (Dickinson ms. 669a, Amherst; L235). While the "Brook" in J1210/Fr1275C adamantly resists the "Sea's" invitation, the "River" in L235, on the other hand, begs to be "taken," swallowed up by the "Sea," and even offers to collect other "Brooks" in return. And although, in her letters to Higginson, Dickinson repeatedly associates her smallness with insignificance and the need for guidance ("My size felt small—to me" [L261; April 1862]), she at the same time correlates smallness with strength and the potential for support and leadership in a letter to Mary Bowles written in spring 1862: "when your life gets faint for it's other life—you can lean on us—We wont break, Mary. We look very small—but the Reed can carry weight" (L262).

38. See also Juhasz, who talks of Dickinson as maintaining "the ritual of compliment and courtship" ("Reading" 183), and suggests that "finally . . . she must have understood that she had chosen poorly. For slowly the urgency goes out of their correspondence" (185).

39. Critical fascination with conventional notions of amorous mysteries has led to a vast body of controversial readings of these letters in an attempt to identify the addressee as Dickinson's elusive "lover," whose existence was first hinted at by her sister-in-law Susan Gilbert, and later enshrined by Martha Dickinson Bianchi. Two of the most frequently advanced candidates for "Master" are Samuel Bowles, editor of the *Springfield Republican*, and the pulpit orator Reverend Charles Wadsworth. Dickinson's authoritative biographer Richard Sewall identifies Bowles as the possible addressee, a view also shared by, among others, George Frisbee Whicher, David Higgins, Ruth Miller, Theodora Ward, Thomas H. Johnson, and, most recently, Bill Arnold. John Evangelist Walsh, Barton Levi St. Armand, and Cynthia

Griffin Wolff have suggested Judge Otis Lord; Benjamin Lease relates Dickinson's crisis in the "Master" letters to a crisis in Wadsworth's life and argues that these letters stylistically echo passages from Wadsworth's sermons (10). Wadsworth had been advanced earlier by William H. Shurr, who offers a marriage narrative complete with pregnancy and possible abortion. Lillian Faderman and Adalaide Morris, on the other hand, were the first to challenge the assumption that the recipient of the "Master" letters is necessarily male. Characteristic of many of these critical positions is a pervasive ambivalence about the nature of "Master," ranging from insistence on a concrete, identifiable referent to reading him/her as a self-referential and/or literary construct (the latter position is shared by Albert Gelpi, Wendy Martin, Joanne Feit Diehl, Betsy Erkkila, Judith Farr, Susan Howe, and Martha Nell Smith, among others). Although Dickinson's reference to her "Master's" "beard" as well as her use of masculine pronouns suggests a male identity, we cannot be sure whether this is merely an epistolary construct to highlight that person's "male" qualities. Examining the manuscript version of the line "but if I had the Beard on my cheek—like you" (L233), Martha Nell Smith even comes to the conclusion that the phrase that clearly identifies the letter's addressee as male ("like you") has only been added on as a kind of "afterthought": "the handwriting is different enough from the inked script of the main body of the letter to suggest that the addition was made at a much different time—chronologically or psychically" (*Rowing* 113). Although Smith is "most comfortable with the conclusion that Dickinson made the revision herself" (240 n. 17), she nevertheless surmises that "anxiety" over the potentially lesbian interpretation may also have prompted someone else to insert this revisionary phrase.

40. Although Johnson and Ward list this as the third of the "Master" letters, Franklin has argued that L248 was most likely written before L233.

41. Cf. also "Low at the knee that bore her once unto . . . wordless rest . . . Daisy . . . kneels a culprit—tell her her . . . fault—Master—if it is . . . small eno' to cancel with her life, . . . she is satisfied—but punish . . . dont banish her—shut her in prison, Sir—only pledge that you will forgive—sometime—before the grave, and Daisy will not mind" (L248).

42. See also *Comic Power in Emily Dickinson*, by Juhasz, Miller, and Smith, which is the first book-length study that emphasizes the playful aspects in Dickinson's poetry.

43. Johnson and Ward comment on this character in *David Copperfield* as "one who remained nameless" (*Letters* 609). In the second letter (L820), "Brooks of Sheffield" refers to the as yet unborn (and thus unnamed) baby that Elizabeth Holland's daughter Kate was expecting.

44. Johnson and Ward explain that "Samuel Nash, the first editor of the *Hampshire and Franklin Express*, died in 1861. His name therefore would recall the past" (*Letters* 852).

45. See Salska, who has pointed out that Dickinson's letters create a bond between writer and addressee "against the others" ("Letters" 14).

46. As Suzanne Juhasz, Cristanne Miller, and Martha Nell Smith have pointed out in the context of their discussion of comic strategies in Dickinson's poetry, functioning as a means of defamiliarization, "Dickinson's comic vision destabilizes, subverts, and reimagines cultural situations"; it "challenge[s] all manners of orthodoxy" (25, 137).

47. Phaeton's father's epithet, "Phoebus" ("the bright one"), recalls his association with Apollo, patron of poetry and music, in Virgil's *Eclogues*. Cf. also J1009/Fr1009: "I was a Phoebe—nothing more— | a Phoebe— nothing less— . . . A Phoebe makes a little print | Upon the Floors of Fame—." Farr has pointed out that "literature and art in the 1860s linked the heroic white male with Apollo" (*Passion* 183).

48. See also Martha Nell Smith, who has suggested that Dickinson's gender roles become fluid (*Rowing* 114).

49. In this way she also challenges any easy correlation between gender and sex. As Butler has emphasized: "The presumption of a binary gender system implicitly retains the belief in a mimetic relation of gender to sex whereby gender mirrors sex or is otherwise restricted by it. When the constructed status of gender is theorized as radically independent of sex, gender itself becomes a free-floating artifice" (*Gender* 6).

CHAPTER 5. MANIPULATING MULTIPLE VOICES

1. See also Barthes: "The text is a tissue of quotations drawn from innumerable centres of culture" ("Death" 146). And Frow explains that "texts are therefore not structures of presence but traces and tracings of otherness. They are shaped by the repetition and the transformation of other textual structures" (45).

2. This has been noted by Manfred Pfister (6).

3. See also his summary in *The Dialogic Imagination:* "In the majority of poetic genres (poetic in the narrow sense), as we have said, the internal dialogization of discourse is not put to artistic use, it does not enter into the work's 'aesthetic object,' and is artificially extinguished in poetic discourse. In the novel, however, this internal dialogization becomes one of the most fundamental aspects of prose style and undergoes a specific artistic elaboration" (284).

4. Reading Dickinson's writings through the theories of Bakhtin is a very recent development in Dickinson criticism. In his survey of Bakhtinian analyses of Dickinson's poetry, Paul Crumbley stresses that "only a few works have made the application of Bakhtinian thought a central theoretical concern" ("Dialogic" 11). The two major critics to use such an approach are Crumbley and Erika Scheurer.

5. The allusion is to the beginning of Dickinson's J303/Fr409: "The Soul selects her own Society— | Then—shuts the Door— | To her divine Majority— | Present no more—."

6. Crumbley observes that several critics have discussed dialogic features in Dickinson's poems without explicitly referring to Bakhtin. Most of these critics have focused on the stylistic indeterminacy of Dickinson's manuscript variants, thus illustrating how a "dialogic voice . . . grows from this constant negotiation of linguistic possibilities" (Crumbley, "Dialogic" 5). According to Crumbley, in addition to Gary Lee Stonum, Barton Levi St. Armand, Martha Nell Smith, and Cynthia Griffin Wolff, Sharon Cameron, in her *Choosing Not Choosing*, illustrates how Dickinson's stylistic and linguistic indeterminacy, her resistance to creating "final" versions of her poems, denies "monological exclusivity." For those critics, therefore,

Dickinson's "voice is always plural, [her] speakers polyvocal" (Crumbley, "Dickinson's Dialogic Voice" 102).

7. By "chirography," Crumbley here alludes to Dickinson's playfully "animated" handwriting; she, for example, turns "o's" into faces that look back at her reader, or tilts "s's" sideways to suggest waves when discussing water imagery. This quotation appears in an earlier manuscript version of Crumbley's essay "Dickinson's Dialogic Voice" in *The Emily Dickinson Handbook*.

8. Scheurer does stress the monologic aspects of Dickinson's "oral" voice, though: "I think it is important to emphasize the oral qualities of this voice and the closure that can come with it" (90). Ultimately, however, she too comes to the conclusion that "while Dickinson did not value writing over speech, she did value dialogic writing and speech over monologic writing and speech" (93).

9. For the purposes of this discussion, I use the term *direct quotation* for utterances enclosed by quotation marks, irrespective of their degree of accuracy. Words or phrases transposed verbatim into the host text without quotation marks (a very rare occurrence in Dickinson's correspondence) shall be referred to by Herman Meyer's term *borrowings*. All other visually unmarked but identifiable elements from other texts shall be called *allusions*, whereas substantive transformations of larger textual units will be discussed as *creative rewritings* and *paraphrases*. In the vast majority of cases, however, Dickinson prefers direct quotations to any other forms of intertextuality. Based on Genette's range of transtextual relationships (intertextuality, paratextuality, metatextuality, architextuality, and hypertextuality), I am thus principally concerned with what he has defined as "intertextuality" (i.e., the presence of one text within another [8]). Genette includes quotation and allusion, among others, under the category of intertextuality. Since Dickinson also embeds some of her quotations in a dialogic structure or comments on them critically, I shall also analyze what Genette has termed metatextual relations (i.e., one text's—often critical—evocation of or comment upon another without quoting it directly [10]). Occasionally, Dickinson's modifications of discursive formations reveal an architextual relationship (i.e., an evocation of general discursive or generic features [7]). And finally, some of her rewritings fall under the category of hypertextuality (i.e., the simple or indirect transformation of an earlier text that Genette also refers to as "imitation" [14]).

10. Laurent Jenny calls this the "elimination of combinatorial incompatibilities": "To typographical coherence must be joined the elimination of combinatorial incompatibilities of texts which often have quite heterogeneous origins. Sometimes a borrowed fragment is linked to its new context by syntactic means, in a sentence whose grammaticality enhances its plausibility" (52).

11. For detailed definitions of these six terms, see Pfister 26–29.

12. See also Laurent Jenny, who emphasizes "the work of assimilation and transformation which characterizes all intertextual processes" (37).

13. It might be argued that some of what I refer to as "assimilations" and "manipulations" are indeed mere "inaccuracies" or the results of quoting from memory. And it is true that some

"misquotations," especially misspellings of names, might be interpreted as such. Once, for example, Dickinson cites Burns's poem "John Anderson, My Jo" as " 'John Anderson my Joe' " (L99), and refers to "Mr Brooks of Sheffield," a character in Dickens's *David Copperfield*, as "Mr Brown of Sheffield" (L204). In the ensuing discussion, however, I am primarily concerned with the textual effects of these modifications and their consequences for the reader, irrespective of the question of intentionality. Additionally, in specific groups of texts, Dickinson's manipulative strategies display a high degree of systematization, which, together with her repeated insistence on accuracy in quotations, renders them significant.

14. Johnson and Ward explain that "William S. Robinson ('Warrington') was the Boston correspondent for the *Springfield Republican*. . . . A collection of his writings, *Pen-Portraits* . . . (Boston 1877), was issued by his wife" (*Letters* 828).

15. According to Diepeveen, a direct quotation also implies that one cannot paraphrase texture (18).

16. See also Ruth 1:16 ("for whither thou goest, I will go"), which is quoted as, " 'Where thou goest, *we* will go—' " (L732). Psalms 127:2 ("*for* so he giveth his beloved sleep") becomes, " 'He giveth *our* Beloved Sleep' " (L796). In L45, the changes to Psalms 137:5 ("If I forget thee, O Jerusalem, let my right hand forget *her cunning*") are deemed too substantial for using quotation marks: "if you forget me now your right hand *shall* it's cunning" (L45).

17. A good example is the manuscript of L873.

18. Allusions, on the other hand, provide no visual dislocation and thus contribute to a predominantly monologic reading experience (Diepeveen 10).

19. Focusing on Dickinson's poetry, critics have noted the highly assimilative quality of her quotations. Lease, for example, has argued that "Dickinson responded to men and books creatively. She transformed their messages into her own message" (xi). Capps, even more forcefully, claims that in Dickinson's poems, the "incorporation of such material [as quotations] is not always obvious, primarily because her assimilation was nearly always complete" (5). Similarly, Richard Sewall stresses the liberties Dickinson takes even in seemingly direct quotations: "Her freedom with the text is characteristic of a lifelong habit. Her quotations are seldom exact" (*Life* 695). Although it is true that, generally speaking, in her poetry Dickinson engages in more drastic modifications and revisionist rewritings of her borrowed texts (Vivian Pollak, for example, has counted merely 51 poems that contain direct quotations foregrounded by quotation marks ["Literary Allusions" 60]), her poems actually mailed to correspondents display a higher degree of dialogicity, expressed through a disproportionately high number of direct quotations.

20. The Dickinson family library contains no copy of Brontë's poems. The exact source of this quotation thus remains unknown.

21. In Dickinson's manuscript, "suns" can also be interpreted as capitalized, whereas "Thee" might be in lower case.

22. Since the manuscript of this letter is privately owned, my transcription follows Johnson and Ward's edition.

23. All of her modifications, for example, occur *within* quotation marks.

24. Some of the more general discussions include Richard Sewall's chapter "Emily Dickinson's Books and Reading" as well as Benjamin Lease's *Emily Dickinson's Readings of Men and Books*, which both attempt to trace the "sources" for many passages in Dickinson's oeuvre. Lease argues that "Shakespeare, the King James Bible, Watts, and some notable seventeenth-century writers of devotional prose and poetry served as catalysts to release Dickinson's distinctive voice and vision—a voice and vision that transformed these sacred texts to serve her own religious quest and dedicated artistry" (35). Cristanne Miller's *Poet's Grammar* approaches the question of "influence" from a linguistic perspective, analyzing "various stylistic, theoretical, and thematic influences on Dickinson's writing, [and] examining probable models or sources for the most striking of her language techniques and ideas" (131). Focusing especially on the Bible, Miller concludes that the "Biblical style, in its King James version and as modified by seventeenth-century writers and Americans generally, provided a model for the extreme compression, parataxis, and disjunction of Dickinson's style" (131). More specific discussions of Higginson's and Shakespeare's "influence" on Dickinson will be referred to below.

25. She defines intertextuality as "the transposition of one or more *systems* of signs into another, accompanied by a new articulation of the enunciative and denotative position" (*Revolution* 15).

26. For the identification of specific referents for Dickinson's quotations and allusions, I am particularly indebted to Jack L. Capps (*Emily Dickinson's Reading*), Thomas H. Johnson (his annotations to *Poems* and *Letters*), and Jay Leyda (*The Years and Hours of Emily Dickinson*), who have undertaken comprehensive and systematic attempts to identify the vast number of Dickinson's literary and scriptural allusions. Yet since I am primarily interested in the *function* of intertextual references within Dickinson's correspondence, I am not concerned with tracing and identifying additional, hitherto unnoticed "sources," "echoes," or "influences" in either poems or letters. For the most recent addition in this latter category, see Marcy Tanter's dissertation, which focuses specifically on British writers.

27. St. Armand comments: "In her unpublished 'Life' of Emily Dickinson, Martha Dickinson Bianchi states: 'when Colonel Higginson's article, 'The Procession of the Flowers' appeared in the *Atlantic* Sue ran over with it to Emily the hour it arrived. They read it together and apart, and frequently went back to it' (529–530)" (340 n. 10).

28. Johnson and Ward point out that this could refer to either "The Door Unlatched" or "The Gate Unlatched," both published in *The Woman's Journal* (in January and July 1870, respectively).

29. Johnson and Ward explain that, in his reply, Higginson "evidently suggested that the essay of his she might have in mind was 'A Shadow'. . . . She here makes clear that she had read 'A Shadow' " (*Letters* 482).

30. Johnson and Ward explain: "ED correctly guessed that Higginson wrote the unsigned review of Lowell's *Among My Books: Second Series* for the March 1876 issue of *Scribner's*

Monthly. . . . The review of Emerson's *Letters and Social Aims* in the April issue, likewise unsigned, may be Higginson's but has not been so identified" (*Letters* 552).

31. Higginson's version differs morphologically in two instances, as well as in capitalization: "Such being the majesty of the art you seek to practise, you can at least take time and deliberation before dishonoring it" (403).

32. Ruth Miller has cited its announcement in the "Books, Authors & Art" column of the *Springfield Republican*, to which the Dickinsons were regular subscribers: "The *Atlantic Monthly* for April is one of the best numbers ever issued. . . . Its leading article, Thomas Wentworth Higginson's 'Letter to a Young Contributor,' ought to be read by all the would-be authors of the land. . . . It is a test of latent power. Whoever rises from its thorough perusal strengthened and encouraged, may be reasonably certain of ultimate success" (qtd. in Miller 42).

33. Cf. the discussion of these two examples below.

34. Johnson prints two draft versions of Dickinson's poem, both of which are longer than the version she eventually mailed to Higginson: "Lay this Laurel on the one | Triumphed and remained unknown— | Laurel—fell your futile Tree— | Such a Victor could not be— | Lay this Laurel on the one | Too intrinsic for Renown— | Laurel—vail your deathless Tree— | Him you chasten—that is he—." Johnson comments on this draft: "It is impossible to know whether ED intended the poem finally to be two stanzas or one" (*Poems* 962).

35. This example had been noted by St. Armand.

36. That Dickinson's opinion of several of Higginson's famous literary protégées was indeed highly ambivalent manifests itself in some of her letters. About Spofford, for example, she is less than enthusiastic: "I read Miss Prescott's 'Circumstance,' but it followed me in the Dark—so I avoided her—" (L261). And her comments on Helen Hunt Jackson are fraught with double-voiced ambivalence. After Jackson's death, Higginson had written a commemorative sonnet, a copy of which he mailed to Dickinson, who thanks him twice: "Thank you for 'the Sonnet'—I have lain it at her loved feet" (L1042); and "Dear friend. The beautiful Sonnet confirms me—Thank you for confiding it" (L1043). Yet an earlier (discarded) draft of L1043 had started with an almost accusatory undertone, challenging Higginson's literary preferences: "Dear friend—No 'Sonnet' had George Eliot. The sweet Acclamation of Death is forever bounded" (Johnson and Ward, *Letters* 904–905). A similarly ambivalent evaluation of Jackson had already appeared in a much earlier letter to Higginson, embedded in Dickinson's response to his *Short Studies of American Authors:* "Of Poe, I know too little to think—Hawthorne appalls, entices—Mrs Jackson soars to your estimate lawfully as a Bird, but of Howells and James, one hesitates—Your relentless Music dooms as it redeems" (L622). Dickinson's choice of "lawfully" can be interpreted as a condemnation of Jackson's poetry (the "Bird's" song) as merely conforming or rising to the expectations of her mentor's poetic precepts, with which Dickinson herself clearly disagreed.

37. Lease has drawn attention to the fact that there were nineteen Bibles in the Dickinson household.

38. Additional examples include Matthew 18:20 ("For where two or three are gathered together in my name"), which is quoted as: "that 'two or three' are gathered in your name" (L77). In L947, Matthew 11:11 ("he that is least in the kingdom of heaven") is tailored to Mrs. James S. Cooper's granddaughter Margaret: "She that is 'least in the kingdom of Heaven'" (L947). With Proverbs 14:10 ("The heart knoweth his own bitterness"), Dickinson changes the pronoun "his" to the more usual "its," yet carefully excludes both her conjunction ("but") as well as her substitution for "bitterness" ("Whim") from the quoted environment: "but 'the Heart knoweth its own' Whim" (L750). Her quotation of 2 Corinthians 4:17 ("worketh for us a far more exceeding *and* eternal weight of glory") becomes "it shall work out for us a far more exceeding and 'eternal weight' of *presence*" (L52). Ephesians 2:9 ("Not of works, lest any man should boast") is quoted as "Lest any Bee should boast" (no quotation marks) in L850, and, "'Lest any' Hen 'should boast'" in L852. In L52, Dickinson writes to her brother: "we're 'with you alway, even unto the end'!," a quotation based on Matthew 28:20: "I am with you alway, *even* unto the end of the world." Dickinson's changed subject ("we're") has carefully been excluded from the quotation marks.

39. The second letter, signed "Paul," quotes this as a separate syntactical unit: "'We shall not all sleep, but we shall all be changed'" (L885).

40. In the transcript produced by Frances and Louise Norcross, quotation marks are omitted.

41. In Milton's *Paradise Lost*, these words are also attributed to Adam only: "and of thy voice / Afraid, being naked, hid myself" (10.116f).

42. Cf. also Luke 4:10: "For it is written, He shall give his angels charge over thee, to keep thee."

43. A variant of this line can be found in L991 to Mrs. Sweetser: "only a kiss and a gratitude, and every grace of being, from your loving niece. 'I give his angels charge!'"

44. Stonum's observation that Dickinson "never refers to [Shakespeare's] sonnets" but "attends overwhelmingly to the tragedies, referring primarily to characters and dramatic speeches rather than to theme or style" ("Literary Background" 54) helps to confirm this thesis.

45. Finch therefore argues that "Dickinson offers an especially good subject for the study of how meter encodes information about a poem's relation to contemporaneous influences, traditions, and societal attitudes and to the poetic past and its supporting social structures" ("Patriarchal Meter" 174). Cf. also Easthope: "In an unbroken continuity from the Renaissance to 1900 and beyond, a poem within the metrical tradition [of iambic pentameter] identifies itself (in Puttenham's words) with polish and reformed manners as against poetry in another metre which can be characterized as rude, homely, and in the modern sense, vulgar" (65).

46. See also Joanne Feit Diehl's "Dickinson and Bloom," in which she states: "[Dickinson's] precursor is composite, . . . an amalgam of poetic identities . . . which the woman poet identifies with the collective powers of the poetic tradition as well as with the male deity of the Old and New Testaments. . . . The precursor as a composite figure represents to the woman not simply

a poet of astonishing authority but the other male personifications of power, the father and God the Father" (423–424).

47. Finch illustrates how iambic pentameter is associated with "Christianity" in J959/Fr1072 ("A loss of something ever felt I") and with "masculine power" in J616/Fr454 ("I rose—because He sank"), and she comments on Dickinson's subversive use of "split pentameters" in J320/Fr282 ("We play at Paste"), a poem mailed to Higginson.

48. This example has also been noted by Shurr (*New Poems* 81).

49. This example has also been noted by Fried, who observes that "a number of the repeated Shakespearean tags in the letters are three-beat lines." Fried lists three additional examples: " 'Leave that which leaves itself'; 'Love's remainder biscuit'; 'An envious silver [*sic*] broke' " (155 n. 16).

50. Additional examples include L430 and L978, which shorten "Egypt, thou knew'st too well / My heart was to thy rudder tied by the strings, / And thou shouldst tow me after" (*Antony and Cleopatra*) to " 'Egypt—thou knew'st' " and " 'You knew, Oh Egypt' said the entangled Antony," respectively. L678 further truncates the trimeter from L1006 (" 'An envious Sliver broke' ") to: "it [your hand] has saved too many to be assailed by an 'envious sliver—.' " The following passage from *Hamlet*, "ay, marry, is't; crowner's-quest law," becomes "her Maker must be her 'Crowner's Quest' " (L979). Similarly, "For who would bear the whips and scorns of time" (*Hamlet*) is shortened to "and the 'Whips of Time' felt a long way off" (L547). See also L31, L8, and L73 (*Macbeth*); L544 (*Lear*); L746 (*Romeo and Juliet*); and L545 and L882 (*As You Like It*) for further examples.

51. The lineation of L538 (" 'I here do give thee that with all my heart, which, but thou hast already, with all my heart I would keep from thee' " [*Othello*]), could not be verified, as the manuscript of this letter is missing.

52. A similar example is the statement "Nothing in his life / Became him like the leaving it" (*Macbeth*), which is cited (albeit without quotation marks) as "That nothing in | her Life became | her like it's last | event, it is probable—" (Houghton MS Am 1118.3 [H84]; L882).

53. Additional examples can be found in L546 (Dryden), L950 (Barrett Browning), L31 (Gray), L29 and L1038 (Milton), L337 and L477 (Browning), L873 (E. Brontë), L506 (Tennyson), L11 (Young), L1029 (Byron), and L544 and L888 (Waller).

54. A similar idea has been expressed by Pfister (2).

55. See also Dickinson's declaration of her own sense of "ownership" in L271: "I marked a line in One Verse—because I met it after I made it—and never consciously touch a paint, mixed by another person—I do not let go it, because it is mine."

56. In her quoting practices as well as in her explicit comments on her readings, Dickinson grants equal "authority" to "high" and "popular" literature. Earlier critics have occasionally expressed dissatisfaction with this democratization. Sewall, for example, deplores Dickinson's references to the "tearful effusions of the sub-poets": "Although Emily's reading sobered considerably as time went on (the allusions to sub-literature diminish rapidly after the mid-1860s), she never lost her taste for sentiment" ("Books and Reading" 42). Similarly, Capps

calls Dickinson's literary "taste" into question: "Emily Dickinson had a high regard for established literary masters, but her taste in contemporary literature was often erratic" (6); furthermore, "Dickinson's apparently omnivorous literary taste and her fallible critical evaluations cast some doubt on her standards of criticism" (23). Pollak is somewhat less harsh in her verdict, observing that many of Dickinson's allusions "hover between literary sources on the one hand and the popular culture of an avid nineteenth-century reader on the other" ("Literary Allusions" 55).

57. " 'Taken Captivity Captive' " at the same time also evokes X. B. Saintine's novel *Picciola*, subtitled *The Prisoner of Fenestrella or, Captivity Captive*, to which Dickinson refers in L27.

58. In L513 to Higginson, to whom Dickinson had also mailed a copy of this poem, she referred to it as "a Word to a Friend."

59. According to Johnson and Ward's description, the illustration "represents the letter 'T' in the alphabet: 'Young Timothy / Learnt sin to fly,' and shows a youth pursued by an upright wolf-like creature with forked tail" (*Letters* 360). They explain that "to the note is another attached by Mrs. Bianchi: 'Sent over the morning after a revel—when my Grandfather [Dickinson's father] with his lantern appeared suddenly to take Emily home the hour nearing indecent midnight' " (360).

60. Martha Nell Smith describes this manuscript thus: "When Dickinson sent this poem next door to her sister-in-law, she appended a picture of Little Nell being comforted by her grandfather to the top of the poem with pink thread; then, also with pink thread, she bound a cutout of Little Nell being ferried to heaven by a host of angels to the bottom of the poem. This appears to have been attached in such a way so that when the missive was unfolded, the bottom picture of Little Nell among the seraphs popped up—like a pop-up greeting card—to the reader" (*Comic Power* 78). Smith goes on to emphasize how these textual gestures change the reader's response to an otherwise overly sentimental poem: "In this context calling attention to her appropriation of Dickens' work and the poem's hyperbolic overstatement, a lyric that might be either disregarded or read earnestly as religious or romantic sentiment becomes the cartooning play of one writer responding to another. . . . What might be read all too solemnly when divorced from the illustrations Dickinson attached cannot be read without humor with her original context restored" (*Comic Power* 78, 80).

61. Johnson describes this poem thus: "Pasted onto the center of the front half of the half-sheet of notepaper on which the poem is written there is an unused three-cent postage stamp of the issue of 1869. Beneath one side of the stamp are two small strips clipped from [a review published in] *Harper's Magazine* for May 1870. One bears the name 'George Sand' and the other 'Mauprat'—the title of the novel by George Sand published in 1836" (*Poems* 816). This poem and its enclosure have been discussed by Jeanne Holland as an emblem for "Dickinson's polymorphously sexed body-image" ("Scraps" 159).

62. Johnson and Ward comment on this letter: "On 11 March the *Springfield Republican* mentions that Higginson had spent a fortnight in South Carolina" (*Letters* 607).

63. Holland's reading confirms that "the stamp and its two 'legs' are an integral part of the text" ("Scraps" 146).

64. In his essay on Dryden, Lowell had quoted from Dryden's *Aurengzebe:* "And this single verse from 'Aurengzebe': 'Live still! oh live! live even to be unkind!' "

65. See also L315, which introduces a quotation from Wordsworth's *Elegiac Stanzas* thus: "Here is the 'light' the Stranger said 'was not on land or sea.' "

CONCLUSION: DICKINSON'S LETTERS TO THE WORLD

1. Since the version actually mailed to the Norcross cousins (including plural pronouns throughout) is lost, I am quoting here from the earlier of the two surviving manuscripts.

2. Both extant copies of J494/Fr277 are signed "Emily," thus sporting an epistolary feature and embodying as well as enacting epistolary discourse in addition to thematizing it.

3. In his introduction to *The Manuscript Books of Emily Dickinson,* Franklin explains that Dickinson "organized the largest portion" of her nearly eighteen hundred poems in forty manuscript booklets, which constituted "her own form of bookmaking: selected poems copied onto sheets of letter paper that she bound with string" (1:ix). The fascicles do not contain any letters or letter-drafts.

4. The problem of organizational principles is central; because Dickinson "did not number or otherwise label the fascicles, did not index them or apparently maintain them in a particular order, one may wonder how she found her way among them" (Franklin, *Manuscript Books* 1:x).

5. Franklin continues: "Her earliest goal appears to have been a systematic and comprehensive record of completed poems. But variants developed as she made copies for friends, and about 1861, some three years after she began assembling manuscript books, alternative readings became abundant in the fascicles" (*Manuscript Books* 1:x).

6. This view is also shared by Martha Nell Smith (*Rowing* 11–16) and Sharon Cameron, among others. In contrast to Smith, however, Cameron emphasizes the speculative nature of all theories developed about Dickinson's fascicles: "an alternative speculation is that the fascicles were a form of private publication" ("Dickinson's Fascicles" 139).

7. Ruth Miller was the first to advance the hypothesis that the fascicles display a narrative pattern analogous to Francis Quarles's organization of *Emblems, Divine and Moral.* Rosenthal and Gall have discerned a similarly coherent narrative pattern, regarding fascicles 15 ("The Poetry of Psychic Trauma") and 16 ("A New Start") as interdependent formations of "an epic of the subjective life" (53). Most controversially, in *Emily Dickinson's Fascicles: Method and Meaning,* Dorothy Huff Oberhaus reads fascicle 40 as "an architectural tour de force, a three-part meditation, a letter addressed to the reader, a garland of praise, and a conversion narrative, as well as the triumphant conclusion of the protagonist's account of her poetic and spiritual pilgrimage from renunciation to illumination to union and finally, after many conflicts, to contentment with this union" (168). Franklin himself, Barton Levi St. Armand, and

Sharon Cameron, however, are more cautious. Franklin views the fascicles primarily as tools to reduce disorder in her manuscripts and cannot detect any particular order across fascicle boundaries (*Poems* 1:8), and St. Armand can only find "a seemingly random patchwork pattern" (9). Finally, in *Choosing Not Choosing: Dickinson's Fascicles,* Cameron argues for a deliberate subversion of the concepts of structure and closure on Dickinson's part by considering an entire fascicle book as a unit of sense (15). Cameron convincingly demonstrates the extent to which Dickinson's fascicles thematize a refusal to make choices on a textual, formal, thematic, and philosophical level, and call into question the very concept of structure by "redetermin[ing] our very understanding of how the identity of a poetic structure is to be construed" (18). For a more recent discussion of this topic, see her article in the *Emily Dickinson Handbook.* Bruce W. Clary's *Emily Dickinson's Menagerie: The Fascicles as Poetic Scrapbooks* is the most recent book-length study of the fascicles. Occupying a position somewhere between structure advocates and structure rejecters (with strong leanings toward the latter group), Clary concludes "that the Dickinson fascicles are neither random 'workbooks' of lyrics as Franklin described them nor are they artfully organized poetic wholes" (8). What characterizes them best, he claims, is a kind of "loose" organization of "assorted groups of items, gathered by a variety of principles" (11), including a "balance or unity between her opening and closing poems" (233), or "pairs and clusters of poems" (247). Additionally, Clary observes that "it is possible that early in her fascicle-making project Dickinson was classifying poems by purpose and type as well as by length" (249). He draws attention to fascicle 1, for example, which contains eleven poems sent to friends with flowers (248). Ultimately, however, Clary concludes that space remains Dickinson's main consideration in sequencing her poems (12), and that each fascicle poem "remains a discrete lyric, a self-contained and autonomous expression" (5).

8. Franklin himself, among others, has emphasized the draft-like quality of most poems in the later fascicles: "What started out as a comprehensive record of completed poems, serving as a source for additional copies, broadened to include intermediate stages and became in a sense a continuing workshop" (*Manuscript Books* 1:x; cf. also Martha Nell Smith, "Manuscripts" 114). In his 1998 edition of *Poems,* Franklin gives a detailed account of the various stages of fascicle production, beginning with only completed fair-copy poems admitted before 1860 (*Poems* 1:19–20), shifting to "less careful" transcriptions of texts with unresolved readings that were "not intended for others" by early 1861 (i.e., fascicle 9; *Poems* 1:20–22), and ending with the temporary abandoning of the fascicle method by early 1862 (1:22). Dickinson then resumed fascicle making in the summer of 1862 (1:24), continuing until early 1864 (1:25), and often including poems from earlier times, "as though Dickinson were cleaning up the workshop once again" (1:26). All in all, Dickinson's fascicle production thus spans the years 1858 to 1865, whereas she made sets between 1870 and 1875.

9. Smith in this context also speaks of "provocative experimentations with a poet's contract with readers' expectations" ("Manuscripts" 126). See also Sharon Cameron's *Choosing Not Choosing.*

10. This term was used by both Franklin and Clary.

11. The poem in question is "Safe in their alabaster chambers" (J216/Fr124). Cf. Smith (*Rowing*) and Hart and Smith (*Open Me*). Yet even the draft quality of this poem has been contested by Franklin, who argues that "all of the versions of ["Safe in their alabaster chambers"] . . . that Susan received in 1861 were fair copies, one in ink, one in pencil, each on a bifolium of her notepaper with messages added to them" (*Poems* 1:31). For a refutation of Franklin's interpretation, see Smith and Hart's "Gifts & Ghosts" (30).

12. In 1885, for example, Jackson had written to Dickinson: "I wish I knew what your portfolios, by this time, hold" (L976a).

13. This might also explain the presence of poems from different years within one fascicle (although any other [thematic] organizational principle might, of course, do so as well).

14. This number also includes the fifteen unbound manuscript booklets commonly referred to as "sets."

15. Juhasz comments on the phallocentricity of the "frustrated spinster" approach, which implies that: "(a) Emily Dickinson wrote poetry because she did not have a sex life or (b) the only explanation for such poetry was an active (albeit secret) sex life. Both interpretations lodge the male at the center of a woman's creativity" (*Naked and Fiery Forms* 10).

16. Variants on this position are currently shared by many feminist critics. Budick, for example, suggests that Dickinson "decided to cut herself off from the social interactions of life in this world" and chose to withdraw into the symbolic realm of language (n.p.); Paula Bennett maintains that Dickinson had to reject the traditional New England female socialization in order to pursue the "life of self-indulgence and self-gratification associated with writing poetry" (*My Life* 17).

17. Bennett's view is also shared by Erkkila.

Works Cited and Consulted

Aids to Epistolary Correspondence, or: Familiar Directions for Writing Letters on Various Subjects. Also: Rules of Punctuation. Quebec: G. E. Desbarats, 1865.

Allardyce, Paul. *"Stops," or, How to Punctuate.* London: T. Fisher Unwin, n.d.

Altman, Janet Gurkin. *Epistolarity: Approaches to a Form.* Columbus: Ohio State UP, 1982.

——. "The Letter Book as a Literary Institution 1539–1789: Toward a Cultural History of Published Correspondences in France." *Yale French Studies* 71 (1986): 17–62.

Anderson, Charles R. *Emily Dickinson's Poetry: Stairway of Surprise.* New York: Holt, 1960.

Anderson, Howard, Philip B. Daghlian, and Irvin Ehrenpreis, eds. *The Familiar Letter in the Eighteenth Century.* Lawrence: U of Kansas P, 1966.

Anderson, Howard, and Irvin Ehrenpreis. "The Familiar Letter in the Eighteenth Century: Some Generalizations." Anderson, Daghlian, and Ehrenpreis 269–282.

Anderson, Peggy. "The Bride of the White Election: A New Look at Biblical Influence on Emily Dickinson." Nathan 1–11.

Anderson, Susan M. " 'Regard(ing) a Mouse' in Dickinson's Poems and Letters." *The Emily Dickinson Journal* 2.1 (1993): 84–102.

Angenot, Marc. "L'intertextualité: Enquête sur l'émergence et la diffusion d'un champ notionnel." *Revue des Sciences Humaines* 60.189 (1983): 121–135.

Anthony, Mary. "Emily Dickinson's Scriptural Echoes." *Massachusetts Review* 2 (1961): 557–561.

Aristotle. *Poetics*. Ed. and trans. S. H. Butcher. 4th ed. London: Macmillan, 1925.

Ashley, Kathleen, Leigh Gilmore, and Gerald Peters, eds. *Autobiography and Postmodernism*. Amherst: U of Massachusetts P, 1994.

Auerbach, Nina. *Communities of Women: An Idea in Fiction*. Cambridge: Harvard UP, 1978.

Bain, Alexander. *English Composition and Rhetoric*. American ed., revised. New York: Appleton, 1867.

Bakhtin, Mikhail. *The Dialogic Imagination*. Trans. Caryl Emerson and Michael Holquist. Ed. Holquist. Austin: U of Texas P, 1981.

——. *Problems of Dostoevsky's Poetics*. Ed. and trans. Caryl Emerson. Minneapolis: U of Minnesota P, 1984.

——. *Speech Genres and Other Late Essays*. Trans. Vern W. McGee. Ed. Caryl Emerson and Michael Holquist. Austin: U of Texas P, 1986.

Barker, Wendy. *Lunacy of Light: Emily Dickinson and the Experience of Metaphor*. Carbondale: Southern Illinois UP, 1987.

Barthes, Roland. *Camera Lucida: Reflections on Photography*. New York: Noonday, 1981.

——. "The Death of the Author." *Image, Music, Text*. By Barthes. Trans. Stephen Heath. New York: Noonday, 1977. 142–149.

——. *S/Z*. Trans. Richard Miller. New York: Hill and Wang, 1974.

Baym, Nina. "Melodramas of Beset Manhood: How Theories of American Fiction Exclude Women Writers." *American Quarterly* 33 (1981): 123–139.

Beauchamp, Virginia Walcott. "Letters and Diaries: The Persona and the Real Woman—A Case Study." Hoffmann and Culley 40–47.

——. "Letters as Literature: The Prestons of Baltimore." Hoffmann and Culley 29–39.

Bennett, Betty T. "Feminism and Editing Mary Wollstonecraft Shelley: The Editor And? / Or? the Text." Bornstein and Williams 67–96.

Bennett, John. *Letters to a Young Lady, on a variety of useful and interesting subjects: calculated to improve the heart, to form manners, and enlighten the understanding*. 8th American ed. New York: Lang, 1824.

Bennett, Paula. " 'By a Mouth That Cannot Speak': Spectral Presence in Emily Dickinson's Letters." *Emily Dickinson Journal* 1.1 (1992): 76–99.

——. *My Life a Loaded Gun: Female Creativity and Feminist Poetics*. Boston: Beacon, 1986.

——. " 'The Orient Is in the West': Emily Dickinson's Reading of *Antony and Cleopatra*." *Women's Revisions of Shakespeare*. Ed. Marianne Novy. Urbana: U of Illinois P, 1990. 108–123.

Ben-Porat, Ziva. "The Poetics of Allusion—A Text-Linking Device—In Different Media of Communication." *A Semiotic Landscape*. Ed. Seymour Chatman et al. The Hague: Mouton, 1979. 588–593.

——. "The Poetics of Literary Allusions." *PTL* 1.1 (1976): 105–128.

Benstock, Shari. "From Letters to Literature: *La Carte Postale* in the Epistolary Genre." *Genre* 18 (1985): 257–295.

——, ed. *The Private Self: Theory and Practice of Women's Autobiographical Writings*. Chapel Hill: U of North Carolina P, 1988.

Benveniste, Emile. *Problems in General Linguistics*. Trans. Mary Elizabeth Meek. Coral Gables: U of Miami P, 1971.

Bergland, Betty. "Postmodernism and the Autobiographical Subject: Reconstructing the 'Other.'" Ashley, Gilmore, and Peters 130–166.

Bianchi, Martha Dickinson. *Emily Dickinson Face to Face: Unpublished Letters with Notes and Reminiscences*. Boston: Houghton, 1932.

——. *The Life and Letters of Emily Dickinson*. Boston: Houghton, 1924.

Bilworth, H. W. *The Complete Letter Writer: or Young Secretary's Instructor Containing a Great Variety of Letters*. Baltimore: Warner, 1819.

Bingham, Millicent Todd. *Ancestors' Brocades: The Literary Debut of Emily Dickinson*. New York: Harper, 1945.

——. *Emily Dickinson: A Revelation*. New York: Harper, 1954.

——. *Emily Dickinson's Home: Letters of Edward Dickinson and His Family*. New York: Harper, 1955.

Bornstein, George. Introduction. Bornstein and Williams 1–6.

Bornstein, George, and Ralph G. Williams, eds. *Palimpsest: Editorial Theory in the Humanities*. Ann Arbor: U of Michigan P, 1993.

Bové, Mastrangelo Carol. "The Text as Dialogue in Bakhtin and Kristeva." *University of Ottawa Quarterly* 53 (1983): 117–124.

Brodzki, Bella, and Celeste Schenck, eds. *Life/Lines: Theorizing Women's Autobiography*. Ithaca: Cornell UP, 1988.

Broich, Ulrich. "Formen der Markierung von Intertextualität." Broich and Pfister 31–47.

Broich, Ulrich, and Manfred Pfister, eds. *Intertextualität: Formen, Funktionen, anglistische Fallstudien*. Tübingen: Max Niemeyer, 1985.

Buckingham, Willis J., ed. *Emily Dickinson's Reception in the 1890s: A Documentary History*. Pittsburgh: U of Pittsburgh P, 1989.

——. "Poetry Readers and Reading in the 1890s: Emily Dickinson's First Reception." *Readers in History: Nineteenth-Century American Literature and the Context of Response*. Ed. James L. Machor. Baltimore: Johns Hopkins UP, 1993. 164–179.

Budick, E. Miller. *Emily Dickinson and the Life of Language: A Study in Symbolic Poetics*. Baton Rouge: Louisiana State UP, 1985.

Butler, Judith. *Bodies That Matter*. New York: Routledge, 1993.

——. *Gender Trouble: Feminism and the Subversion of Identity*. New York: Routledge, 1990.

Cameron, Deborah, ed. *The Feminist Critique of Language*. London: Routledge, 1990.

Cameron, Sharon. *Choosing Not Choosing: Dickinson's Fascicles*. Chicago: U of Chicago P, 1992.

——. "Dickinson's Fascicles." Grabher, Hagenbüchle, and Miller 138–160.

——. *Lyric Time: Dickinson and the Limits of Genre*. Baltimore: Johns Hopkins UP, 1979.

Capps, Jack L. *Emily Dickinson's Reading 1836–1886*. Cambridge: Harvard UP, 1966.

Chase, Richard. *Emily Dickinson*. New York: Dell, 1951.

Cherewatuk, Karen, and Ulrike Wiethaus. "Introduction: Women Writing Letters in the Middle Ages." *Dear Sister: Medieval Women and the Epistolary Genre*. Ed. Karen Cherewatuk and Ulrike Wiethaus. Philadelphia: U of Pennsylvania P, 1993. 1–19.

Clary, Bruce W. *Emily Dickinson's Menagerie: The Fascicles as Poetic Scrapbooks*. Diss. Kansas State U, 1998. Ann Arbor: UMI, 1998. 9833774.

Cody, John. *After Great Pain: The Inner Life of Emily Dickinson*. Cambridge: Belknap P of Harvard UP, 1971.

Cohen, Ralph. "Do Postmodern Genres Exist?" *Genre* 20 (1987): 241–258.

Constable, Giles. *Letters and Letter-Collections*. Typologie des Sources du Moyen Age Occidental. Fasc. 17. Turnhout: Editions Brepols, 1976.

Conway, Katherine E. *A Lady and Her Letters*. 2nd ed. Boston: Pilot, 1895.

Cott, Nancy F. *The Bonds of Womanhood: "Woman's Sphere" in New England, 1780–1835*. New Haven: Yale UP, 1977.

Crecelius, Kathryn J. "Authorship and Authority: George Sand's Letters to Her Mother." Goldsmith 257–272.

Crumbley, Paul. "Art's Haunted House: Dickinson's Sense of Self." *The Emily Dickinson Journal* 5.2 (1996): 78–84.

——. "The Dialogic Voice." Unpublished essay, 1996.

——. "Dickinson's Dialogic Voice." Grabher, Hagenbüchle, and Miller 93–109.

——. "The Dickinson *Variorum* and the Question of Home." *The Emily Dickinson Journal* 8.2 (1999): 10–23.

——. *Inflections of the Pen: Dash and Voice in Emily Dickinson*. Lexington: UP of Kentucky, 1997.

Culler, Jonathan. *The Pursuit of Signs: Semiotics, Literature, Deconstruction*. Ithaca: Cornell UP, 1981.

Davis, Herbert. "The Correspondence of the Augustans." Anderson, Daghlian, and Ehrenpreis 1–13.

Davis, Thomas M., ed. *14 by Emily Dickinson with Selected Criticism*. Chicago: Scott, 1964.

Day, Robert Adams. *Told in Letters: Epistolary Fiction before Richardson*. Ann Arbor: U of Michigan P, 1966.

De Bruyn, Frans. "Genre Criticism." *Encyclopedia of Contemporary Literary Theory*. Gen. ed. and comp. Irena R. Makaryk. Toronto: U of Toronto P, 1993. 79–85.

Decker, William Merrill. "A Letter Always Seems to Me Like Immortality: The Correspondence of Emily Dickinson." *Emerson Society Quarterly* 39 (1993): 77–104.

D'Emilio, John, and Estelle B. Freedman. *Intimate Matters: A History of Sexuality in America.* New York: Harper, 1988.

Derrida, Jacques. *Limited, Inc.* Evanston: Northwestern UP, 1977.

——. "Signature Event Context." Trans. Jeffrey Mehlman and Samuel Weber. *Glyph* 1 (1977): 172–196.

DeShazer, Mary K. *Inspiring Women: Reimagining the Muse.* New York: Pergamon, 1986.

Dickenson, Donna. *Emily Dickinson.* Leamington Spa: Berg, 1985.

Dickie, Margaret. "Dickinson in Context." *American Literary History* 7.2 (1995): 320–333.

——. *Lyric Contingencies: Emily Dickinson and Wallace Stevens.* Philadelphia: U of Pennsylvania P, 1991.

Diehl, Joanne Feit. "Dickinson and Bloom: An Antithetical Reading of Romanticism." *Texas Studies in Literature and Language* 23.3 (1981): 418–441.

——. *Dickinson and the Romantic Imagination.* Princeton: Princeton UP, 1981.

Diepeveen, Leonard. *Changing Voices: The Modern Quoting Poem.* Ann Arbor: U of Michigan P, 1993.

Dobson, Joanne. *Dickinson and the Strategies of Reticence: The Woman Writer in Nineteenth-Century America.* Bloomington: Indiana UP, 1989.

Doriani, Beth Maclay. *Emily Dickinson: Daughter of Prophecy.* Amherst: U of Massachusetts P, 1996.

Eakin, Paul John. *Fictions in Autobiography: Studies in the Art of Self-Invention.* Princeton: Princeton UP, 1985.

——. Introduction. *American Autobiography: Retrospect and Prospect.* Ed. Eakin. Madison: U of Wisconsin P, 1991. 3–22.

Easthope, Antony. *Poetry as Discourse.* London: Methuen, 1983.

Eberwein, Jane Donahue. *Dickinson: Strategies of Limitation.* Amherst: U of Massachusetts P, 1985.

Edelstein, Tilden G. "Emily Dickinson and Her Mentor in Feminist Perspective." Nathan 37–43.

——. *Strange Enthusiasm: A Life of Thomas Wentworth Higginson.* New Haven: Yale UP, 1968.

Elliott, Brent. "The Victorian Language of Flowers." *Plant-Lore Studies.* Ed. Roy Vickery. London: Folklore Society, 1984. 61–65.

Emerson, Ralph Waldo. "Quotation and Originality." *The Complete Works of Ralph Waldo Emerson.* Vol. 8. New York: AMS, 1968. 175–204.

Erasmus. *De conscribendis epistolis: Anleitung zum Briefschreiben.* Ed. Kurt Smolak. Darmstadt: Wissenschaftliche Buchgesellschaft, 1980.

Erkkila, Betsy. "Dickinson and Rich: Toward a Theory of Female Poetic Influence." *American Literature* 56 (1984): 541–559.

——. "Emily Dickinson and Class." *American Literary History* 4 (Spring 1992): 1–27.

——. "Homoeroticism and Audience: Emily Dickinson's Female 'Master.'" Orzeck and Weisbuch 161–180.

——. *The Wicked Sisters: Women Poets, Literary History, and Discord.* New York: Oxford UP, 1992.

Ernst, Katharina. *'Death' in the Poetry of Emily Dickinson.* Heidelberg: Winter, 1992.

Ezell, Margaret J. M., and Katherine O'Brien O'Keeffe, eds. *Cultural Artifacts and the Production of Meaning: The Page, the Image, and the Body.* Ann Arbor: U of Michigan P, 1994.

Faderman, Lillian. "Emily Dickinson's Letters to Sue Gilbert." *Massachusetts Review* 18 (1977): 197–225.

——. *Surpassing the Love of Men: Romantic Friendship and Love between Women from the Renaissance to the Present.* New York: Morrow, 1981.

Farr, Judith, ed. *Emily Dickinson: A Collection of Critical Essays.* Englewood Cliffs, NJ: Prentice, 1996.

——. "Emily Dickinson's 'Engulfing' Play: *Antony and Cleopatra.*" *Tulsa Studies in Women's Literature* 9 (1990): 231–250.

——. *The Passion of Emily Dickinson.* Cambridge: Harvard UP, 1992.

Fast, Robin Riley, and Christine Mack Gordon, eds. *Approaches to Teaching Dickinson's Poetry.* New York: MLA, 1989.

Favret, Mary A. *Romantic Correspondence: Women, Politics, and the Fiction of Letters.* Cambridge: CUP, 1993.

Ferlazzo, Paul J. *Emily Dickinson.* Boston: Twayne, 1976.

Fetterley, Judith. *The Resisting Reader: A Feminist Approach to American Fiction.* Bloomington: Indiana UP, 1978.

Finch, Annie R. C. "Dickinson and Patriarchal Meter: A Theory of Metrical Codes." *PMLA* 102 (1987): 166–176.

——. *The Ghost of Meter: Culture and Prosody in American Free Verse.* Ann Arbor: U of Michigan P, 1993.

Finnerty, Páraic. "'No Matter—now—Sweet—But when I'm Earl': Dickinson's Shakespearean Cross-Dressing." *The Emily Dickinson Journal* 7.2 (1998): 65–94.

Fleming, C. A. *A Business Letter: A Manual for Use in Colleges, Schools, and for Private Learners.* Owen Sound: Northern Business College Steam, 1890.

Foster, Thomas. "Homelessness at Home: Placing Emily Dickinson in (Women's) History." *Engendering Men: The Question of Male Feminist Criticism.* Ed. Joseph A. Boone and Michael Cadden. New York: Routledge, 1990. 239–253.

Foucault, Michel. "What Is an Author?" Trans. Josué V. Harari. *Textual Strategies: Perspectives in Post-Structuralist Criticism.* Ed. Harari. Ithaca: Cornell UP, 1979. 141–160. Trans. of "Qu'est-ce qu'un auteur?" *Bulletin de la Société française de Philosophie* 63.3 (1969): 73–104.

Franklin, R. W. *The Editing of Emily Dickinson: A Reconsideration.* Madison: U of Wisconsin P, 1967.

——. "Emily Dickinson to Abiah Root: Ten Reconstructed Letters." *The Emily Dickinson Journal* 4.1 (1995): 1–43.

——, ed. *The Manuscript Books of Emily Dickinson*. 2 vols. Cambridge: Belknap P of Harvard UP, 1981.

——, ed. *The Master Letters of Emily Dickinson*. Amherst: Amherst College P, 1986.

——, ed. *The Poems of Emily Dickinson*. 3 vols. Cambridge: Belknap P of Harvard UP, 1998.

Fried, Debra. *Valves of Attention: Quotation and Context in the Age of Emerson*. Diss. Yale U, 1983. Ann Arbor: UMI, 1983. 8329252.

Frow, John. "Intertextuality and Ontology." Worton and Still 45–55.

Garbowsky, Maryanne M. *The House without the Door: A Study of Emily Dickinson and the Illness of Agoraphobia*. Rutherford: Associated University Presses, 1989.

Gardiner, John Hays, George Lyman Kittredge, and Sarah Louise Arnold. *Manual of Composition and Rhetoric*. Boston: Ginn, 1907.

Gelpi, Albert. *The Tenth Muse: The Psyche of the American Poet*. Cambridge: Harvard UP, 1975.

Genette, Gérard. *Palimpsestes: La littérature au second degré*. Paris: Edition du Seuil, 1982.

Gilbert, Sandra M. "The American Sexual Poetics of Walt Whitman and Emily Dickinson." *Reconstructing American Literary History*. Ed. Sacvan Bercovitch. Cambridge: Harvard UP, 1986. 123–154.

Gilbert, Sandra M., and Susan Gubar. *The Madwoman in the Attic: The Woman Writer and the Nineteenth-Century Literary Imagination*. New Haven: Yale UP, 1979.

Gilmore, Leigh. "The Mark of Autobiography: Postmodernism, Autobiography, and Genre." Ashley, Gilmore, and Peters 3–18.

Giuliani, Maria Teresa. "Il Vocabolario delle Lettere de Emily Dickinson." *Studi Americani* 12 (1966): 89–124.

Goldsmith, Elizabeth C. "Authority, Authenticity, and the Publication of Letters by Women." Goldsmith 46–59.

——, ed. *Writing the Female Voice: Essays on Epistolary Literature*. Boston: Northeastern UP, 1989.

Goodwin, James. *Autobiography: The Self Made Text*. Studies in Literary Themes and Genres 2. New York: Twayne, 1993.

Goody, Jack. *The Culture of Flowers*. Cambridge: Cambridge UP, 1993.

Grabher, Gudrun, Roland Hagenbüchle, and Cristanne Miller, eds. *The Emily Dickinson Handbook*. Amherst: U of Massachusetts P, 1998.

Grahn, Judy. *The Highest Apple: Sappho and the Lesbian Poetic Tradition*. San Francisco: Spinster's Ink, 1985.

Greetham, D. C. "Editorial and Critical Theory: From Modernism to Postmodernism." Bornstein and Williams 9–28.

Gregory, Elizabeth Lee. *Quotation and Modern American Poetry: Eliot, Williams, and Moore*. Diss. Yale U, 1989. Ann Arbor: UMI, 1990. 9010657

Griffith, Clarke. *The Long Shadow: Emily Dickinson's Tragic Poetry.* Princeton: Princeton UP, 1964.

Guillén, Claudio. "Notes toward the Study of the Renaissance Letter." Lewalski 70–101.

Gunn, Janet Varner. *Autobiography: Toward a Poetics of Experience.* Philadelphia: U of Pennsylvania P, 1982.

Gusdorf, Georges. "Conditions and Limits of Autobiography." Trans. James Olney. Olney 28–48.

Hagenbüchle, Roland. *Emily Dickinson: Wagnis der Selbstbegegnung.* Tübingen: Stauffenburg, 1988.

——. "Precision and Indeterminacy in Emily Dickinson's Poetry." *Emerson Society Quarterly* 20 (1974): 33–56.

Hall, Florence Howe. *Social Customs.* Boston: Estes and Lauriat, 1897.

Hamill, Sam. "Epistolary Poetry: The Poem as Letter; the Letter as Poem." *Northwest Review* 19.1–2 (1981): 228–234.

"Handlist of Books Found in the Home of Emily Dickinson at Amherst, Massachusetts, Spring 1950." Harvard Reading Room Index D560. Cambridge, Mass., 1951.

Hart, Ellen Louise. "The Elizabeth Whitney Putnam Manuscripts and New Strategies for Editing Emily Dickinson's Letters." *Emily Dickinson Journal* 4.1 (1995): 44–74.

——. "The Encoding of Homoerotic Desire: Emily Dickinson's Letters and Poems to Susan Dickinson, 1850–1886." *Tulsa Studies in Women's Literature* 9 (1990): 251–272.

Hart, Ellen Louise, and Martha Nell Smith, eds. *Open Me Carefully: Emily Dickinson's Intimate Letters to Susan Huntington Dickinson.* Ashfield, Mass.: Paris, 1998.

Hebel, Udo, comp. *Intertextuality, Allusion, and Quotation: An International Bibliography of Critical Studies.* New York: Greenwood, 1989.

Heilbrun, Carolyn G. *Writing a Woman's Life.* New York: Ballantine, 1988.

Helsinger, Elizabeth K., Robin Lauterbach Sheets, and William Veeder. *The Woman Question.* 3 vols. Chicago: U of Chicago P, 1983.

Henderson, Judith Rice. "Erasmus on the Art of Letter-Writing." J. Murphy 331–355.

Herrmann, Anne. *The Dialogic and Difference: 'An / Other Woman' in Virginia Woolf and Christa Wolf.* New York: Columbia UP, 1989.

Higgins, David. *Portrait of Emily Dickinson: The Poet and Her Prose.* New Brunswick: Rutgers, 1967.

Higginson, Thomas Wentworth. *Army Life in a Black Regiment.* 1870. Boston: Beacon, 1962.

——. "Emily Dickinson's Letters." *The Atlantic Monthly* 68 (October 1891): 444–456. Rpt. in Buckingham, *Reception,* item 221.

——. "Letter to a Young Contributor." *The Atlantic Monthly* 9 (April 1862): 401–411.

——. "The Life of Birds." *The Atlantic Monthly* 10 (September 1862): 368–376. Rpt. in *The Procession of the Flowers and Kindred Papers.* By Higginson. New York: Longmans, 1897. 129–158.

——. *Women and the Alphabet.* Boston: Houghton, 1881.

——. "Women's Letters." *Women and Men.* By Higginson. New York: Harper, 1888. 110–114.

Higginson, Thomas Wentworth, and Henry Walcott Boynton. *A Reader's History of American Literature.* Boston: Houghton, 1903.

Higginson, Thomas Wentworth, and Mabel Loomis Todd, eds. *Poems by Emily Dickinson.* Boston: Roberts Brothers, 1890.

——, eds. *Poems by Emily Dickinson.* Second Series. Boston: Roberts Brothers, 1891.

Hill, David W. "Words Doing: Dickinson's Language as Autonomous Action." Turco 129–146.

Hill, Thomas E. *Never Give a Lady a Restive Horse: A Nineteenth-Century Handbook of Etiquette.* 1873. Excerpts compiled by David MacKenzie and W. B. Blankenburg. Berkeley: Diabolo, 1967.

Himelhoch, Myra, and Rebecca Patterson. "The Dating of Emily Dickinson's Letters to the Bowles Family, 1858–1862." *Emily Dickinson Bulletin* 20 (1972): 1–28.

Hinz, Evelyn J. "Mimesis: The Dramatic Lineage of Auto/Biography." Kadar 195–212.

Hoffmann, Leonore, and Margo Culley, eds. *Women's Personal Narratives: Essays in Criticism and Pedagogy.* New York: MLA, 1985.

Holland, Jeanne. "'Knock with / tremor': When Daughters Revise 'Dear Father.'" Turco 84–97.

——. "Scraps, Stamps, and Cutouts: Emily Dickinson's Domestic Technologies of Publication." Ezell and O'Keeffe 139–181.

The Holy Bible, Containing the Old and New Testaments. Philadelphia: J. B. Lippincott, 1843.

Homans, Margaret. *Women Writers and Poetic Identity.* Princeton: Princeton UP, 1980.

Horan, Elizabeth. "To Market: The Dickinson Copyright Wars." *The Emily Dickinson Journal* 5.1 (1996): 88–120.

Hornbeak, Katherine Gee. *The Complete Letter Writer in English 1568–1800.* Smith College Studies in Modern Languages 15. 3–4. Ed. Caroline B. Bourland et al. Northampton: Collegiate, 1934.

Howe, Susan. *The Birth-Mark: Unsettling the Wilderness in American Literary History.* Hanover: Wesleyan UP, 1993.

——. *My Emily Dickinson.* Berkeley: North Atlantic, 1985.

——. "Some Notes on Visual Intentionality in Emily Dickinson." *HOW(ever)* 3.4 (1986): 11–13.

——. "These Flames and Generosities of the Heart: Emily Dickinson and the Illogic of Sumptuary Values." *Sulfur* 28 (Spring 1991): 134–155.

——. "Women and Their Effect in the Distance." *Ironwood* 28 (1986): 58–91.

Imbrie, Ann E. "Defining Nonfiction Genres." Lewalski 45–69.

Jay, Paul. "Posing: Autobiography and the Subject of Photography." Ashley, Gilmore, and Peters 191–211.

Jeffreys, Mark. "Ideologies of Lyric: A Problem of Genre in Contemporary Anglophone Poetics." *PMLA* 110 (1995): 196–205.

Jehlen, Myra. *American Incarnation: The Individual, The Nation, and The Continent.* Cambridge: Harvard UP, 1986.

Jelinek, Estelle C., ed. *Women's Autobiography: Essays in Criticism.* Bloomington: Indiana UP, 1980.

Jenny, Laurent. "The Strategy of Form." *French Literary Theory Today.* Ed. Tzvetan Todorov. Trans. R. Carter. Cambridge: Cambridge UP, 1982. 34–63.

Jensen, Katharine Ann. "Male Models of Feminine Epistolarity; or, How to Write Like a Woman in Seventeenth-Century France." Goldsmith 25–45.

——. *Writing Love: Letters, Women, and the Novel in France, 1605–1776.* Carbondale: Southern Illinois UP, 1995.

Johnson, Nan. *Nineteenth-Century Rhetoric in North America.* Carbondale: Southern Illinois UP, 1991.

Johnson, Thomas H. *Emily Dickinson: An Interpretive Biography.* Cambridge: Harvard UP, 1963.

——. "Establishing a Text: The Emily Dickinson Papers." *Studies in Bibliography* 5 (1952–1953): 31–32.

——. Introduction. Johnson and Ward xv–xxii.

——, ed. *The Poems of Emily Dickinson.* 3 vols. Cambridge: Belknap P of Harvard UP, 1955.

Johnson, Thomas H., and Theodora van Wagenen Ward, eds. *The Letters of Emily Dickinson.* 3 vols. Cambridge: Belknap P of Harvard UP, 1958.

Johnston, Nancy C. "The Literary Production of *Poems by Emily Dickinson (1890)*: A Sociology of Texts." Diss. York U, Toronto, 1995.

Juhasz, Suzanne, ed. *Feminist Critics Read Emily Dickinson.* Bloomington: Indiana UP, 1983.

——. "Materiality and the Poet." Grabher, Hagenbüchle, and Miller 427–439.

——. *Naked and Fiery Forms: Modern American Poetry by Women: A New Tradition.* New York: Harper, 1976.

——. "Reading Emily Dickinson's Letters." *Emerson Society Quarterly* 30 (1984): 170–191.

Juhasz, Suzanne, Cristanne Miller, and Martha Nell Smith. *Comic Power in Emily Dickinson.* Austin: U of Texas P, 1993.

Kadar, Marlene. "Coming to Terms: Life Writing—from Genre to Critical Practice." Kadar 3–16.

——, ed. *Essays on Life Writing: From Genre to Critical Practice.* Toronto: U of Toronto P, 1992.

——. "Whose Life Is It Anyway? Out of the Bathtub and into the Narrative." Kadar 152–161.

Kamuf, Peggy. *Fictions of Feminine Desire: Disclosures of Héloïse.* Lincoln: U of Nebraska P, 1982.

Kaplan, Deborah. "Representing Two Cultures: Jane Austen's Letters." Benstock 211–229.

Kauffman, Linda S. *Discourses of Desire: Gender, Genre, and Epistolary Fictions.* Ithaca: Cornell UP, 1986.

———. "Special Delivery: Twenty-First Century Epistolarity in *The Handmaid's Tale.*" Goldsmith 221–244.

Kauffman, Linda S., and Catharine R. Stimpson. *Special Delivery: Epistolary Modes in Modern Fiction.* Chicago: U of Chicago P, 1991.

Keller, Lynn, and Cristanne Miller, eds. *Feminist Measures: Soundings in Poetry and Theory.* Ann Arbor: U of Michigan P, 1994.

Kirkby, Joan. *Emily Dickinson.* Women Writers Series. Gen. eds. Eva Figes and Adele King. London: Macmillan, 1991.

Knight, Philip. *Flower Poetics in Nineteenth-Century France.* Oxford: Clarendon, 1986.

Kolodny, Annette. *The Lay of the Land: Metaphor as Experience and History in American Life and Letters.* Chapel Hill: U of North Carolina P, 1975.

Kristeva, Julia. "The Bounded Text." Kristeva, *Desire in Language* 36–63.

———. *Desire in Language: A Semiotic Approach to Literature and Art.* Ed. Leon S. Roudiez. Trans. Thomas Gora, Alice Jardine, and Leon S. Roudiez. New York: Columbia UP, 1980.

———. *Revolution in Poetic Language.* Trans. Margaret Waller. New York: Columbia UP, 1984.

———. "Word, Dialogue, and Novel." Kristeva, *Desire in Language* 64–91.

Krohn, Violet-Marie. "Emily Dickinson's Literary Background as Indicated in Her Letters: Emphasizing Her Relationship to Her Favorite Authors." MA, U of Chicago, 1940.

Lambert, Robert Graham, Jr. *A Critical Study of Emily Dickinson's Letters: The Prose of a Poet.* Lewiston: Mellen UP, 1996.

Lawrence, Robert R. "The Mind Alone: The History of the Publication and Criticism of the Letters of Emily Dickinson. Part One: Discovery, 1890–1913." *Emily Dickinson Bulletin* 15 (1970): 94–102.

———. "The Mind Alone: The History of the Publication and Criticism of the Letters of Emily Dickinson. Part Two: Distortion, 1914–1930." *Emily Dickinson Bulletin* 17 (1971): 34–44.

Lazer, Hank. "The Letter Poem." *Northwest Review* 19.1–2 (1981): 235–245.

Lease, Benjamin. *Emily Dickinson's Readings of Men and Books: Sacred Soundings.* London: Macmillan, 1990.

Lenz, Bernd. "Intertextualität und Gattungswechsel." Broich and Pfister 158–178.

Levine, George, and William Madden, eds. *The Art of Victorian Prose.* Oxford: Oxford UP, 1968.

Lewalski, Barbara Kiefer. "Introduction: Issues and Approaches." Lewalski 1–12.

———, ed. *Renaissance Genres: Essays on Theory, History, and Interpretation.* Cambridge: Harvard UP, 1986.

Leyda, Jay. *The Years and Hours of Emily Dickinson.* 2 vols. New Haven: Yale UP, 1970.

Lindberg-Seyersted, Brita. *The Voice of the Poet: Aspects of Style in the Poetry of Emily Dickinson.* Cambridge: Harvard UP, 1968.

Loeffelholz, Mary. "The Incidental Dickinson." *NEQ* (September 1999): 456–472.

Longsworth, Polly. *Austin and Mabel: The Amherst Affair and Love Letters of Austin Dickinson and Mabel Loomis Todd.* New York: Holt, 1984.

——. "'Was Mr Dudley Dear?': Emily Dickinson and John Langdon Dudley." *Massachusetts Review* 26 (1985): 360–372.

——. *The World of Emily Dickinson.* New York: Norton, 1990.

Lowenberg, Carlton. *Emily Dickinson's Textbooks.* Ed. Territa A. Lowenberg and Carla L. Brown. Berkeley, CA: West Coast Print Center, 1986.

Lucas, Dolores Dyer. *Emily Dickinson and Riddle.* DeKalb: Northern Illinois UP, 1969.

Lunettes, Henry. *The American Gentleman's Guide to Politeness and Fashion.* Rev. ed. Philadelphia: J. B. Lippincott, 1864.

Malroux, Claire. "Emily Dickinson: Lettres à T. W. Higginson (1862–1870)." *Po&sie* 48 (1989): 3–12.

Mann, John Stuart. "Dickinson's Letters to Higginson." Fast and Gordon 39–46.

——. "Dickinson's Letters to Higginson: Motives for Metaphor." *Higginson Journal of Poetry* 22 (1979): 1–79.

Mansell, Darrel. "Unsettling the Colonel's Hash: 'Fact' in Autobiography." *The American Autobiography.* Ed. Albert E. Stone. Englewood Cliffs, NJ: Prentice, 1981. 61–79.

Martin, Wendy. *An American Triptych.* Chapel Hill: U of North Carolina P, 1984.

McCabe, James D. *The National Encyclopedia of Business and Social Forms.* London: Schuyler Smith, 1879.

McCall, Anne E. "Of Textual Demise and Literary Renewal: George Sand and the Problematics of Epistolary Autobiography." *Auto/Biography Studies* 9.2 (1994): 212–230.

McGann, Jerome J. *Black Riders: The Visible Language of Modernism.* Princeton: Princeton UP, 1993.

——. "Composition as Explanation (of Modern and Postmodern Poetries)." Ezell and O'Keeffe 101–138.

——. *A Critique of Modern Textual Criticism.* Charlottesville: U of Virginia P, 1992.

——. "Emily Dickinson's Visible Language." Farr 248–259.

——. *The Textual Condition.* Princeton: Princeton UP, 1991.

McKinstry, S. Jaret. "'How Lovely Are the Wiles of Words!'—or, 'Subjects Hinder Talk': The Letters of Emily Dickinson." *Engendering the Word: Feminist Essays in Psychosexual Poetics.* Ed. Temma F. Berg. Urbana: U of Illinois P, 1989. 193–207.

Meyer, Herman. *The Poetics of Quotation in the European Novel.* Princeton: Princeton UP, 1968.

Miller, Cristanne. *Emily Dickinson: A Poet's Grammar.* Cambridge: Harvard UP, 1987.

——. "A Letter Is a Joy of Earth: Dickinson's Communication with the World." *Legacy* ns 5.3 (1986): 29–39.

——. "Whose Dickinson?" *American Literary History* 12.1–2 (2000): 230–253.

Miller, Nancy K. "Changing the Subject: Authorship, Writing, and the Reader." *Feminist Studies/Critical Studies.* Ed. Teresa de Lauretis. Bloomington: Indiana UP, 1986. 102–120.

Miller, Ruth. *The Poetry of Emily Dickinson.* Middletown: Wesleyan UP, 1968.

Mitchell, Domhnall. "Emily Dickinson, Ralph Franklin and the Diplomacy of Translation." *The Emily Dickinson Journal* 8.2 (1999): 39–54.

——. "Revising the Script: Emily Dickinson's Manuscripts." *American Literature* 70.4 (1998): 705–737.

Monroe, Jonathan. *A Poverty of Objects: The Prose Poem and the Politics of Genre*. Ithaca: Cornell UP, 1987.

Monteiro, George. "Emily Dickinson's Business." *Literature and Belief* 10 (1990): 24–42.

Morawski, Stefan. "The Basic Functions of Quotations." *Sign, Language, Culture*. Ed. A. J. Greimas et al. The Hague: Mouton, 1970. 690–705.

Morgan, Thaïs E. "Is There an Intertext in This Text?: Literary and Interdisciplinary Approaches to Intertextuality." *American Journal of Semiotics* 3.4 (1985): 1–40.

Morris, Adalaide. " 'The Love of Thee—a Prism Be': Men and Women in the Love Poetry of Emily Dickinson." Juhasz 98–113.

Morse, Jonathan. "Daguerrotype." *The Emily Dickinson Encyclopedia*. Ed. Jane Donahue Eberwein. Westport, CT: Greenwood, 1998. 61–62.

Mossberg, Barbara Antonina Clarke. *Emily Dickinson: When a Writer Is a Daughter*. Bloomington: Indiana UP, 1982.

Mowitt, John. Foreword. *Discerning the Subject*. Theory and History of Literature 55. By Paul Smith. Minneapolis: U of Minnesota P, 1988. ix–xxiii.

Mudge, Jean McClure. "Emily Dickinson and 'Sister Sue.' " *Prairie Schooner* 52 (Spring 1977): 90–108.

——. *Emily Dickinson and the Image of Home*. Amherst: U of Massachusetts P, 1975.

Mukarovsky, Jan. *Structure, Sign, and Function: Selected Essays by Jan Mukarovsky*. Ed. and trans. John Burbank and Peter Steiner. New Haven: Yale UP, 1978.

Mulvihill, John. "Why Dickinson Didn't Title." *Emily Dickinson Journal* 5.1 (1996): 71–87.

Murphy, James J., ed. *Renaissance Eloquence: Studies in the Theory and Practice of Renaissance Rhetoric*. Berkeley: U of California P, 1983.

Murphy, Margueritte S. *A Tradition of Subversion: The Prose Poem in English from Wilde to Ashbery*. Amherst: U of Massachusetts P, 1992.

Nathan, Rhoda B., ed. *Nineteenth-Century Women Writers of the English-Speaking World*. New York: Greenwood, 1986.

Neuman, Shirley. "Autobiography: From Different Poetics to a Poetics of Differences." Kadar 213–230.

The New Complete [American] Letter Writer: or, The Art of Correspondence. Philadelphia: Spotswood, 1792.

Newman, Samuel Phillips. *Practical System of Rhetoric, or the Principles and Rules of Style, Inferred from Examples of Writing, to Which Is Added a Historical Dissertation on English Style*. 5th ed. Andover, MA: Gould, 1835.

Norton, Charles Eliot. *The New Life of Dante*. Cambridge, MA: Houghton, 1859.

Nussbaum, Felicity A. "Eighteenth-Century Women's Autobiographical Commonplaces." Benstock 147–171.

Oberhaus, Dorothy Huff. *Emily Dickinson's Fascicles: Method and Meaning*. University Park: Pennsylvania State UP, 1995.

——. "In Defense of Sue." *Dickinson Studies* 48 (1983): 1–25.

O'Keefe, Martha. "Primal Thought." *Dickinson Studies* 35 (1979): 8–11.

Olney, James. "Autobiography and the Cultural Moment: A Thematic, Historical, and Bibliographical Introduction." Olney 3–27.

——, ed. *Autobiography: Essays Theoretical and Critical*. Princeton: Princeton UP, 1980.

Ong, Walter. *Orality and Literacy: The Technologizing of the Word*. London: Routledge, 1982.

Orzeck, Martin. "Dickinson's Letters to Abiah Root: Formulating the Reader as 'Absentee.'" Orzeck and Weisbuch 135–160.

Orzeck, Martin, and Robert Weisbuch, eds. *Dickinson and Audience*. Ann Arbor: U of Michigan P, 1997.

Ostriker, Alicia. *Stealing the Language: The Emergence of Women's Poetry in America*. Boston: Beacon, 1986.

Paglia, Camille. *Sexual Personae: Art and Decadence from Nefertiti to Emily Dickinson*. New York: Vintage, 1991.

Patterson, Rebecca. "On Dating Dickinson's Poems." *American Notes and Queries* 12 (1974): 84–86.

——. *The Riddle of Emily Dickinson*. Boston: Houghton, 1951.

Perri, Carmela. "On Alluding." *Poetics* 7 (1978): 289–307.

Perry, Ruth. *Women, Letters, and the Novel*. New York: AMS, 1980.

Pfister, Manfred. "Konzepte der Intertextualität." Broich and Pfister 1–30.

Phillips, Elizabeth. *Emily Dickinson: Personae and Performance*. University Park: Pennsylvania State UP, 1988.

Pollak, Vivian R. "Dickinson, Poe, and Barrett Browning: A Clarification." *New England Quarterly* 54 (1981): 121–124.

——. *Dickinson: The Anxiety of Gender*. Ithaca: Cornell UP, 1984.

——. "Emily Dickinson's Early Poems and Letters." Diss. Brandeis U, 1969.

——. "Emily Dickinson's Literary Allusions." *Essays in Literature* 1 (1974): 54–68.

——. *A Poet's Parents: The Courtship Letters of Emily Norcross and Edward Dickinson*. Chapel Hill: U of North Carolina P, 1988.

——. "The Second Act: Emily Dickinson's Orphaned Persona." Nathan 159–169.

Porter, David. *The Art of Emily Dickinson's Early Poetry*. Cambridge: Harvard UP, 1966.

——. "Emily Dickinson: A Disabling Freedom." *Massachusetts Studies in English* 7–8 (1981): 80–87.

——. "Review Essay." *Emily Dickinson Journal* 4.1 (1995): 126–128.

Pratt, Annis. *Archetypal Patterns in Women's Fiction*. Bloomington: Indiana UP, 1981.

Prioli, Carmine A. "Emily Dickinson's Reading of Francis Quarles." *Dickinson Studies* 35 (1979): 3–7.

Quackenbos, G. P. *Advanced Course of Composition and Rhetoric.* New York: Appleton, 1866.

Rabinowitz, Peter J. " 'What's Hecuba to Us?' The Audience's Experience of Literary Borrowing." *The Reader in the Text: Essays on Audience and Interpretation.* Ed. Susan R. Suleiman and Inge Crosman. Princeton: Princeton UP, 1980. 241–263.

Redford, Bruce. *The Converse of the Pen: Acts of Intimacy in the Eighteenth-Century Familiar Letter.* Chicago: U of Chicago P, 1986.

Renza, Louis A. "The Veto of the Imagination: A Theory of Autobiography." Olney 268–295.

Reynolds, David S. *Beneath the American Renaissance: The Subversive Imagination in the Age of Emerson and Melville.* Cambridge: Harvard UP, 1989.

Rich, Adrienne. " 'I am in Danger—Sir—.' " *Necessities of Life.* New York: Norton, 1966. 33.

——. "Vesuvius at Home: The Power of Emily Dickinson." *Parnassus: Poetry in Review* 5.1 (1976): 49–74.

Richardson, Samuel. *Clarissa.* 2 vols. London: Everyman's Library, 1962.

Riffaterre, Michael. "Compulsory Reader Response: The Intertextual Drive." Worton and Still 56–78.

Rosenthal, Margaret F. "A Courtesan's Voice: Epistolary Self-Portraiture in Veronica Franco's *Terze Rime.*" Goldsmith 3–24.

Rosenthal, M. L., and Sally M. Gall. *The Modern Poetic Sequence.* Oxford: Oxord UP, 1983.

Rothman, Ellen K. *Hands and Hearts: A History of Courtship in America.* Cambridge: Harvard UP, 1987.

Saintsbury, George. *A Letter Book.* London: Bell, 1922.

Salska, Agnieszka. "Dickinson's Letters." Grabher, Hagenbüchle, and Miller 163–180.

——. "Emily Dickinson's Letters: The Making of a Poetics." *Crossing Borders: American Literature and Other Artistic Media.* Ed. Jadwiga Maszewska. Warszawa: PWN, 1992. 4–19.

——. "Letters." Unpublished essay, 1996.

Schappes, Morris U. "The Letters of Emily Dickinson." *Symposium* III (April 1932): 260–269.

Scharnhorst, Gary. "A Glimpse of Dickinson at Work." *American Literature* 57.3 (1985): 483–485.

Schenck, Celeste. "All of a Piece: Women's Poetry and Autobiography." Brodzki and Schenck 281–305.

Scheurer, Erika. "Near But Remote: Emily Dickinson's Epistolary Voice." *The Emily Dickinson Journal* 4.1 (1995): 86–107.

Sewall, Richard B. "Emily Dickinson's Books and Reading." Farr 40–52.

——. *The Life of Emily Dickinson.* 2 vols. London: Faber and Faber, 1974.

——. *The Lyman Letters: New Light on Emily Dickinson and Her Family.* Amherst: U of Massachusetts P, 1965.

Shakespere [sic], William. *The Comedies, Histories, Tragedies, and Poems of William Shakespere.* Ed. Charles Knight. 8 vols. Boston: Little, 1853.

Shay, Mary Irmina. "Emily Dickinson's Prose: A Study of Her Letters." MA, Boston College, 1935.

Sherwood, William R. *Circumference and Circumstance: Stages in the Mind and Art of Emily Dickinson.* New York: Columbia UP, 1968.

Shevelow, Kathryn. "The Production of the Female Writing Subject: Letters to the *Athenian Mercury*." *Genre* 19 (1986): 385–407.

Shillingsburg, Peter L. "Polymorphic, Polysemic, Protean, Reliable, Electronic Texts." Bornstein and Williams 29–43.

Showalter, Elaine. *A Literature of Their Own: British Women Novelists from Brontë to Lessing.* Princeton: Princeton UP, 1977.

Shurr, William H. "Editing the *New Poems of Emily Dickinson*." *The Emily Dickinson Journal* 4.1 (1995): 118–125.

——, ed. *New Poems of Emily Dickinson.* Chapel Hill: U of North Carolina P, 1993.

Smith, Barbara Herrnstein. *On the Margins of Discourse: The Relation of Literature to Language.* Chicago: U of Chicago P, 1978.

Smith, Martha Nell. " 'Because the Plunge from the Front Overturned Us': The Dickinson Electronic Archives Project. ⟨http://jefferson.village.virginia.edu/dickinson/⟩. *Studies in the Literary Imagination* 32.1 (Spring 1999): 133–151.

——. "Dickinson's Manuscripts." Grabher, Hagenbüchle, and Miller 113–137.

——. "Electronic Resources on Emily Dickinson." *Emily Dickinson International Society Bulletin* 12.2 (Nov.–Dec. 2000): 13; 26.

——. "Gender Issues in Textual Editing of Emily Dickinson." *Women's Studies Quarterly* 19.3–4 (Fall–Winter 1991): 78–111.

——. "The Importance of a Hypermedia Archive of Dickinson's Creative Work." *The Emily Dickinson Journal* 4.1 (1995): 75–85.

——. " 'Open Me Carefully': Emily's Book for Susan." *Emily Dickinson International Society Bulletin* 10.1 (May–June 1998): 12–13; 22–23.

——. *Rowing in Eden: Rereading Emily Dickinson.* Austin: U of Texas P, 1992.

——. "To Fill a Gap." *San Jose Studies* 13.3 (1987): 3–25.

Smith, Martha Nell, and Ellen Louise Hart. "On Franklin's Gifts & Ghosts." *The Emily Dickinson Journal* 8.2 (1999): 24–38.

Smith, Martha Nell, ed., with Ellen Louise Hart, Laura Lauth, Marcy Tanter, and Lara Vetter. *Writings by Susan Dickinson: A Critical Online Edition.* ⟨http://jefferson.village.virginia.edu/dickinson/susan⟩.

Smith, Paul. *Discerning the Subject.* Theory and History of Literature 55. Minneapolis: U of Minnesota P, 1988.

Smith, Sidonie. *A Poetics of Women's Autobiography.* Bloomington: Indiana UP, 1987.

Smith-Rosenberg, Carroll. *Disorderly Conduct: Visions of Gender in Victorian America.* New York: Knopf, 1985.

———. "The Female World of Love and Ritual: Relations between Women in Nineteenth-Century America." *Signs* 1.1 (1995): 1–29.

Spacks, Patricia Meyer. "Female Resources: Epistles, Plot, and Power." Goldsmith 63–76.

Spengeman, William C., ed. *The Forms of Autobiography: A Collection of Critical Essays.* Englewood Cliffs, NJ: Prentice, 1981.

Sprinker, Michael. "Fictions of the Self: The End of Autobiography." Olney 321–342.

Stanton, Domna C., and Jeanine Parisier Plottel, eds. *The Female Autograph.* New York: New York Literary Forum, 1984.

St. Armand, Barton Levi. *Emily Dickinson and Her Culture: The Soul's Society.* Cambridge: Cambridge UP, 1984.

Stedman, Edmund Clarence. *The Nature and Elements of Poetry.* Boston: Houghton Mifflin, 1892.

Stevens, Elizabeth C. "Dickinson's Language of Flowers." *Emily Dickinson International Society Bulletin* 2.2 (Nov.–Dec. 1990): 3–5.

Stone, Albert R. *The American Autobiography: A Collection of Critical Essays.* Englewood Cliffs, NJ: Prentice, 1981.

Stonum, Gary Lee. "Dickinson's Literary Background." Grabher, Hagenbüchle, and Miller 44–60.

———. *The Dickinson Sublime.* Madison: U of Wisconsin P, 1990.

Sullivan, David. "Suing Sue: Emily Dickinson Addressing Susan Gilbert." *The Emily Dickinson Journal* 5.1 (1996): 45–70.

Swenson, May. " 'Big My Secret, but It's Bandaged.' " *Parnassus* 12–13 (1985): 16–44.

Taggard, Genevieve. "Poet as Letter Writer." *New York Herald Tribune Books,* 13 Dec. 1931.

Tanselle, G. Thomas. "The Varieties of Scholarly Editing." *Scholarly Editing: A Guide to Research.* Ed. D. C. Greetham. New York: MLA, 1995. 9–32.

Tanter, Marcy L. " 'Behind the wall of sense': Emily Dickinson and Her Nineteenth-Century British Writers." Diss. U of Massachusetts, Amherst, 1996.

Terris, Virginia Rinaldy. *Emily Dickinson and the Genteel Critics.* Diss. New York U, 1973. Ann Arbor: UMI, 1973. 7319976.

Tingley, Stephanie A. " 'A Letter Is a Joy of Earth': Emily Dickinson's Letters and Victorian Epistolary Conventions." Second International Emily Dickinson Conference. U of Innsbruck (Austria). 4–6 August 1995.

———. " '*My* Business is to *Sing*': Emily Dickinson's Letters to Elizabeth Holland." Orzeck and Weisbuch 181–199.

Todd, Janet. *Women's Friendship in Literature.* New York: Columbia UP, 1980.

Todd, John Emerson. *Emily Dickinson's Use of the Persona.* The Hague: Mouton, 1973.

Todd, Mabel Loomis. "Emily Dickinson's Letters." *Bachelor of Arts* 5.1 (May 1895): 39–66.

——. Introductory. Todd 1: v–xii. Rpt. in Buckingham, *Reception*, item 418.

——, ed. *Letters of Emily Dickinson.* 2 vols. Boston: Roberts Brothers, 1894.

——, ed. *Letters of Emily Dickinson.* New and enlarged ed. New York: Harper, 1931.

Todorov, Tzvetan. *Mikhail Bakhtin: The Dialogical Principle.* Minneapolis: U of Minnesota P, 1984.

Tuckerman, Henry T. *Characteristics of Literature, Illustrated by the Genius of Distinguished Writers.* 2nd series. New York: Books for Libraries, 1851.

Turco, Lewis. *Emily Dickinson: Woman of Letters. Poems and Centos from Lines in Emily Dickinson's Letters.* New York: State U of New York P, 1993.

——. "Iron Pyrites in the Dickinson Mine." *Emily Dickinson Journal* 4.1 (1995): 108–117.

Villani, Jim, ed. *The Epistolary Form and the Letter as Artifact.* Youngstown: Pig Iron, 1991.

Walker, Cheryl. "Feminist Literary Criticism and the Author." *Critical Inquiry* 16 (Spring 1990): 551–571.

Walker, Nancy. " 'Wider Than the Sky': Public Presence and Private Self in Dickinson, James, and Woolf." Benstock 272–303.

Walsh, John E. *The Hidden Life of Emily Dickinson.* New York: Simon, 1971.

Ward, H[arrietta] O[xnard]. *Sensible Etiquette of the Best Society, Customs, Manners, Morals, and Home Culture.* Philadelphia: Porter, 1878.

Ward, Theodora van Wagenen. *The Capsule of the Mind: Chapters in the Life of Emily Dickinson.* Cambridge: Harvard UP, 1961.

——, ed. *Emily Dickinson's Letters to Dr. and Mrs. Josiah Gilbert Holland.* Cambridge: Harvard UP, 1951.

Weimann, Robert. "Text, Author-Function, and Appropriation in Modern Narrative: Toward a Sociology of Representation." *Critical Inquiry* 14 (Spring 1988): 431–447.

Weisbuch, Robert. *Emily Dickinson's Poetry.* Chicago: U of Chicago P, 1972.

Weisbuch, Robert, and Martin Orzeck. "Introduction: Dickinson the Scrivener." Orzeck and Weisbuch 1–8.

Wells, Anna Mary. "ED Forgeries." *Dickinson Studies* 35 (1979): 12–16.

——. "The Soul's Society: Emily Dickinson and Colonel Higginson." Nathan 221–229.

Wells, Henry W. *Introduction to Emily Dickinson.* Chicago: Packard, 1947.

Welter, Barbara. *Dimity Convictions: The American Woman in the Nineteenth Century.* Athens: Ohio UP, 1976.

Werner, Marta L. *Emily Dickinson's Open Folios: Scenes of Reading, Surfaces of Writing.* Ann Arbor: U of Michigan P, 1995.

——, ed. *Radical Scatters: Emily Dickinson's Late Fragments and Related Texts, 1870–1886.* Electronic Archive. ⟨http://www.hti.umich.edu/d/dickinson/⟩ Ann Arbor: U of Michigan P, 1999.

——. "The Shot Bird's Progress: Emily Dickinson's Master Letters." Turco 147–152.

Wheeler, Michael. *The Art of Allusion in Victorian Fiction.* London: Macmillan, 1979.

Whicher, George Frisbie. *This Was a Poet: A Critical Biography of Emily Dickinson*. Ann Arbor: U of Michigan P, 1965.

Wider, Sarah. "Corresponding Worlds: The Art of Emily Dickinson's Letters." *The Emily Dickinson Journal* 1.1 (1992): 19–38.

Williams, Ralph G. "I Shall Be Spoken: Textual Boundaries, Authors, and Intent." Bornstein and Williams 45–66.

Wolff, Cynthia Griffin. *Emily Dickinson*. New York: Knopf, 1986.

——. "[Im]pertinent Constructions of Body and Self: Dickinson's Use of the Romantic Grotesque." Farr 119–129.

Wolosky, Shira. "Emily Dickinson's Manuscript Body: History/Textuality/Gender." *The Emily Dickinson Journal* 8.2 (1999): 87–99.

Wood, Alphonso. *A Class-book of Botany*. Claremont: Claremont Manufacturing, 1853.

Worton, Michael, and Judith Still, eds. *Intertextuality: Theories and Practices*. Manchester: Manchester UP, 1990.

Wylder, Edith. *The Last Face: Emily Dickinson's Manuscripts*. Albuquerque: U of New Mexico P, 1971.

Yaeger, Patricia. *Honey-Mad Women: Emancipatory Strategies in Women's Writing*. New York: Columbia UP, 1988.

The Young Lady's Book of Classical Letters. Consisting of epistolary selections: designed to improve young ladies and gentlemen in the art of letter-writing, and in those principles which are for respectability and success in life. Philadelphia: Desilver, 1836.

The Young Lady's Own Book: A manual of intellectual improvement and moral deportment by the author of the young man's own book. Philadelphia: Desilver, 1836.

Index of First Lines of Poems

Unless otherwise noted, poems are cited here and throughout the text in the form(s) in which they were incorporated into or enclosed with a letter; whenever available, the respective letter number has been added for easier reference.

Index of Letters

The numbers and dates follow Thomas H. Johnson and Theodora Ward, *The Letters of Emily Dickinson* (Cambridge: Harvard UP, 1958).

General Index

LaVergne, TN USA
21 March 2010
176620LV00002B/2/P